SONS OF DARKNESS
&
SONS OF LIGHT

by

Rayvn Navarro

Egregore Press
Denver, CO

"Sons of Darkness ~ Sons of Light" copyright © 2006: Rayvn Navarro
Front cover "Master of Metal" copyright © Rayvn Navarro, 2006

Published by:
Egregore Press
Denver, CO. 80231
June, 2007
egregore@semjaaza.com

All rights reserved.

No part of this book may be reproduced or utilized in any form or by any means, electronic or mechanical, including photocopying, recording, or by any information storage and retrieval system, without written permission from the publisher.

ISBN: 978-0-6151-4989-9

Printed and bound in the United States

- Quote on dedication page from the song "Pazuzu" on the album "Zoon" by The Nefilim. Lyric by Carl McCoy

This book is dedicated to
Fields of the Nephilim fans everywhere

*Many thanks to those who were supportive of
this effort and bore with it's birth-pangs with
their suggestions and enthusiasm.
Special thanks to Cobweb, Zoonshe,
Nightvision, Nefi, Endy, Leviathan and
the Angel in the Ratty Ol' Hat.*

No one here remembers the bending of our minds...
Pazuzu – *Zoon* by The Nefilim

TABLE of CONTENTS

THE ORIGINS OF ENOCH 7
    THE LINEAGE OF ENOCH 9
    THE MAN WHO WALKED WITH GOD 11
    A HISTORY OF THE BOOKS OF ENOCH 17
    A BRIEF HISTORY OF THE TIMES 22
    THE AUTHORS OF ENOCH 28
THE BOOK OF THE WATCHERS 33
    Chapters 1-5 35
    Chapter 6 38
    Chapter 7 44
    Chapter 8 53
    Chapter 9 55
    Chapter 10 61
    Chapter 11 69
    Chapter 12 70
    Chapter 13 73
    Chapter 14 77
    Chapter 15 83
    Chapter 16 97
    Chapters 17-19 100
    Chapters 20-21 104
    Chapters 22-36 108
    Chapter 69 109
THE YAHAD 117
    JUDGES, ASSASSINS & WATCHERS 119
THE WATCHERS 129
    THE NAMES OF THE WATCHERS 131
GEMATRIA 161
    GEMATRIC TABLE OF HEBREW LETTERS 163
    THE SYMBOLOGY OF HEBREW LETTERS 165
BRANCHES, KNOTS & SPIRALS 169
    TWO PROPHETS AND A KING NAMED HAZAEL 171
    THE STORY OF SAMSON 176
        A NAZARITE FROM BIRTH 176
        THE JAWBONE OF AN ASS 180
        DELILAH 181
    THE STORY OF SOLOMON AND SHEBA 186
    THE SONS OF DAN 188
        THE MYCENAEANS 188
        THE SEA PEOPLE 189
        THE TUATHA DE DANANN 193
    THE DIVINE FEMININE 196
        LIONS, BEES & SERPENTS 196
        THE GORGON 200
    THE PRIMORDIAL SERPENT DEITIES 207
        TIAMAT 207
        TYPHON 208
        WATER, FIRE & BLOOD 210
        THE GENESIS OF GODS & RELIGION 211
        THE SUN & THE SERPENT 212
    THE WATCHERS OF "THE MYSTERIES" 215
BIBLIOGRAPHY 219

THE ORIGINS OF ENOCH

8

THE LINEAGE OF ENOCH

There are two men in the Bible named Enoch. The first mention of an Enoch is the first-born son of Cain in *Genesis*:

> 17 And Cain knew his wife; and she conceived, and bare Enoch; and he builded a city, and called the name of the city Enoch, after the name of his son, Enoch. 18 And unto Enoch was born Irad: and Irad begat Mehujael: and Mehujael begat Methushael: and Methushael begat Lamech. (Genesis 4)

The second mention of a man called Enoch occurs again in *Genesis*:

> 18 And Jared lived an hundred sixty and two years, and he begat Enoch: 19 And Jared lived after he begat Enoch eight hundred years, and begat sons and daughters: 20 And all the days of Jared were nine hundred sixty and two years: and he died. 21 And Enoch lived sixty and five years, and begat Methuselah: 22 And Enoch walked with God after he begat Methuselah three hundred years, and begat sons and daughters: 23 And all the days of Enoch were three hundred sixty and five years: 24 And Enoch walked with God: and he was not; for God took him. (Genesis 5)

Continuing through verses 25 to 26, we see that Methuselah lived a hundred and eighty seven years, then begat Lamech.

Comparing the genealogies of the two Enochs reveals that – with a bit of juggling - these two lineages seem to contain individuals with very similar names:

CAIN'S LINEAGE	JARED'S LINEAGE
Enoch	Mahaleleel
Irad	Jared
Mehujael	Enoch
Methushael	Methuselah
Lamech	Lamech
Jabal, Jubal, Tubal-Cain, Namah	Noah

According to biblical scholars, this anomaly occurs because *Genesis* was the combined work of two different writers – one a Yahwist and the other a priest.

It is after Lamech that we see a divergence in the lines. Noah, the hero of the biblical Flood myth, comes from far earlier flood stories from Mesopotamia. The Sumerians called him Ziusudra. The Babylonians called him Atrahasis, and the Assyrians called him Utnapishtim. A similar story is later told by Lucian of Samosata in which Deucalion was the hero of the Flood. The Greek historian Berrosus also wrote of the Flood, calling his hero Xisuthros, which is thought to be a phonetic Greek spelling of Ziusudra.

The tablets of the Old Babylonian text of the *Atrahasis* story can be dated to around 1700 BCE – approximately 400 years before the Hebrews purportedly left Egypt. This text is quite remarkable in that the author is actually named – a rarity in such ancient writings. He was called Ipiq-aya. Ipiq-aya was a scribe who lived during the reign of Ammi-şaduqa, a king of Babylon from approximately 1702-1682 BCE and probably lived in Sippar.

According to one version of the Sumerian king list, Atrahasis is called by his Sumerian name Ziusudra, and is the ruler of the city Shuruppak (land of utmost well-being). His father – also a ruler of Shuruppak – was named Shuruppak...as the city of Enoch was named after Cain's first-born son, Enoch. Clay tablets from the Early Dynastic period in the early third millennium BCE contain a composition called *The Instructions of Shuruppak*. The sage wisdom transmitted from Shuruppak to his son Ziusudra was part of a continuing literary tradition, indicating that Atrahasis had been a figure of note from quite early on in history. The Hebrews most likely heard these stories during the Babylonian captivity. Samuel Noah Kramer posits that the Hebrews *were* the Sumerians. In this case, the stories may have been part of an oral tradition or they were re-heard and re-learned during the Babylonian captivity.

Knowing these facts about the man called "Noah" and the story of the Flood found in the Old Testament, leaves us to ponder the question, "If the story of Noah comes from Sumeria, who then is his progenitor Enoch?"

THE MAN WHO WALKED WITH GOD

What does it mean, Enoch "walked with God: and he was not"? In the context of the story of Enoch further described in the *Books of Enoch*, it appears that Enoch achieved enlightenment while he lived. The phrase 'and he was not' appears suspect here, because Enoch most certainly continued to exist according to Chapters 12 and 65 after, where he appears to Noah. While he spends a great deal of time in the various heavens, conversing with and learning from the angels or Watchers, he also appears before the Watchers, who are on the earth. This question will be further addressed in the next chapter.

Enoch symbolizes the enlightened man, and according to various writings becomes the 'lesser Yahweh', Metatron. According to the Assyrian legend, *The Epic of Izdubar* – Metatron is the "king over all the angels". The authorities of the *Talmud* do not encourage this identification of the patriarch Enoch with Metatron, but do consider him the link between humanity and divinity. As Metatron, he has a twin or half-brother, the angel Sandalphon. Sandalphon is said to have been the prophet Elijah, in his earthly incarnation. Metatron is regarded by some sources to also be the Shekinah or consort of Yahweh, in his feminine aspect. Like Yahweh, Enoch-Metatron has many alternate names, such as El Shaddai (the All Powerful God), Estes, Surya, Yofiel, Tatriel and more. While few have given a satisfactory etymology for the name Metatron, the Greek translation of the name seems to be something like 'visiting the Throne'.

Others see Enoch's origins in the god Mithra of the Persians (Mithras from the Romans). Let us now examine this possibility.

Enoch was said to have lived 365 years. Scholars have remarked on the coincidence between the number of years he lived in the flesh and the number of days in the year of the solar calendar. Whether or not one has any bearing on the other remains to be seen. It is the Julian calendar, which did not exist at the time Enoch was written that is 365 days long. The calendar used by the sect at Qumran was 364 days long and certainly solar-based. It was an edict from God to use the 364 solar-based calendar, rather than the 354 day lunar-based calendar. By the time the Romans took the Holy Land, it was only the Sicarii, the last defenders of the fort at Masada, who still used the 364 day calendar. The Sicarii are mentioned by Josephus in both *Jewish Antiquities* (xx) and *The Jewish War* (vii). They were called thus for their use of a short curved dagger called a *sica* to assassinate Romans and collaborators with Rome. It is possible that Judas 'Iscariot' was in fact a Sicarii and that the Sicarii were one in the same with the Zealots. Iscariot is believed to be a Hellenized corruption of the word.

It is presumed that the Qumran group made adjustments to their year by the use of a kind of 'sun-dial' that marked not the hours of the day, but the day when the sun rose at a certain position in the east – the spring equinox. Such a 'sun-dial' has been found at Khirbit Qumran. According to this mode of thinking, Enoch would have lived a year and a day – the extra day being a recognition that the year is 'reborn' on this intercalary day. But this idea certainly adds credence to the idea of Enoch's origins being tied to the solar deity known variously as Shamash (Babylonia), Mithras (Romans), Mihr (Persia), Mitra (India) and Surya (India). Surya, as you will note from above, is one of Metatron's many names. Further credence is given to this image when contemplating the sigil of Metatron found in S. Liddel MacGregor Mathers *The Greater Key of Solomon the King (Clavicula Salomonis)*. The sigil appears as No. 32, the First Pentacle of the Sun. The text below it appears in *Clavicula Salomonis*:

Figure 1: Metatron as El Shaddai

Figure 32. – The First Pentacle of the Sun. – The Countenance of Shaddai the Almighty, at Whose aspect all creatures obey, and the Angelic Spirits do reverence on bended knees.

Editor's Note. – This singular Pantacle contains the head of the great Angel Methraton or Metatron, the vice-gerent and representative of Shaddai, who is called the Prince of Countenances, and the right-hand masculine Cherub of the Ark, as Sandalphon is the left and feminine. On either side is the Name "El Shaddai." Around is written in Latin: - "Behold His face and form by Whom all things were made, and Whom all creatures obey."

It is interesting to note here the rays emanating from Metatron's head, and his horns. The rays are indicative of the divine radiance or another form of the halo. The horns are also symbolic of divinity, as evidenced by the horned head-dresses of the Sumerian gods. The greater the number of horns in their caps, the greater their status in Anu's Heaven. Like the drawing of Metatron above, Mitra is sometimes depicted with a crown of rays emanating from around his head. It is also pertinent to take note of the first spelling of the name here – Methraton.... Mithraton?

In Sumerian mythology, the god of the sun was Utu (also called Babbar). Utu was the twin brother or brother of Inanna (Venus). He was the upholder of laws and justice. After Utu came Shamash, who was Utu's Babylonian counterpart. Like Utu before him, Shamash was the twin of the goddess now called Ishtar. In some stories, she is also his consort. Their children were Kittum (truth) and Mesharum (justice). In Sippar and Larsa, Shamash was also known as a god of divination. Shamash is thought to be an ancient Semitic god that was introduced into Mesopotamia by the Akkadians. Shemesh or Shamash is a general Semitic name for the sun, whether as a personification or as 'the light of the sun'.

Mitra is both a Persian and a Hindu solar deity. Mitra is counted as one of the sons of Aditi, the self-formed 'Mother of Worlds'. The Adityas (sons of the goddess Aditi) were thought to be Persian in origin and migrated into India with the so-called Aryan invasions. Aditi is also called Deva-Matri – 'the Mother of the Gods' and is often equated with the goddesses Vach and Danu. As Danu, she is the wife of Mitra-Varuna and her sons are the Dānavas, which are giants. As Diti (Bounded), the earth goddess, her mate is Kaśyapa (Vision) and her sons are the Daityas, which are genii. The attribution of being giants and genii is common to the Nephilim and the Watchers.

In India, the Dānavas were equated with the *asuras* or anti-gods. As the story is told, they were once virtuous, but became degraded in their ways:

> *In the course of time, on account of their change of heart, I saw that the Divine Law had disappeared from them, who were animated by passion and rage. (Mahābhārata 13.8360.[210])*
>
> *The* daityas *and* dānavas *are supernatural beings who dwell in the lower worlds yet enjoy heavenly pleasures. They are among the first children of Vision (Kaśyapa) and are thus counted among the* asuras, *the elder brothers of the gods. They are said to have been relegated to an inferior status because they were proud, cruel, and seekers of pleasure. (Vijayānanda Tripāthi, "Devatā Tattva.")*

Things were not always this way. In the oldest portions of the *Rig Veda* the Supreme Spirit was called *asura*, which is the equivalent of the Zoroastrian Ahura Mazda. Across the mountains, to the west in Iran/Persia, the *asuras* are the gods and not the anti-gods. It is possible that the Dānavas were in fact the Greeks who came into

India during the campaign of Alexander the Great on his mission to conquer the world.

There are twelve Adityas or 'sovereign principles' and these are generally equated to the twelve signs of the zodiac. The twelve tribes of Israel are also said to represent the twelve signs of the zodiac. Mitra is the guardian of the day and his brother Varuna is the guardian of the night. Together, they are called the 'champions of justice'. In pre-Zoroastrian times in the *Rig Veda*, Mitra was known as the 'giver and guardian of cattle'. He was a giver of light, loyal and obedient as the sun's course in the heavens. Later, after Zoroaster, Mitra became one of the twenty-eight Izeds (angels) surrounding the throne of Ahura Mazda, the Supreme God of the Zoroastrians. He was also known as *Dae-pa-Meher*, a *hamakar* or assistant of Ahura Mazda. The appearance of Mithra and other pre-Zoroastrian deities in Zoroastrianism would seem to be an incorporation of popular and older pagan deities into the ontology as lesser spirits – specifically archangels and angels, or Izeds.

Bulls were sacrificed to Mitra to seal covenants and pacts between nations. He is thus known as 'the god of the contract'. He is the protector of truth and the enemy of lies. According to Zoroastrian legend, Ahura Mazda created Mitra to assist him in the endless battle with his evil brother, the Lord of Darkness, Angira Mainyu. Mithra is said to have brought forth the sun and the moon from his light and heat. In some versions of the legend, he also brought forth the female principle as Anahita, the goddess of the waters. Anahita is sometimes equated with Venus/Inanna/Ishtar. In other versions of his birth, Mithra is the son of Anahita, who like Aditi is the 'Mother of Worlds/Gods'. Some forms of Mithra show him as androgynous, where he is called Mithra-Anahita. Mithra-Anahita or Sabazius-Aniatis was a prominent goddess figure in several Anatolian mystery cults. Much like the Sumerian Tiamat, Anahita is the one born of the primal waters, the pool of creation, and from her womb comes the Light Bringer.

Surya is the Brahmanic version of the Hindu sun god. He is the remover of darkness, and the nourisher of mortal life. In the *Vedas*, he is celebrated as the Supreme Soul. Surya sees and makes note of all things from his position in the heavens and is therefore the Lord of Fate.

Mithraism arrived fully developed in Rome with the return of the Roman legions from the Holy Land in the first century BCE. This form of Mithraism seems only somewhat relevant to the pre-Aryan and Aryan/Zoroastrian Mithra. Here, he was the god of warriors and soldiers and only men could join in his mysteries. Women were excluded. Mithras was worshipped as the supreme mediator between God and Man. In the theological doctrine of Mithraism, the movement of the sun from solstice to solstice is symbolic of the movement of the soul through the cosmos – from its unbounded state, to entrapment in the flesh, and rebirth beyond the flesh into an afterlife. These ideas are often considered to be neo-Platonic in origin, but have a great deal of basis in the Egyptian mysteries. The neo-Platonists flourished in Alexandria, where the knowledge of those mysteries was well known.

One thing that most of these solar deities have in common is that they represent 'truth and justice' as well as 'the law'. The most apparent reason for this is that the sun is quite predictable in its movement, establishing a rhythm of life and a 'law' of the cosmos as it turns round the sky. The 366 books that were supposed to have been written by Enoch were books of laws. The light of the sun bares all falsehoods and glamours; strips away the shadows and the darkness. From its lofty position in the heavens, it is easy to see where the sun might be considered 'visiting' the throne of God or ascending into heaven to the Throne. Symbolically speaking, as the brightest object in the heavens, the sun is the 'lesser face of God' – a magnificent simulacrum that nevertheless fails to convey the actual glorious (and blinding) brilliance of the true limitless Light of the Supreme God – Ain. Without the sun to warm our planet, nothing would grow. There would be no life as we know it. The Earth would be just another lump of ice coursing through the heavens. The sun regulates our actions each day, and nourishes life. The Latin caption beneath the sigil of Metatron must be read in this regard - *"Behold His face and form by Whom all things were made, and Whom all creatures obey."*

The sun reigns supreme in the sky, blotting out all the other stars that are still there. Yet the sun is another star – from the vantage of man, the greatest star in the heavens. The writer of Enoch equates angels and stars in this passage from Chapter 18:

> *13 I saw there seven stars like great burning mountains, 14 and to me, when I inquired regarding them, The angel said: 'This place is the end of heaven and earth: this has become a prison for the stars and the host of heaven. And the stars which roll over the fire are they which have transgressed the commandment of the Lord in the beginning of 16 their rising, because they did not come forth at their appointed times. And He was wroth with them, and bound them till the time when their guilt should be consummated (even) for ten thousand years.'*

One interpretation of the *Sefer Yetzirah* says:

> *In answering these questions, the commentaries note that the angels are like souls to the stars. …There is therefore a one-to-one relationship between the stars and angels. Each star*

> has its own particular angel, and each angel has its own star. (Kaplan, pg.172- 173).

In this light, it is easy to understand how Enoch-Metatron might be called the 'king of the angels'.

If you are still not convinced that Enoch-Metatron may have derived from a syncretism of the sun gods of earlier Mesopotamian cultures and the Indo-Persian solar deities, there is more. Like Mithras as a mediator, Enoch functions as a mediator between the fallen Watchers and God. As Metatron has a twin in the angel Sandalphon, the solar deities named above also have a twin or a counter-part in either a goddess or god representing Venus or the moon. In Ginzberg's *The Legends of the Jews*, Enoch is taken up into heaven by a "fiery chariot drawn by fiery chargers". Rabbi Eleazar credits the invention of astronomy and arithmetic to Enoch. The sun is the 'ruler' of the skies in more ways than one. It marks the hours of the days, the turning of the seasons, the precession of the zodiac and the length of the solar year.

A HISTORY OF THE BOOKS OF ENOCH

The *Books of Enoch* consist of five major sections:
   The Book of Watchers (1 Enoch 1 - 36) – mid 2nd century BCE
   The Book of Parables (1 Enoch 37 - 71) – 1st century CE
   The Book of Luminaries (1 Enoch 72 - 82) – 3rd century BCE
   The Dreams of Enoch (1 Enoch 83 - 90) – 2nd century BCE
   The Epistle of Enoch (1 Enoch 91 - 108) – early 2nd century BCE

Many scholars consider these sections to have once been independent works that were only later compiled into what we now know as the *Books of Enoch*. This line of thinking is of course refuted by others, who maintain that there is a consistent 'literary integrity' amongst the various segments. This latter view completely ignores the writing style of the *Book of Parables* (a.k.a. the *Book of Similitudes*), which purports to contain some fragment of the Book of Noah at Chapter 60. Here God is consistently referred to as the "Lord of Spirits", which is the translation of the name of the Sumero-Babylonian god Ellil or Enlil – *el* or *en* meaning 'lord' and *lil* meaning 'spirits'. This epithet of God is not used in any other portion of the books.

What was thought to be the *Book of the Prophesies of Enoch* arrived in Europe in the second half of the 17th century. The man who received it from Ethiopia was Nicholas Claude Fabri (1580-1637), the Seigneur of Peiresc in Aix en Provençe. Peiresc maintained correspondence with friends and officials in Ethiopia, as he was keenly interested in their history, religion and customs. He'd heard of the phenomenal exploits of a man called Vermillius of Montpellier there. Vermillius was a jeweler, who had become a soldier. He won a great battle for the King of Ethiopia and the King made him the Commander-in-Chief of his army. Vermillius then wrote to some friends in Marseilles and asked them to send him some books from Europe to assist in developing his strategies. Peiresc heard of this request and knew that Vermillius' friends would not go to the trouble. So, he took it upon himself to send Vermillius a large number of mathematical books, and books concerning military and civil architecture. After this, Peiresc felt comfortable in asking Vermillius to send him some books from Ethiopia. Little was known about this land in Europe at the time. There is no proof that Vermillius complied with Peiresc's request, but it is probable that he did.

Some time around 1633, a Capuchin monk named Gilles de Loches went to Aix to visit Peiresc, who was his patron. The monk had been traveling in Egypt for seven years and had visited many of the libraries and monasteries there. He confided in Peiresc that he'd found a manuscript entitled *Mazhafahat Einok (the Book of the Prophecy of Enoch)*, which contained an account of everything which would happen up to the end of the world. De Loches told Peiresc that this lost book was written in Ethiopic script and that it was preserved in its integrity in Ethiopia.

Peiresc then determined that he was going to get a copy of this book come what may – no matter the expense. It is certain that Peiresc must have then written to his friend Vermillius and requested that he send him a copy of this incredible find. Sometime between 1633 and 1637 Peiresc did receive a book from Ethiopia – presumably from Vermillius.

Word of this spectacular find spread throughout Europe. The great Ethiopian scholar Hiob (Job) Ludolf was anxious to see the manuscript. He spared no expense to obtain copies of the manuscript from Peiresc. Ludolf traveled from Frankfort to Aix only to find that Peiresc was dead and his famous library had been purchased by Cardinal Mazarin. Mazarin removed the library to Paris. Ludolf went to Paris in 1683 to look at the manuscript in the Cardinal's library and found it had been transferred to the Bibliotheca Regia. It was there that he finally got his hands on it.

Upon examining the text, Ludolf found that what he was reading had been written by someone named Bakhayla Mîikâ'êl, also known as Zôsîmâs. Much of what he saw there was identical to what the scholar Joseph Scaliger had found in the book of George Syncellus. The book of Syncellus was also called the *Book of Enoch*. Scholars have chalked it up to scribal error that both of these books were so named. The book contained similar stories as written in *Enoch*, and a chapter about Enoch's birth, but it was not the lost *Book of Enoch*. Deeply disappointed, Ludolf pronounced what he'd read as "a collection of foolish fables and silly stories which were so absurd that he could hardly bear to read them. What he had in-hand was a book called *The Book of the Mysteries of the Heavens and Earth*.

Nothing is known about the author of this book, Bakhayla Mîikâ'êl. E. A. Wallis Budge, who compiled these works and translated them for publication, is of the opinion that Bakhayla Mîikâ'êl lived and wrote in the 15th century, but that parts of the book may be older. Bakhayla Mîikâ'êl states that what is written in this book was revealed to him by Gabriel. It reads rather like a *mishnah* of many events and ideas presented in both the Old and New Testaments of the Bible. While it is *not* the *Book of Enoch*, it provides an interesting insight into the Ethiopian mind and religion.

The influences on Ethiopian religious literature, architecture and art were Jewish, Alexandrian and Syrian. Jewish apocryphal works such as *Jubilees*, *Enoch*, and *Baruch* are found in the canonical Ethiopic Old Testament. We also find Alexandrian patristic texts as part of their literature. One of the most important Ethiopic texts, the *Didascalia*, derives from early Syrian theological works. Their literary tradition was not confined, however, to re-working imported texts. There is a considerable body of legendary histories, the lives of saints and apocalyptic works. Their ideas about angels are clearly borrowed from the Jewish tradition. The Ethiopian religion is a curious blend of Judaism and Christianity.

Enoch seems to have been adopted by the Ethiopian Church as their great patriarch to replace Moses as the spokesman for their own brand of faith. The chapters that concern the Watchers in *The Book of the Mysteries of the Heavens and Earth* are quite prosaic and even a little naïve when compared to what is said of the Watchers in both *Enoch* and *Jubilees*, which were written in a far earlier and distant time.

The famous explorer James Bruce spent six years in Abbysinia (Ethiopia) searching for the source of the Blue Nile and somewhere in the process came upon copies of the lost Book of Enoch. He returned in 1773 with three Ethiopic copies of the book. In 1821 Richard Laurence published the first English translation. The famous R.H. Charles edition was published in 1912. In the following years several portions of the Greek text surfaced in Italy and Greece.

In 1947 a young Bedouin shepherd boy searching for a lost goat came upon a cave containing seven scrolls. This was Cave 1. As the years passed, eleven caves in all were discovered – primarily between 1951 and 1956 - all containing fragments of scrolls secreted away in earthenware jars. Seven fragmentary copies of the Aramaic text of the *Books of Enoch* were discovered in Cave 4. Cave 4 was a treasure trove of material containing 15,000 fragments from approximately six hundred composite texts. The remnants of a settlement were also found in this area, a settlement known today as Khirbit Qumran – the Ruin of Qumran. The scrolls found at Qumran are thought to be the remains of the library of the Essenes, a Jewish sect mentioned by such scholars as Josephus, Philo of Alexandria and Pliny the Elder. Archeological evidence indicates that Qumran was founded in the second half of the second century B.C.E., during the time of the Maccabean dynasty.

The *Books of Enoch* are what is known as pseudepigraphical texts. What does this word mean?

> *Pseudepigraphia: 1. Spurious writings; specifically writings falsely attributed to Biblical characters or times. 2. A body of Jewish religious texts written between 200 BC and 200 AD and spuriously ascribed to various prophets, patriarchs and kings of Hebrew literature.*

The bulk of the scrolls found in the area of Qumran were written on the skins of various animals (i.e. parchment) with carbon-based ink. A few scrolls were written on papyrus. Parchment is known to be more durable than papyrus, and so was more commonly used. One scroll was 'written' on a sheet of copper. They were written from right to left in the traditional Hebrew manner, with no punctuation other than an occasional indentation for a paragraph. There were no periods, commas, quotation marks or question marks. In some cases, there are not even spaces between the words – thus translating them has been a difficult process and one fraught with inconsistencies that have only been rectified by finding other copies of the same document. The scrolls are written in several languages, primarily Hebrew and Aramaic, and half a dozen different scripts. Some scrolls were written in crypto-scripts, meant to be read by only certain people who knew the code. It is now thought that the scrolls were not written at Qumran, but that the site acted as a repository for them.

The fragments found at Qumran contained at least one copy of every book of the Jewish Bible (Old Testament), with the exception of the *Book of Esther*. Other scrolls contain 'interpretations' or 'renditions' of these books, which vary greatly from how we know them today. There were two decidedly different texts of the *Book of Jeremiah* – one about 15 percent shorter than the 'traditional' one we see in the Bible, and with the contents in a different order. Several versions of *Psalms* were found, all differing from one another. There were also scrolls found that contained a sort of 'anthology' of several books of the Bible and 're-written Bible'. The *Book of Jubilees*, the *Book of Giants*, the *Book of the Patriarchs* and the *Books of Enoch* were all found amongst the *Dead Sea Scrolls*. These were most likely written within the same span of time...that is from around 165 BCE to about 70 CE, from the Seleucid (Greek) occupation of the Holy Land, to when Jerusalem and the surrounding country fell to the Romans. A scroll titled *The Healing of King Nabonidus* was also found at Qumran, which may have been a source of inspiration for the writer of the *Book of Daniel*, which is thought to have been written around the same period as the *Book of the Watchers*. The story in this scroll is a more primitive version of the story of Nebucchadneezer found in *Daniel* 4. The *Book of the Watchers* is generally thought to have been written between 165 and 150 BCE.

This sect called themselves 'the Yahad' in the scrolls that pertained to their community. This is translated to mean 'unity'. The debate as to just who were these people rages on today. Theories abound and are often debunked as new evidence comes to light with each new translation or new discovery. Some scholars think that they were a group of Hasidim or traditional Hebrews trying desperately to uphold and live the Laws of Moses, which were being eroded and corrupted by the rule and influx of both the Greeks and the Romans. Still others believe that they were Gnostic Hebrews, whose belief system was a syncretism of both traditional Mosaic Judaism and the ideas learned from the Egyptian Jews in Alexandria – whose influences included the belief systems of the Egyptians, the Persians, the Zoroastrians, the Vedics, the Buddhists, and the Medes, as well as the Greek philosophers and mystery schools. Certainly, they were separatists whose mode of life included strict adherence to their faith and beliefs. The fact that the *Books of Enoch* are considered a part of the Ethiopic canon of holy books would give credence to the later idea – that they were a sect of Gnostic Hebrews. So would the fact that they believed in angels, and even considered themselves as angels – the Sons of Light, as seen in the famous *War Scroll*. Still others believe them to have been a group of Christian Jews. More likely than this is that they were Messianic-Jews. There is a difference between the two. Other scholars believe that the references to the "Son of Man" were a gloss, added later by Christian copiests. Possibly, it is something else entirely. As the revelations to be found in Enoch unfold, we might come to a bit different idea of their identity that is nonetheless inclusive of many of these possibilities.

Whoever they were, it is important when reading the *Books of Enoch* to understand the intricate inter-weavings of the religio-socio-political climate of the times in which these verses were written. With that in mind, let us proceed to investigate the circumstances that led up to one of the most profoundly troubled periods in Jewish history.

A BRIEF HISTORY OF THE TIMES

Much of the material contained in the *Books of Enoch* appears to refer to the socio-religio-political climate current at the time of the Maccabean revolt against the Seleucid Greeks who, along with the Ptolemies, had 'inherited' portions of the Holy Land from the reign of Alexander the Great. The Ptolemies controlled Palestine from their seat in Egypt from approximately 323 to 198 BCE. Ptolemy I, Sotor relocated many Jews to Egypt and Alexandria became an important and influential Jewish cultural center. Greek became their new 'native language'. He annexed Cyrenaica, Syria and Phoenicia to improve his access to the Mediterranean and defend himself against his rivals Antigonus and Seleucus. Jewish writers and scholars flourished in Alexandria, most all of them anxious to persuade their fellow Jews and the gentiles alike that the Jewish traditions fit in well with those of the people by whom they were ruled. Jewish scholars were highly influenced by the philosophies of the neo-Platonists, the Hermeticists, Greek mystery cults, Magian knowledge, and the teachings of the Far East. The latter had come to Alexandria via the Silk Road and maritime commerce from all over the known world. It is important to keep this fact in mind for later.

The Jewish scriptures were translated into Greek during the reign of Ptolemy II, Philadelphus and became known as *The Septuagint*. In 280 BCE General Seleucus I, Nicator was murdered and his son Antiochus I, Sotor took over his empire, which at the time included Syria and Babylonia. Antiochus I and his son Antiochus II, Theos fought more or less continuously with Philadelphus, attempting to wrest control of Palestine from Ptolemaic reign. After nearly thirty years of war, a peace agreement was reached between the house of Ptolemy II and the house of Antiochus II, wherein Philadelphus offered the hand of his daughter Berenice in marriage to Antiochus II, thus joining the two houses.

Antiochus II and Ptolemy II died about the same time. The half-sister and wife of Antiochus II, Laodice, had other ideas about the son of Berenice ascending the throne after her husband. Laodice wanted her son to assume the throne after the death of Antiochus II and slew Berenice and her son. Philadelphus was succeeded by his son, Ptolemy III, Euergetes I. This enraged the Ptolemies and the Laodicean Wars broke out, wherein the Ptolemies took control of a large part of the Seleucid empire, including Syria. However problems in Egypt called Euergetes back from the battlefield. Seleucus II used this to his advantage, taking back many of his lost territories, but he failed to re-take Palestine. Euergetes and Seleucus II came to an accord of peace in 240 BCE.

Seleucus II, Callinicus was succeeded by his son Seleucus III, who only reigned for three years before being poisoned. He was succeeded by his younger brother, Antiochus III, Megas (the Great).

In 221, Euergetes died and was succeeded by his son Ptolemy IV, Philopater. Philopater hated the Jews and wanted them gone from Egypt. He systematically began persecuting them with the thought of driving them from his seat of power. He hated them and their God so much, he even tried to force his way into the Holy of Holies in the Second Temple and defile it.

Ptolemy V, Epiphanes was the last of the Ptolemies to rule over Palestine. In 198 BCE, Antiochus III wrested Palestine from the Ptolemies in the Battle of Panion in the Jordan Valley. The Seleucids 'officially' held control of Palestine until the coming of the Romans in 63 BCE, however their hold on the region was never stable. The Jews were happy with this turn of events, seeing it as an end to the long and bitter struggle between the two empires. Little did they realize that in the end the Seleucid kings would be their worst nightmare realized.

Things began well enough, with Antiochus III granting the Jews the freedom to live in accordance with traditional Mosaic Jewish law. However, there were other Jews who sought to promote Hellenistic culture amongst their brethren, seeing it as far superior to their own. In *I Maccabees*, these men are portrayed as "lawless men who misled many".

Hannibal Barca, the great military commander of Carthage had the grand dream of conquering Rome. He was defeated by the Romans at the Battle of Zama. His defeat forced the Carthaginian Senate to send him into exile. He sought refuge in the court of Antiochus III, where he functioned as a military advisor in Antiochus' own battle against Rome. The Romans defeated Antiochus III in 190 BCE, forcing him to pay enormous amounts of tribute. They also took his navy and war elephants. To ensure that Antiochus III continued to make his payments to the Empire, they demanded that he surrender his son, Antiochus IV to them. Antiochus IV lived as a hostage in Rome for twelve years and returned later as Antiochus IV Epiphanes.

A few years after his defeat by the Romans, Antiochus III died. He was succeeded by Seleucus IV, Philopater who was still under orders to pay fantastic amounts of tribute to Rome. He taxed the people of Palestine heavily to this end, creating enemies and dissention amongst the population. Some Jews felt it was their duty to give money to the king. These were led by the High Priest of the Temple at the time, Onias. Other Jews felt that it was sinful and improper to give money to the government. Their side was taken by Jason, the brother of Onias, who wanted nothing more than to be the High Priest of the Temple himself. With this in mind, he took on the cause of the

Jews who opposed the heavy taxation, seeking to further his own nefarious agendas.

Jason met with little success in his efforts until the return of Antiochus IV Epiphanes and death of Seleucus IV – reportedly murdered by Epiphanes himself, or one of his henchmen. Jason obtained the position of High Priest from Epiphanes by promising him a total of 440 talents of silver for the position. Jason promises to pay another 150 talents if he is allowed to set up a gymnasium and a training place for the youth...

> ...to enrol the people of Jerusalem as citizens of Antioch. When the king had consented, and he had taken office, he immediately brought his countrymen over to the Greek way of living. He set aside royal ordinances especially favoring the Jews, secured through John, the father of Eupolemus, who went on the mission to the Romans to establish friendly relations and an alliance with them, and abrogating the lawful ways of living he introduced new customs contrary to the Law. (II Macc. 4:9-12)

Jason understood that the gymnasium and its games were nothing more than a thinly veiled training-ground for soldiers. Being a hero of the games guaranteed a young man - who might have otherwise been just another farmer, craftsman or merchant - a higher ranking in the army of the king. During the time of Epiphanes, the countryside of Judah was populated by garrisons of soldiers, which developed into towns. Presumably, they ate fairly well in the service and name of the king, putting a strain on the resources of the region.

The text goes on to say how the Jews became quite Hellenized, adopting Greek fashion and customs; they preferred to engage in athletic contests, rather than study the ways of their fathers; the priests were no longer earnest about the services and neglected the sacrifices...

> As a result, they found themselves in a trying situation, for those whose mode of life they cultivated, and whom they wished to imitate exactly, became their enemies and punished them. (II Macc. 4:16)

This is only the beginning of a period of dastardly deeds: larceny, betrayal, the darkest religio-political intrigues, desecration, revolution and rampant carnage.

Thoroughly Romanized himself by his captors, Epiphanes would forge the disastrous link between the previous empires of the Ptolemies (Egyptian influence) and Seleucids (Greek/Macedonian influence), and the coming of the Romans.

Three years after installing Jason as the High Priest, Epiphanes is bribed with even more money by Menelaus for the position. Epiphanes ousts Jason and installs Menelaus as the High Priest. The Jews who still held to the Mosaic Law and tradition were enraged by this action – to think that the office of High Priest could be bought and sold in such a manner. They banded together, speaking out against the actions of Epiphanes, dubbing him "Epimanes" – the Madman. These were the early Hasidim, and it is from them that the Hasidic Jews of today trace their origins.

In 169 BCE, Antiochus IV sets out to fulfill his dream of conquering Egypt and ending the dynastic reign of the Ptolemies for good. Reports come back from the front that the king has been killed in battle. Upon receiving this news, Jason returns from his exile and takes back the office of High Priest from Menelaus. However, the news of Epiphanes' death is false. Epiphanes returns from his campaign to Jerusalem, forcibly ousting Jason from the Temple and reinstalling Menelaus as the High Priest. At the same time, Epiphanes helps himself to the treasury there, gathering more wealth to further his campaign to take over Egypt.

In the following year, Epiphanes returns to Egypt, but he is stopped in his tracks by the Roman representative (his former captors and sponsors) Popilius Laenus and told to take himself back home and mind his own empire. He is told never to return to Egypt again. Clearly, the Romans had their own ideas about who would rule the great land of Egypt. The long trip home provides plenty of time for the deep wound to Epiphanes' pride and ambition to fester into something truly mad. Upon his return to Jerusalem, he takes out his wrath and frustration upon the Jews. He begins by tearing down the city walls and slaughtering Jews at will. He orders all Jewish scriptures to be confiscated and consigned to the flames. Given this fact alone, it is entirely understandable why a repository such as the one at Qumran may have been created. Any Jew caught in possession of such works is summarily put to the sword, as well as any Jew caught observing the Sabbath or any other Jewish holy day. He forbids the practice of circumcision. Any Jewish mother found with a circumcised baby boy is put to death, along with her child. The child was then hung around the dead mother's neck. He and his soldiers take prostitutes into the Temple and there have sex with them in the Holy of Holies, defiling the Temple. While this may have seemed standard operating procedure for a Greek, it was horrifying to the Jews. He then sacks the Temple of its treasures again and erects an altar to Olympian-Zeus. On the Altar of Sacrifice, he slaughters a pig to his god. These actions are what has come to be known as the 'Abomination of Desecration' – and what is perhaps the darkest hour *to that point in time* in Jewish history.

In 167 BCE, Epiphanes sends some of his officers to the small village of Modin, which lies some 17 miles to the northwest of Jerusalem.

According to the apocryphal texts of the *Books of the Maccabees*, they were to force the Jews living there to offer up sacrifices to the pagan gods. The elder of the village, one Mattithias – a priest of the one God – was made and example and ordered to offer the first sacrifice. However Mattithias refuses to be bullied into this further desecration. Another Jew steps forward to perform the deed, fearing reprisals against the village if the demands of the king's officers were not met. Zealously, Mattithias kills this man as well as the officers of the king. He then proceeds to tear down the pagan altar and declares:

> *Let everyone who is zealous for the Law and who stands by the covenant follow me! (I Macc. 2:27)*

Thus began the Maccabean revolt, for Mattithias was none other than the patriarch of the Hasmonean family. His sons were Judas, Eleazar, Jonathan and Simon. Between this and the Abomination of Desecration, the Jews had all they could take.

The Hasmoneans were also known as the Maccabeans, which means 'the Hammerers'. These men organized themselves and their sympathizers into a powerful army using guerilla-warfare tactics. Quite familiar with the lands and hills surrounding Jerusalem, they wasted no time launching raids against the towns and villages of the land, tearing down pagan altars, and killing the officials of the king. They also executed those Jews they found worshipping the pagan gods. Jew had turned against Jew, because of the influence of Antiochus Epiphanes and his Hellenized and Romanized minions and supporters.

The revolt was long and bloody and the land was torn apart. Brother fought against brother and families were divided. Eventually, the Hasmoneans took control of Judah and the Temple, establishing themselves as kings and hereditary priests. But the division did not end there. There were still those who refuted the right of the Hasmoneans to hold the office of High Priest, for they were not Cohanim, nor Levites, nor Zadokites – the traditional holders of this office. There were still Jews who remained sympathetic to the Greeks and the slow influx of the Romans, in spite of what had befallen their land. There came to be several factions of Jews during this time. Josephus names them as the Pharisees, the Sadducees and the Essenes in his *History of the Jews*, but neglects to mention any others. Josephus was writing at least two hundred years after the fact with regard to the Greek domination of the Holy Land, using what information was available to him at the time. He was, however, an eyewitness to the later Roman occupation.

Judaism in the last centuries of BCE and the first few centuries of the Common Era was by no means a solidified religious belief system. If nothing else has become evident from the contents of the Qumran scrolls, it is this. The influences of the syncretized Greco-Egyptian gods; the neo-Platonists of Alexandria; the Persians, the Babylonians, the native Philistines, Canaanites and Ammorites, the Phoenicians, and the mysterious Gnostics were all part of the disastrous brew that was compromised yet again in the dawning of the Common Era by the equally fractured and eclectic cult calling themselves Christians.

THE AUTHORS OF ENOCH

The *Books of Enoch* are considered to be 'gnostic' literature by many scholars. The fact that the fallen Watchers teach the daughters of man and others the 'worthless secrets of heaven' attests to this idea. The philosophy of the Hermeticists of Alexandria, such as Porphyry and Plotinus, was that all forms of the knowledge of God's creation – such as mathematics, astronomy, geomancy, etc. – were highly overestimated by the traditional philosophers. The only knowledge worthy of human intellectual investigation was knowledge of the Divine; and even more truly useful, the knowledge of gaining immortality for one's soul through the realization of one's own divinity.

There has been much speculation amongst scholars as to who wrote the *Books of Enoch* and when they were written. Most are of the opinion that they were written by the scribes of the Yahad, beginning in about 165 - 150 BCE. This is the group that Josephus called the Essenes. As for the etymology of the name 'Essenes', the historian of Gnosticism and heresiologist, Hippolytus called them "The Naaseni who specially call themselves 'Gnostics'. But inasmuch as this deception of theirs is multiform and has many heads (a play upon their name of serpent-followers), like the Hydra of fable, if I smite all the heads at once with the wand of Truth, I shall destroy the whole serpent, for all the other sects differ but little from this one in essentials."

> *"Their strange-sounding title "Naaseni"--"Followers of the Naas" (the only way in which the Greek, from its want of aspirate letters, could write the Hebrew Nachash, "Serpent") was literally rendered by "Ophites," the name which has ever since served to designate them."* (King, 82)

The Yahad was set up as a sectarian organization, as evidenced by the scroll known as the *Community Rule* or *Charter of a Jewish Sectarian Association*. However, this *Community Rule* did not apply solely to the group at Qumran. It applied to all the groups of these people scattered throughout Palestine and Judah.

This sect also refers to themselves often within the scrolls as 'the Sons of Light' – another indication that their beliefs were of a Gnostic nature and that they saw themselves on a par with, if not as angelic and illumined beings. There are no overt indications within the *Books of Enoch*, nor in any of the other texts found so far that the authors are aligned with the Ophites, who are said to have developed in Phrygia in Anatolia. It is possible that later writers, particularly those heresiologists of the early Church, had lumped all Gnostics together under the banner of the Ophites. The Yahad appear instead to be a group of rather orthodox followers of Mosaic law, who were nonetheless Jewish Gnostics with their own set of mysteries. These mysteries were revealed to those who rose up within their hierarchy, in much the same way that the secrets and mysteries of modern day occult lodges, temples and covens reveal their mysteries to those who have risen to higher degrees within the group. But wherefrom did these mysteries originate? Possibly, the idea of mysteries was borrowed from the Ophite and Eleusinian mystery schools. But more likely than not, they originated in Egypt.

This hierarchy system is extremely ancient and most likely began within the Magian schools of Persia. The hierarchical system would seem to be borrowed from the teachings of Zoroaster, with his Kingdoms of Light and Darkness and the Izeds or Yazads (angels) who gathered about the throne of Ahura Mazda, the Lord of Light and the descending orders of lesser angels.

The writings of the Yahad appear to display a significantly Jewish mythology and basis. In the light of diligent study, however, the mythology of the Jews is an unimaginable mish-mash of Sumerian, Egyptian, Canaanite, Assyrian, Babylonian, Persian, Greek and possibly Hindu mythico-religious concepts. Their writings also reflect the despair of a people distressed by the invasion and rule of alien overlords whose persecution of their beliefs and ways has torn their land apart and caused a major rift between the various factions of Jews. However, the Jews were no less violent in their usurpation of the 'promised land' and toward their oppressors in later times.

They are outraged by and condemnatory of the Gentiles and their pagan ways. Yet, the Jews are not without their sins in this matter, as we shall see.

They have been deceived repeatedly by the foreign kings, who offered reconciliation and freedom, then turned upon them yet again, slaying and persecuting them without discrimination. In the stories of the Jews, we see that they too have recourse to deceptive methods to attain their goals. This may be a case of 'fighting fire with fire'.

These works – and especially the *Books of Enoch* – display a distinct influence and reference to the very mythologies and belief systems of their oppressors. This is not without precedent, for what little information we now possess about the Gnostics is contained within the writings of the heresiologists and early Church Fathers who were condemning the Gnostics.

> *"Because these stories involve sociopolitical satire laced with religious polemic, some historians have recently asked to what specific historical situations they refer. Are Jews who thus embellish the story of angels that mate with human beings covertly ridiculing the pretensions of their Hellenistic rulers? George Nickelsburg points out that from the time of Alexander the Great, Greek kings had claimed to be*

> descended from gods as well as from human women; the
> Greeks called such hybrid beings heroes. But their Jewish
> subjects, with their derisive tale of Semihazah, may have
> turned such claims of divine descent against the foreign
> usurpers." (Pagels, 50)

Another indicator of the Gnostic leanings of the authors of the *Books of Enoch* is the phrase that Enoch 'walked with God'. The Hermeticists and the Gnostics believed in the Perfect or Essential Man from whose 'template' all other men were created. This being was called Adamas. The Ophites believed that we had 'fallen' from this Primal Man, who exists as the Logos, into the vessel of the body of clay and become servants of the Demiurge. The created, lesser man was given a soul, that through this soul the image of the Man above might suffer and be chastened in this bondage. The divine spark was contained within this vessel of clay, giving man both a divine nature as well as a bestial one. They considered that all of creation was possessed of a soul but only man - God's supreme creation - was capable of realizing his divine nature through a process of revelation, the experience of God and the heavenly realms, and rebirth (*palingenesia*).

> Rebirth is emphatically not a repetition of physical birth, but a
> bursting into a new plane of existence previously unattained,
> even unsuspected, albeit available potentially. It is, in fact, a
> negation of physical birth, in that our first birth imprisons the
> soul in the body, while our rebirth liberates it. (Fowden, 108)

The experience of rebirth was sought *in life* and thought to confer upon one who had accomplished this passage an immortality of the soul. The body did not die at this point, but lived on until it at last wore out. The divine spark/soul or Nous however, did not die with the body. It was absorbed into the being of the Perfect Man/Logos or even into God in Heaven upon the death of the body – depending upon the belief system quoted. It was believed that once having achieved this rebirth, the perfected man had the ability to remain in contact with the Divine worlds. Upon the death of the body, when the Nous was re-absorbed within the Divine, this soul was no longer subject to rebirth on the physical plane...unless it chose to be reborn. These ideas are seen again in Buddhist, Vedantic and Tantric thinking. Buddhists even have a name for the souls who choose to be reborn and return to earth to help others achieve enlightenment or perfection - *bodhisatva*. Buddhist ideas were very much a part of the curriculum of study in Alexandria and known to the Neo-platonists. The souls perfected in life became the teachers, who led others through this difficult process.

The *Corpus Hermeticum* states:

> Man is a divine being, to be compared not with the other
> earthly beings, but with those who are called gods, up in the

> heavens. Rather, if one must dare to speak the truth, the true Man is above even the gods, or at least fully their equal. After all, none of the celestial gods will leave the heavenly frontiers and descend to earth; yet Man ascends even into the heavens, and measures them, and knows their heights and depths, and everything else about them he learns with exactitude. What is even more remarkable, he establishes himself on high without even leaving the earth, so far does his power extend. We must presume then to say that earthly Man is a mortal god, and that the celestial God is an immortal man. And so it is through these two, the world and Man, that all things exist; but they were all created by the One. (C.H. x)

Enoch accomplishes these very things. He ascends into Heaven, takes the grand tour and is shown all the secrets of the sun, moon and stars. He speaks with God and the angels. In Chapter 93 of Enoch, we read the following:

> *11 [For who is there of all the children of men that is able to hear the voice of the Holy One without being troubled? And who can think His thoughts? and who is there that can behold all the works 12 of heaven? And how should there be one who could behold the heaven, and who is there that could understand the things of heaven and see a soul or a spirit and could tell thereof, or ascend and see 13 all their ends and think them or do like them? And who is there of all men that could know what is the breadth and the length of the earth, and to whom has been shown the measure of all of them? 14 Or is there any one who could discern the length of the heaven and how great is its height, and upon what it is founded, and how great is the number of the stars, and where all the luminaries rest ?]*

We shall no doubt come upon more instances of 'gnostic sensibilities' within the commentaries, but these are sufficient for now to underscore the gnostic nature or 'wisdom ethic' of the *Books of Enoch*.

As for the question of who wrote them, it is still open to debate. Had the Books been written in Alexandria, they would have contained much more Hermetic (i.e., syncretic Greco-Egyptian), Magian and Greco-Roman references than they do. Yet, they do contain many elements of gnostic beliefs that indicate they were written by a distinctly Jewish group of gnostics living amongst these influences. Up until the time of the rule of Antiochus Epiphanes IV, the nation of Judah and the Jews themselves had not experienced such dire and bitter circumstances that are laid out within the story. As troubled and harsh as was their history up to that point, these were their darkest days. Had the books been written during the Babylonian captivity or by a member of the Great Assembly, they would have had a more condemnatory and ecclesiastical flavor, and most likely been ascribed to a prophet and not a patriarch.

THE BOOK OF THE WATCHERS

Chapters 1-5

The following is a commentary on the verses of the *Book of the Watchers*, as well as notations on similar verses in the Bible, and other myths, apocryphal or pseudepigraphical works. The version of Enoch seen here is the translation by Rev. R.H. Charles.

What is contained in this commentary are only the chapters of the *Book of the Watchers* and following that, only those that are applicable to the Watchers and the Nephilim.

[Chapter 1] 1 The words of the blessing of Enoch, wherewith he blessed the elect and righteous, who will be 2 living in the day of tribulation, when all the wicked and godless are to be removed. And he took up his parable and said - Enoch a righteous man, whose eyes were opened by God, saw the vision of the Holy One in the heavens, which the angels showed me, and from them I heard everything, and from them I understood as I saw, but not for this generation, but for a remote one which is 3 for to come. Concerning the elect I said, and took up my parable concerning them: The Holy Great One will come forth from His dwelling, 4 And the eternal God will tread upon the earth, (even) on Mount Sinai, [And appear from His camp] And appear in the strength of His might from the heaven of heavens. 5 And all shall be smitten with fear And the Watchers shall quake, And great fear and trembling shall seize them unto the ends of the earth. 6 And the high mountains shall be shaken, And the high hills shall be made low, And shall melt like wax before the flame 7 And the earth shall be wholly rent in sunder, And all that is upon the earth shall perish, And there shall be a judgment upon all (men). 8 But with the righteous He will make peace. And will protect the elect, And mercy shall be upon them. And they shall all belong to God, And they shall be prospered, And they shall all be blessed. And He will help them all, And light shall appear unto them, And He will make peace with them'. 9 And behold! He cometh with ten thousands of His holy ones To execute judgment upon all, And to destroy all the ungodly: And to convict all flesh Of all the works of their ungodliness which they have ungodly committed, And of all the hard things which ungodly sinners have spoken against Him.

The *Book of Enoch* is referenced in the *Epistle of Jude*, which was written some time between 65 and 75 CE. The quote from *Jude* 1:14-15 is quite similar to verse 9:

> *And Enoch also, the seventh from Adam, prophesied of these [men], saying, Behold, the Lord cometh with ten thousands of*

> his saints, To execute judgment upon all, and to convince all that are ungodly among them of all their ungodly deeds which they have ungodly committed, and of all their hard speeches which ungodly sinners have spoken against him.

The writer here and in other chapters is chastising the 'ungodly' who have spoken out against the Holy Great One. He prophesies the coming of God to punish those who have turned against Him and make peace with those who still hold to the Covenant. This would seem to give credence to the idea that at least this portion of Enoch was written during the time of Antiochus Epiphanes IV, when Judah was in great turmoil and the entire fabric of the Jewish way of life and beliefs were rapidly coming unraveled.

This is also the first mention of the Watchers.

[Chapter 2] 1 Observe ye everything that takes place in the heaven, how they do not change their orbits, and the luminaries which are in the heaven, how they all rise and set in order each in its season, and 2 transgress not against their appointed order. Behold ye the earth, and give heed to the things which take place upon it from first to last, how steadfast they are, how none of the things upon earth 3 change, but all the works of God appear to you. Behold the summer and the winter, how the whole earth is filled with water, and clouds and dew and rain lie upon it.

In this chapter, the writer notes the order of the heavens. He points out the rising of the constellations and planets 'each in its season', and that they do not transgress against their appointed order. The seasons also play a part in this cosmic order, as he describes the summer and winter as 'works of God'. This chapter and the chapters to follow are strongly reminiscent of sentiment expressed in *Ecclesiastes 3:1*:

> *To every thing there is a season, and a time to every purpose under the heaven.*

[Chapter 3] Observe and see how (in the winter) all the trees seem as though they had withered and shed all their leaves, except fourteen trees, which do not lose their foliage but retain the old foliage from two to three years till the new comes.

Again, we are prompted to behold the orderliness of the seasons.

[Chapter 4] And again, observe ye the days of summer how the sun is above the earth over against it. And you seek shade and shelter by reason of the heat of the sun, and the earth also

burns with growing heat, and so you cannot tread on the earth, or on a rock by reason of its heat.

This chapter speaks for itself.

[Chapter 5] 1 Observe ye how the trees cover themselves with green leaves and   bear fruit: wherefore give ye heed and know with regard to all His works, and recognize how He that liveth for ever hath made them so. 2 And all His works go on thus from year to year for ever, and all the tasks which they accomplish for Him, and their tasks change not, but according as God hath ordained so is it done. 3 And behold how the sea and the rivers in like manner accomplish and change not their tasks from His commandments'. 4 But ye - ye have not been steadfast, nor done the commandments of the Lord, But ye have turned away and spoken proud and hard words With your impure mouths against His greatness. Oh, ye hard-hearted, ye shall find no peace. 5 Therefore shall ye execrate your days, And the years of your life shall perish, And the years of your destruction shall be multiplied in eternal execration, And ye shall find no mercy. 6a In those days ye shall make your names an eternal execration unto all the righteous, b And by you shall all who curse, curse, And all the sinners and godless shall imprecate by you, 7c And for you the godless there shall be a curse. 6d And all the . . . shall rejoice, 6e And there shall be forgiveness of sins, 6f And every mercy and peace and forbearance: 6g There shall be salvation unto them, a goodly light. 6i And for all of you sinners there shall be no salvation, 6j But on you all shall abide a curse. 7a But for the elect there shall be light and joy and peace, b And they shall inherit the earth. 8 And then there shall be bestowed upon the elect wisdom, And they shall all live and never again sin, Either through ungodliness or through pride: But they who are wise shall be humble. 9 And they shall not again transgress, Nor shall they sin all the days of their life, Nor shall they die of (the divine) anger or wrath, But they shall complete the number of the days of their life. And their lives shall be increased in peace, And the years of their joy shall be multiplied, In eternal gladness and peace, All the days of their life.

Here, the author contrasts the steadfastness of the earth and the 'works of God' seemingly with those who have not remained true to the Mosaic Laws and the Covenant established between YHWH and Moses – i.e., what was wished to be considered 'true' Judaism. These Hebrews considered nature as God's handiwork – the antithesis of the mythopoeic religions of the Sumerians, Akkadians, Babylonians, Egyptians, Canaanites, Greeks and Romans who anthropomorphized aspects of nature into gods and goddesses.

Chapter 6

[Chapter 6] 1 And it came to pass when the children of men had multiplied that in those days were born unto 2 them beautiful and comely daughters.

This is undoubtedly the most often quoted verse of Enoch. It is also seemingly a precursor or a take-off on *Genesis 6*, which reads:

> *And it came to pass, when men began to multiply on the face of the earth, and daughters were born unto them 2 That the sons of God saw the daughters of men that they were fair; and they took them wives of all which they chose.*

Although the first five books of the Old Testament were said to be written by Moses, the *Book of Jubilees* would seem to indicate that these books and others of the Old Testament were going through a period of refinement and even being re-written. *Jubilees* does not begin with the words "In the beginning..." as does the canonical *Genesis*, describing God's creation of the angels, heavens, earth, animals, fish, birds and man – but begins with a description of how Moses led the Israelites out of Egypt. One might be tempted to then say, "*Jubilees* is merely a precursor to *Exodus*". However, the Creation is then described in Chapter 2 of *Jubilees*. Some scholars have suggested that it was a sort of rough draft of what later became the version of *Genesis* accepted by the Church and the Temple. There are many such fragments found in the Qumran scrolls that fall into this category of 're-written Bible'. *Jubilees* actually contains a much more detailed account of creation, as well as the genealogy of the patriarchs. Most biblical scholars are of the opinion that *Jubilees* was written by a Pharisee some time between the year that John Hyrcanus became the high priest in 135 BCE and 105 BCE when Hyrcanus died. Some years before his death, Hyrcanus purportedly had a falling out with the Pharisees. John Hyrcanus was of the Hasmonean line.

However, we know that some form of the *Torah* did exist before *Jubilees* was written, because Antiochus Epiphanes IV ordered that all copies of this document were to be burned, and that anyone caught with a copy of the *Torah* was to be put to the sword. This earlier version of the *Torah* was most likely established during the period of the Great Assembly.

The Great Assembly was also called The Great Synagogue and consisted of 120 post-exilic rabbis. They are considered the link between the Prophets and Rabbinical Judaism. It is believed that three of their number – Haggai, Zechariah and Malachi received the *Torah* from the Prophets. These Prophets were presumably Daniel and Jeremiah. They in turn passed on this knowledge to the others of the Great Assembly, led by Ezra and Nehemiah. This Great Assembly is thought to have begun in the early years of the Second Temple which was completed in about 515 BCE. The last survivor of the Great Synagogue, Simeon the Just, was said to have met Alexander the Great, in about 330 BCE.

The fact that the *Torah* is being re-written – as seen in *Jubilees* - in these later times by a Pharisee only solidifies the idea that Judaism was going through a period of splinter groups, upheaval and modification. A fact that was surely distressing to those struggling to maintain or even codify the 'old ways'.

And the angels, the children of the heaven, saw and lusted after them, and said to one another: 'Come, let us choose us wives from among the children of men 3 and beget us children.'

In the days of Alexander's conquest of the 'world', the Macedonian ruler often left groups of his soldiers behind to marry local women and manage the governments of the conquered lands. Alexander's aim was to Hellenize the world. It was to this end that he did this, by intermingling his soldiers, their language, customs and gods with the native populations. Is it possible that the idea of the angels choosing wives from amongst the 'children of men' springs from this? Recall the earlier reference "that from the time of Alexander the Great, Greek kings had claimed to be descended from gods as well as from human women". Alexander was made pharaoh of Egypt by its inhabitants when he conquered this land, and was declared to be the 'son of Amon' – a son of the high god. Of course, all pharaohs were seen to be divinely born and functioned as a representative of the gods. During the time that the *Books of Enoch* were most likely written, the Hebrews were still very much under the government of their Hellenist conquerors and subject to their whims. The Hellenic soldiers would have taken whatever women they chose, being the conquering forces.

And Semjaza, who was their leader, said unto them: 'I fear ye will not 4 indeed agree to do this deed, and I alone shall have to pay the penalty of a great sin.' And they all answered him and said: 'Let us all swear an oath, and all bind ourselves by mutual imprecations 5 not to abandon this plan but to do this thing.' Then sware they all together and bound themselves 6 by mutual imprecations upon it. And they were in all two hundred; who descended in the days of Jared on the summit of Mount Hermon, and they called it Mount Hermon, because they had sworn 7 and bound themselves by mutual imprecations upon it. And these are the names of their leaders: Samiazaz, their leader, Arakiba, Rameel, Kokabiel, Tamiel, Ramiel, Danel, Ezeqeel, Baraqijal, 8 Asael, Armaros, Batarel, Ananel, Zaqiel, Samsapeel, Satarel, Turel, Jomjael, Sariel. These are their chiefs of tens.

There is a lot going on in the remainder of Chapter 6, but the last line is highly significant and so we shall begin at the end. "These are their chiefs of tens." The phrase "chiefs of tens" or "rulers of tens" appears only in the current version of *Exodus*, Chapter 18, in both verses 21 and 25 (KJV) and is considered a 'military terminology':

> *21 Moreover thou shalt provide out of all the people able men, such as fear God, men of truth, hating covetousness; and place each over them, to be rulers of thousands, and rulers of hundreds, rulers of fifties, and rulers of tens.*
>
> *25 And Moses chose able men out of all Israel, and made them heads over the people, rulers of thousands, rulers of hundreds, rulers of fifties, and rulers of tens.*

However, the phrase "chiefs of tens" has a particular significance to those of the Yahad. This idea appears in one of the *Dead Sea Scrolls* entitled *Charter of a Jewish Sectarian Association*. In this document, as put forth in the rules and regulations of the sect, we are told:

> *By these rules they are to govern themselves wherever they dwell, in accordance with each legal finding that bears upon communal life. Inferiors must obey their ranking superiors as regards work and wealth. They shall eat, pray, and deliberate communally. Wherever ten men belonging to the society of the Yahad are gathered, a priest must always be present....*

Each local chapter of this association contained at least ten men, who were led by a priest called the Instructor. The Instructor was the 'chief of ten'. They ate together and studied what then comprised the Old Testament together under the tutelage of the Instructor. Once a year, a full review of the membership was conducted. At this time, a man's rank within the organization might rise or fall, dependent upon his adherence to the rules of the association and his understanding of the scriptures. That there existed a hierarchy within the Yahad is clear, and that hierarchy was seen as a reflection of the hierarchy of Heaven.

The Jews who did not adhere to the Laws of Moses, along with the Gentiles were considered 'Men of Perversity' or the Children/Sons of Darkness, i.e. demons. This is particularly evident in the famous *War Scroll*, wherein Sariel – one of the fallen 'chiefs of tens' mentioned in Chapter 6 is also seen as the Wing Commander of the Third Tower.

If one adds up the two-hundred plus their chiefs of tens, the result is 220. This is one of many puns contained in the *Books of Enoch*, for the word 'nephilim' adds up to 220 in gematria.

The most well known system of gematria today is Hebrew gematria, but it was originally developed by the Greeks. The letters of the alphabet are assigned numeric values, which remain constant. All words that add up to the same number are said to be relative to one another and this reveals hidden connections and correlations between words, letters and numbers. Each letter of the Hebrew alphabet also has its own symbology and interpretive meanings, as we shall later discover with the names of the Watchers. For more information on Hebrew gematria, see GEMATRIA chapter.

Let us now proceed to the matter of the geographical location of this descent.

And they were in all two hundred; who descended in the days of Jared on the summit of Mount Hermon, and they called it Mount Hermon, because they had sworn 7 and bound themselves by mutual imprecations upon it.

These fallen angels or Watchers/Grigori come down upon Mt. Hermon. Situated at the northern boundary of the Promised Land, Mt. Hermon is the highest point – the ultimate watchtower and the closest geographical location to Heaven in the Anti-Lebanon range at 9230 feet above sea level (2814 m.). It was near here that the battle with the giant kings Og and Sihon of Bashan was said to have taken place in the time of Joshua *(Deut.3:1-10)*.

From this high point, all things descend, including the run-off of the snows that crown Mt. Hermon and provide the waters of the Jordan River and the Dead Sea. The name of the patriarch Jared here serves as a pun on this fact – the word *yar-ad* meaning 'descended, came down', or figuratively 'to fall' *(Strong, 3381)*. Mt. Hermon was called Sirion by the Sidonians and Shenir by the Amorites *(Deut. 3:9)*. In *Deut. 4:48*, it is called Sion. The remains of more than twenty temples, thought to be Hittite, Hivite and/or Canaanite, have also been found on the heights of Mt. Hermon.

The writer of this portion of Enoch indicates that Mt. Hermon was called thus because it was there that the fallen Watchers swore oaths, implying that 'hermon' means 'oath'. By definition, an 'imprecation' is a curse. According to R. H. Charles, Mount Hermon derives its name from the Hebrew word *herem,* a curse. This could be viewed as a commentary that a) any oath sworn in this place is a curse, or that b) these angels cursed themselves by these oaths. One definition of 'hermon' is given as 'anathema' or 'devoted to destruction' (*Hitchcock's Bible Names*). Interestingly the modern Hebrew word 'harmon' means 'harem' – and it is from here that the fallen Watchers gathered unto themselves the wives, all of whom they chose.

In Judges 3:3, Mt. Hermon is referred to as 'mount Baal-hermon'. It is interesting to note that in verses 5 and 6 of *Judges*, we find the following information:

> 5 And the children of Israel dwelt among the Canaanites, Hittites, and Amorites, and Perizzites, and Hivites, and Jebusites:
>
> 6 And they took their daughters to be their wives, and gave their daughters to their sons, and served their gods.

Baal or Ba'al is a title that means 'lord' or 'possessor'. There were many Baals or *ba'alim*, who were 'lords' of certain areas of Canaan – such as Baal-Zephon, Baal-Zebub and Baal-Hermon. The suffix after the Baal name indicated the area in which that Baal presided, i.e., Baal-Hermon was the local *ba'al* at Mt. Hermon. The same was true of Ashteroth. In general usage, the word *ba'al* implied one who was the possessor or master of 'things' or regions, and not men. 'The Baal' was the Baal of Tyre, a god called Melkart, who is often associated with Hercules. Baal is derived from the ancient name of Bel, which was one of the many names of the Babylonian god Marduk. Bel's name, however, implies lordship over men. The supreme god of the peoples named in verses 5 and 6 of Judges was El, who may have derived from the more ancient Sumerian god Enlil or Ellil, whose name means 'Lord of the Spirits'. Baal the thunder, rain and vegetation god was the son of El, as Marduk was the son of Enlil. El was the supreme god of the general Semitic pantheon and has many similarities to Yahweh, the One God of the Hebrews. While there may have been some overlap between El and Yahweh, Yahweh and El are probably *not* the same god. El was often represented as a bull, which was also the sacred animal of Mithraism. Many of the angelic names, including those of the fallen Watchers end in the suffix '-el' to denote that they are 'divine' or 'of god'.

The Hebrew letters *aleph* and *lamed* which spell the name of El have some significance in all of this. The *aleph* is said to represent the union of the higher and lower realities, as represented by the two *yods* which comprise the upper and lower 'arms' of the letter.

א

The *lamed* is the only Hebrew letter to rise above the upper boundary of the line of script, and is thus compared with a watchman in his tower, or a watchtower.

This brings us back to the names of the fallen Watchers listed as the 'chiefs of tens' in Chapter 6:

And these are the names of their leaders: Samiazaz, their leader, Arakiba, Rameel, Kokabiel, Tamiel, Ramiel, Danel,

Ezeqeel, Baraqijal, 8 Asael, Armaros, Batarel, Ananel, Zaqiel, Samsapeel, Satarel, Turel, Jomjael, Sariel.

We are told in verse 6 of Chapter 6 that there were two hundred angels who came down to Mount Hermon at the behest of Shemyaza...yet, if you count the named 'chiefs of tens' there are only 19 chiefs named. One of the chiefs is missing. This may or may not be because the twentieth chief is named later on in Chapter 8.

> *The names of the leading angels are mentioned, which appear to be of Hebrew origin, but corrupted by Greek pronunciation. (King, 19)*

King may or may not be correct in his assertion regarding the names of these angels – that they are corrupted by Greek pronunciation. This may be so – particularly in light of the fact that the writers of Enoch are generally thought to be wholly Judaic, but very much aware of Greek culture and mythology, as well as the other cultures and mythologies that surrounded them. It is entirely possible, that the writers of Enoch were striving to impart a generous flavor of Hellenic spice to the names of the Watchers, in light of what is written previously.

It is important to note that the names of these chiefs of tens change – sometimes subtly and sometimes not so subtly throughout the narrative. Some appear to even be duplicates spelled slightly differently. In order to address these issues a separate section will be devoted to the names of the Watchers.

Chapter 7

[Chapter 7] 1 And all the others together with them took unto themselves wives, and each chose for himself one, and they began to go in unto them and to defile themselves with them, and they taught them charms 2 and enchantments, and the cutting of roots, and made them acquainted with plants.

A group of Essenes living at Lake Mareotis in Egypt called themselves 'The Theraputae' or 'The Healers' – the *Rapha*. They used herbs, roots and decoctions of various plants as well as the 'laying on of hands' to effect their healing. According to modern Essene/Nassorean sources, it was with these Essenes that the family of Jesus, Mary and Joseph stayed when they fled to Egypt to escape Herod's extermination. There was another group of Essenes at Mt. Carmel in Israel (Samaria) who were also healers. Clearly then, the Essenes themselves knew these 'secrets' and may have learned them from the Egyptians. From early times, healing was connected with religion and the healing profession was practiced by the priesthood. The first 'hospitals' were located within the precincts of the Egyptian temples. Strabo speaks of the treatment of disease in the Temple of Serapis. Galen also observes there was healing done at a temple at Memphis, called the Hephaestium. It is therefore not unreasonable to associate angels with this knowledge. Charms and amulets against various diseases, demonic spirits, and insect and serpent bites were used as far back as Sumerian times and were also applied by the healer-priests.

And they 3 became pregnant, and they bare great giants, whose height was three thousand ells:

Chapter 5 of the *Book of Jubilees* begins with a couple of similar verses:

> *1 And it came to pass when the children of men began to multiply on the face of the earth and daughters were born unto them, that the angels of God saw them on a certain year of this jubilee, that they were beautiful to look upon; and they took themselves wives of all whom they 2 chose, and they bare unto them sons and they were giants.*

The term used for 'giants' is 'nephilim'. In *Genesis* 6:4, the King James version of the *Bible* states:

> There were **giants** in the earth in those days....

The Anchor Bible on the other hand says:

> The **Nephilim** were on the earth in those days....

There has been a great deal of argument amongst biblical scholars as to which word is correct and which should be used; and who or what were these giants/Nephilim. It has been suggested that the word 'nephilim' comes from the Akkadian word *napalum* which means 'destroyers'. This would certainly fit in with the ideas about the giants put forth in this chapter. The epithet "The Destroyer" also applies to Angira Mainyu, the twin of Ahura Mazda and personification of evil.

There is however another explanation. The Greek word for giants is 'gigantes' which refers to the Titans, who were the sons of the sky-god Uranus and the goddess of the earth, Gaea. The Titans preceded the Olympian gods and were often depicted as half-human and half-serpent. The word 'gigantes' means 'earth-born' because they were born of Gaea, who is the personification of the earth and who is said to have sprung forth from Chaos. We find ourselves in the middle of a great layering of puns here. Life for the Hebrews in the Hasmonean times was certainly chaotic – a time of darkness and dis-order. Also, the fact that the offspring of the Watchers are born on the earth renders them as 'earth-born' as opposed to 'heaven-born' like their sires. The idea that the Titans were half-human and half-serpent comes back to the Gnostics – more specifically the Ophites, who were beyond a doubt human beings, but considered themselves the children of The Serpent of Wisdom. The Gnostic god Abraxas or Abrasax is commonly shown as a lion-headed human with serpentine legs:

Figure 2: Gnostic Gemstone, circa 3rd century CE depicting Abraxas. The shield he carries is the shield of Sophia or Wisdom. Amulets like this were worn to repel or exercise evil spirits.

The name Abraxas is said to have been created to take the place of the unmentionable name of the Gnostics' Supreme God, much the same as the Hebrews used the Tetragrammaton (YHWH). The head of Abraxas is often depicted as being surrounded by rays, like the representations of Metatron. Abraxas was also a Persian sun-god and in Syria was known as IAO (Yahweh). These facts relate to what was earlier discussed regarding Enoch-Metatron. The great Gnostic teacher Basilides posited that between this world and the Father of All existed 365 heavens, corresponding to the days of the year. In Gematria, the name of Abraxas adds up to 365. This is the number of years that Enoch lived before he 'walked with God'.

A Mesopotamian god named Nirah was worshipped in the city of Dēr near the northern border with Elam, east of the Tigris river. Nirah was the minister of a god called Iśtaran, whose primary function seems to have been the adjudicator of border disputes. Gudea, the king of Lagaś installed a shrine to Iśtaran at the temple of Ningirsu and speaks of the god being associated with justice. However, it is Nirah in whom we should be most interested for his physical attributes:

Figure 3: Mesopotamian god Nirah. Nirah was probably worshiped well into the Middle Babylonian period. Was he the model for Abraxas?

What is an ell? There are several variations of the measurement of an 'ell'. The Mosaic ell was equal to six handbreadths (56.018658 cm or approximately 22 inches). There are two other ells mentioned in the *Misnah* (Kelim xvii. 9). One of these is a half a finger's breadth longer than the Mosaic or 'mean ell' (57.185375 cm or approximately 22 and one half inches). The other was a full finger's breadth longer than the 'mean ell' (58.352 cm or approximately 23 inches). The *Mishnah* (Tamid iii. 6) mentions a fourth ell, which was measured from the tip of the middle finger to the armpit. This is around 70 cm or 37 inches. According to the text, the giants were 3000 ells tall. Using even the smallest Mosaic ell, this would make them over a mile tall – about 5500 feet! Even as new-born infants, they would be bigger than an adult human.

Clearly, no real human woman could bear such a monstrosity without dying in the process. Some scholars have proposed that "3000 ells" is a mis-translation and that certainly something else must have been meant. Perhaps the idea here was yet another pun, this time upon the term 'nephilim'. The Hebrew word *nefallem* means 'aborted fetus' and the word *nefel* means 'aborted'. In Elaine Pagels' view that the *Books of Enoch* were written in a spirit of ridiculing socio-political satire, the author or authors of Enoch were effectively calling the offspring of the Watchers 'abortions' – a term that is used even today in a derogatory sense for something that is perceived as malformed, under-developed or incomplete.

Who consumed 4 all the acquisitions of men. And when men could no longer sustain them, the giants turned against 5 them and devoured mankind.

It was earlier mentioned that the numerous garrisons of soldiers of the Seleucid kings in the times of the Maccabees put a tremendous strain on the resources of Judea and Israel (Samaria). The armies, being under the dominion of the Greek rulers more than likely had precedence over the native population, when it came to these resources. If the army required more sustenance, it was taken from the inhabitants of these lands without thought for their welfare or sustenance. The same was true of the gold and other riches possessed by these people, as we have seen above. The Seleucid rulers simply took what they wanted or needed – no permission asked. They took their women, their food, their towns and villages, and their treasures as well – "the acquisitions of men". Raping, pillaging and plundering were an on-going activity.

As we have seen in a previous chapter, the Seleucid rulers of Judea, Israel and Palestine often turned on their hapless subjects, slaughtering them at the slightest provocation. This is possibly what is meant, that they "devoured mankind". However, there is an interesting myth of Pelasgian origin which has to do with a man named Lycaon. This myth has been reported by such ancient authors Ovid, Pausanius and Apollodorus, to mention a few:

Lycaon was the son of Pelasgus, living in the region of Arcadia, which was called Pelasgia in ancient times. According to tradition, he raised civilization in this region to a higher level than previously during the period of his father's reign. He also was the founder of the town Lycosoura in the mountains of Lycaeon and there he became the first king, and started the cult of Zeus Lycaeus and the Lycaean Games.

It is said that Lycaon was the father fifty sons. All of his sons were known as the founders of numerous towns in Pelasgia. Lycaon had also one daughter Callisto, who became one of the loves of Zeus and the mother of Arcas, after whom Arcadia was named.

According to some versions of the story Lycaon made Zeus very angry because he sacrificed on the god's altar a boy in honor to Zeus himself. Other writers said that he invited Zeus to a banquet and offered him a meal, containing meat from a roasted human being. There is also a story about the sons of Lycaon, who cooked soup from the entrails of a sheep and a goat, together with the entrails of their brother Nyctimos. They presented this meal to Zeus, who was visiting them as a simple traveler. Outraged, Zeus transformed Lycaon and his sons into wolves (in Greek *lykos* means 'wolf'). He also he sent a thunderbolt which struck Lycaon's house. Other versions of the story claim that because of the actions of Lycaon and his 'impious sons' Zeus sent the great Flood in the time of Deucalion to punish mankind for their actions.

The story of Lycaon has been interpreted in various ways. According to some scholars, he was an old Pelasgian or pre-Hellenic god, offered human sacrifices. Other scholars consider that the sacrifices offered to the Zeus-Lycaeus in Arcadia were originally cannibal feasts of a wolf-tribe, who recognized the wolf as their totem. Still others identify Lycaon with Zeus-Lycaeus, the god of light, who slays his son Nyctimos (the dark) or is succeeded by him, in allusion to the perpetual succession of night and day. Another take on the story is that Lycaon was a priest of Zeus-Lycaeus and that the 'simple traveler' was in fact Olympian-Zeus – an updated and 'kinder and gentler' version of the god, who was appalled at the primitive actions of the worshippers of Zeus-Lycaeus. In *Genesis* 49:27, Jacob says:

> Benjamin shall ravin as a wolf: in the morning he shall devour the prey, and at night he shall divide the spoil.

Readers of Greek myths might notice the common theme that this man or that man was the father of 'fifty sons'. This attribute is generally indicative that the father is one of the sea-going Greek tribes. Greek ships were more often than not manned by fifty sailors. This same idea is present in the story of Jason and the Argonauts, for there were fifty argonauts.

Here, we have a couple of ideas that fit in with the story of the Watchers and their offspring: God sent the Flood to wipe the earth clean of the sons of the Watchers, and the idea of the giants "devouring mankind". The concept that Lycaon raised civilization to a higher level than was previously experienced also fits in with the ambitions and goals of Alexander the Great and the subsequent heirs to his empire. While the Seleucid kings were generally given to war, greed and general chaos, the Ptolemies of Egypt did continue with

Alexander's dream, building the Great Library and Museum, the Lighthouse at Alexandria, Alexandria itself and many other monuments to man's ingenuity. It also fits with what may have been the Watchers' thought in teaching their wives and extended human families the 'worthless secrets of heaven' – to make life better, richer for those to whom the knowledge was imparted. However, neither man nor angel can foretell what man will do with the knowledge that he is given.

And they began to sin against birds, and beasts, and reptiles, and 6 fish, and to devour one another's flesh, and drink the blood. Then the earth laid accusation against the lawless ones.

Here, it is uncertain who "they" are. Is it the Watchers or their offspring the giants who begin to sin against the birds, beasts and reptiles and fish and to "devour one another's flesh and drink the blood"? This is one of those anomalies we often find in biblical, extra-biblical and pseudepigraphical texts that leaves one scratching his or her head.

Presumably, the Watchers/angels in coming down to earth have taken on the mantle of the flesh. Or have they? We are never specifically told, but it is an assumption that most people make. Otherwise, how would they 'defile' themselves with human women? In the book *The Mysteries of Heaven and Earth*, we are told exactly what happened:

> Let us come back once again to the people of the Flood. And in those days the Watchers (i.e. angels) came down from heaven, and after they had put on the flesh (or, bodies) of men, the madness of sin seized them, and they were thrust aside from the mysteries which they had seen in heaven. (Budge, pg. 26)

In light of what is written later in the *Books of Enoch*, it would seem that the Watchers are still around, so it seems fairly unlikely that they are the 'they' of whom the author here speaks. Oftentimes, people tend to presume that the 'they' means the giant offspring of the Watchers. Yet, in another pseudepigraphical text that is thought to have been written about the same time as the *Book of the Watchers* called the *Book of Giants*, we are told:

> 1Q23 Frag. 1 + 6 [... two hundred] 2 donkeys, two hundred asses, two hundred [... rams of the] 3 flock, two hundred goats, two hundred [... beast of the] 4 field from every animal, from every [bird ...] 5 [...] for miscegenation [...]

It is quite evident here that this text is badly fragmented. However, the translators of this text tend to assume that because the number two hundred is used, that these lines apply to the two hundred Watchers or fallen angels. If these lines are indeed talking about the

Watchers and not the giants, then we have an abrupt sort of non-sequitur in the text where first the author is talking about the giants and suddenly shifts to speak of the Watchers. In the assemblage of these bits and pieces of this work, this fragment is followed by another that reads:

> 4Q531 Frag. 2 [...] they defiled [...] 2 [... they begot] giants and monsters [...] 3 [...] they begot, and, behold, all [the earth was corrupted ...] 4 [...] with its blood and by the hand of [...] 5 [giant's] which did not suffice for them and [...] 6 [...] and they were seeking to devour many [...] 7 [...] 8 [...] the monsters attacked it.

While the text *implies* several rather questionable ideas if you're reading between the lines and lacunae, one cannot honestly derive any sense of what is truly going on from what is said here. It has been shown time and again that when another fragment is found that fills in the blanks of an already translated partial fragment, the entire meaning or gist of what is said may change radically.

What do the last words in the first fragment "for miscegenation" have to do with donkeys, rams and goats? The definition of miscegenation is "the interbreeding of what are presumed to be distinct *human races*". Had 'bestiality' been the intended idea or word here, one would have hoped that the translators would have been more correct in their choice of words. Most assume, however, that this is what is meant.

The term 'miscegenation' may refer back to a common theme in many Jewish texts of fallen Hebrews marrying wives from other pagan peoples who surrounded them and lapsing into the worship of foreign gods. Upon their return from the Babylonian captivity, the prophet Ezra writes these words:

> 10 And now, O our God, what shall we say after this? For we have forsaken they commandments, 11 Which thou hast commanded by they servants the prophets, saying, The land, unto which ye go to possess is, is an unclean land with the filthiness of the people of the lands, with their abominations, which have filled it from one end to another with their uncleanness. 12 Now therefore give not your daughters unto their sons, neither take their daughters unto your sons, nor seek their peace or their wealth for ever... (Ezra 9:10-12)

> 2 And Shechaniah the son of Jehiel, one of the sons of Elam, answered and said unto Ezra, We have trespassed against our God, and have taken strange wives of the people of the land: yet now there is hope in Israel concerning this thing. 3 Now therefore let us make a covenant with our God to put away all the wives, and such as are born of them, according to the

> *counsel of my lord, and of those that tremble at the commandment of our God; and let it be done according to the law. (Ezra 10:2-3)*

It was a problem as far back as Solomon the third king of Israel, who had many pagan wives; and Ahab the seventh king of Israel, who married the Phoenician princess Jezebel and went so far as to prohibit the worship of Yahweh in favor of the worship of Baal. Even before his encounter with the burning bush, Moses was married to a Midianite woman, Zipporah, who was the daughter of Jethro – "a priest of Midian". This particular group of Midianites were known as Kenites – another name for Canaanites, or a group of Canaanites. The Kenites are first mentioned in *Genesis* 15:19 as living in the land that Yahweh promises to Abraham. These particular Canaanites, the Kenites were metal-smiths, whom the Jews may have traced their ancestry back to Tubal-Cain. In *Numbers* 24: 21-22, they are mentioned again, as those who will fall to the will of the Lord and the Scepter of Israel. They later joined with the Moabites against the invasion of the Children of Israel into their lands. We are told:

> *And Israel abode in Shittim, and the people began to commit whoredom with the daughters of Moab. 2 And they called the people unto the sacrifices of their gods: and the people did eat, and bowed down to their gods. 3 And Israel joined himself unto Baal-peor: and the anger of the Lord was kindled against Israel. 4 And the Lord said unto Moses, Take all the heads of the people, and hang them up before the Lord against the sun, that the fierce anger of the Lord may be turned away from Israel. 5 And Moses said unto the judges of Israel, Slay ye every one his men that were joined unto Baal-peor. (Numbers 25:1-5)*

Baal-peor or Belphagor is another name for the Semitic god Chemosh, whose rites were known to have involved the immolation of first-born children upon the god's altar or upon an idol which served as an altar. Chemosh was a sun deity who may have evolved from the earlier Akkadian-Babylonian sun god Shamash. The text above says "hang them up before the Lord *against* the sun".

The mention of such animals as the donkey, ram and goat may be a reference to certain peoples who either incorporated these animals into their pagan rituals of worship, or used these animals as their symbols. In *Genesis, Chapter 49*, Jacob gathers his sons together and tells them *"that which shall befall you in the last days"*. Here, he calls Judah "a lion's whelp"; Issachar is "a strong ass couching down between two burdens"; Dan "shall be a serpent by the way"; Naphtali is "a hind let loose"; and Benjamin "shall ravin as a wolf". As we know, the lion became the standard of Judea, and the hind or roebuck the standard of Naphtali (whose name may be related to the root of the word *nephilim*). The tribe of Dan was depicted as the serpent, but later became an eagle. The ram was symbolic of the Medeo-Persian empire, and the goat symbolic of the Greeks. The ass or donkey may have been symbolic of those who worshipped Baal – specifically Baal-Peor, or the 'ass-eared god' Set. In any case, there are layers of meaning here which could be interpreted in various ways.

While we cannot be certain of what is meant by the fragmentary verses of the *Book of Giants*, clearly the writer of the *Book of the Watchers* was alluding to the sinful practices of the pagan peoples around them and their modes of worship...which included both human sacrifice and bestiality. These practices may have also included the drinking of the blood of the sacrificial victim, for the blood was considered the vehicle of the spirit. It was not uncommon in early times for warriors and to eat the heart of their prey or of a worthy adversary, in order to absorb the characteristics or 'spirit' of the animal or man. There is also a curious reference made to this in another fragment of a pseudepigraphical text called *Tales of the Patriarchs* which was also found at Qumran. The Lord tells Noah:

> 1QapGen: Col 12 You shall eat no blood...

This is echoed in the first and third books of the Old Testament:

> *Every moving thing that liveth shall be meat for you; even as the green herb have I given you all things. 4 But flesh with the life thereof, which is the blood thereof, shall ye not eat. (Genesis 9:3-4)*

> *It shall be a perpetual statute for your generations throughout all your dwellings, that ye eat neither fat nor blood. (Leviticus 3:17)*

The blood of sacrificial bulls, rams and goats in the Hebrew sacrificial rites was often sprinkled over the altar or poured at the base of it by the priest of the sacrifice. The fact that this law was given seems to indicate that either this was their practice at one time, or that it was the practice of the 'others' and not to be imitated by the Hebrews. It could as well have some reference to the Scarlet Women of both Mesopotamia and Egypt, as we shall see in Chapter 15.

Chapter 8

[Chapter 8] 1 And Azazel taught men to make swords, and knives, and shields, and breastplates, and made known to them the metals of the earth and the art of working them, and bracelets, and ornaments, and the use of antimony, and the beautifying of the eyelids, and all kinds of costly stones, and all 2 colouring tinctures. And there arose much godlessness, and they committed fornication, and they 3 were led astray, and became corrupt in all their ways. Semjaza taught enchantments, and root-cuttings, 'Armaros the resolving of enchantments, Baraqijal (taught) astrology, Kokabel the constellations, Ezeqeel the knowledge of the clouds, Araqiel the signs of the earth, Shamsiel the signs of the sun, and Sariel the course of the moon. And as men perished, they cried, and their cry went up to heaven.

Here begins the telling of the 'sins' of the Watchers and the "worthless secrets of heaven" that were taught to mankind. The knowledge of several of the Watchers named here, as we shall see later, is sometimes reflected in their names. What is quite curious about this list is that we know that the Hebrews were quite meticulous about time keeping – that is the knowledge of the movements of the sun and moon. This was important knowledge for them, because the times dictated the proper days upon which their holy days, feasts and sabbaths were held. They also knew the art of war as evidenced by their attacks upon the various indigenous tribes of Canaan as they took the Land of Milk and Honey promised to Abraham by their god. The Old Testament books are replete with tales of war waged between the Hebrews and their various enemies – continually sent against them as punishment for lapsing in their faith.

Both the men and women of Egypt wore cosmetics, painted their eyes with liners and eye-shadows made from malachite and galena. The use of cosmetics was functional, as well as decorative. Oils and ointments helped preserve the skin from the dry climate. The carbon and black oxides used for the kohl eye-liners helped keep the flies away and were also prevalent in concoctions used to prevent diseases of the eyes. Palettes for grinding shadows, lip colors, powders and rouges have been found in Pre-Dynastic tombs (before 3100 BCE). Many Egyptians shaved the hair from their heads as a precaution against lice, and wore wigs. The wigs were often made of human hair. They also wore false eyelashes. The men and women of Babylon also wore cosmetics in much the same fashion. Tweezers, combs and toothpicks have all been found in Babylonian tombs. Jars of white lead make-up were found in the ruins of Pompeii. This was most likely made of stibium or antimony, which is a white lead. Objects described in documents found at Ugarit from around 1300 BCE indicate that cosmetics were as much a part of trade and commerce as were weapons, jewelry, furniture, dishes, oil, animals and timber. Jewelry has been found in the royal tombs of Ur, as well as in the royal tombs of Egypt and Babylon.

Regarding weaponry, the Hittites (Anatolia) held off the armies of Rameses II at Qadesh because of their superior compound bows and iron clad chariots. The Battle of Qadesh occurred some time around 1274 BCE. The Hittites and their neighbors, the Mittani kept their bronze and iron production techniques a big secret to deter others from becoming as powerful in battle. This knowledge was an asset in warfare and not to be shared with potential enemies. It wasn't until about 100 years after Qadesh that iron production techniques began to be more common knowledge. As anyone the slightest bit familiar with the history of the Middle East will be aware, warfare had been a constant specter – and still is – since Sumerian times.

It is of interest to note here that the Mycenaeans, who lived in the northeastern Peloponnese possessed bronze weaponry as early as the 16th century BCE. Weapons such as swords, knives and battle-axes have been found in shaft graves from the Late Helladic I period. The Mycenaeans or Mukanai were a major military power dominating the Mediterranean until about 1100 BCE. It is known that they were a sea-going peoples. A scarab of Queen Tiye, the wife of Amenhotep III was found in the ruins of their citadel at Mycenae. They were also great stone masons, employing what has come to be called 'cyclopean masonry', utilizing huge stones that seemed no one but giants could have built them. We see this same sort of masonry at Baalbek in Lebanon – near Mt. Hermon. King Agamemnon was one of the rulers of the Mycenae, famous for beginning a 10-year war with Troy over the abduction of his brother Menelaus' wife, Helen. These facts are of some import, as we shall later see.

The traditional Hebrew woman did not wear cosmetics, jewelry or dress her hair. This was something that was the province of 'pagan' women – and men. One can imagine that the young women were particularly influenced by the glamour of their pagan neighbors, wearing cosmetics and jewelry.

The remainder of the subjects mentioned in this chapter will be investigated further in the chapter about the Watchers.

Chapter 9

[Chapter 9] 1 And then Michael, Uriel, Raphael, and Gabriel looked down from heaven and saw much blood being 2 shed upon the earth, and all lawlessness being wrought upon the earth. And they said one to another: 'The earth made without inhabitant cries the voice of their cryings up to the gates of heaven. 3 And now to you, the holy ones of heaven, the souls of men make their suit, saying, "Bring our cause 4 before the Most High."' And they said to the Lord of the ages: 'Lord of lords, God of gods, King of kings, and God of the ages, the throne of Thy glory (standeth) unto all the generations of the 5 ages, and Thy name holy and glorious and blessed unto all the ages! Thou hast made all things, and power over all things hast Thou: and all things are naked and open in Thy sight, and Thou seest all 6 things, and nothing can hide itself from Thee. Thou seest what Azazel hath done, who hath taught all unrighteousness on earth and revealed the eternal secrets which were (preserved) in heaven, which 7 men were striving to learn: And Semjaza, to whom Thou hast given authority to bear rule over his associates. And they have gone to the daughters of men upon the earth, and have slept with the 9 women, and have defiled themselves, and revealed to them all kinds of sins. And the women have 10 borne giants, and the whole earth has thereby been filled with blood and unrighteousness. And now, behold, the souls of those who have died are crying and making their suit to the gates of heaven, and their lamentations have ascended: and cannot cease because of the lawless deeds which are 11 wrought on the earth. And Thou knowest all things before they come to pass, and Thou seest these things and Thou dost suffer them, and Thou dost not say to us what we are to do to them in regard to these.'

We begin with the four archangels, Michael, Uriel, Raphael and Gabriel taking note of what is going on down on earth. It is implied here that men are directing their prayers to the archangels to intercede in their behalf with God. This would seem quite out of place in a purely ancient Hebrew text. We do not see Michael mentioned in the Old Testament until the *Book of Daniel* in Chapter 10. The *Book of Daniel* is commonly thought to have been written around 165 BCE – close to the same period in which the *Books of Enoch* were written. Daniel does not pray to Michael to come to him, but sees him in a vision after a fast of three full weeks. Michael is not mentioned again until the New Testament, in the last two books, *Jude* and *Revelations*. Uriel is often thought to be the cherub of the flaming sword placed at the east of Eden to guard the tree of life, but is not specifically named in the KJV. Raphael is not named at all in the Old or New Testaments. Again, in Chapter 8 of *Daniel* we first meet Gabriel, who is sent to interpret a vision for Daniel, who seems to be in a dream state. Gabriel appears again in the same capacity in Chapter 9. It is Gabriel who makes the Annunciation of the birth of John the Baptist in Chapter 1, verse 19 of *Luke* and again makes the Annunciation of the birth of Jesus to Mary in the same chapter, verses 26-33. Angels come and go throughout the Old Testament and the New, serving as messengers. While the Hebrew word for angel is *malach*, the word angel comes from the Greek *angelos*, which means 'messenger'. In fact, Moses forbids any sort of worship of 'the hosts of heaven':

> *16 Lest ye corrupt yourselves, and make you a graven image, the similitude of any figure, the likeness of male or female, 17 The likeness of any beast that is on the earth, the likeness of any winged fowl that flieth in the air, 18 the likeness of any fish that is in the waters beneath the earth: 19 And lest thou lift up thine eyes unto heaven, and when thou seest the sun, and the moon and the stars, even all the host of heaven, shouldest be driven to worship them, and serve them, which the Lord thy God hath divided unto all nations under the whole heaven. (Deuteronomy 4: 16-19)*

We know today that Michael and Gabriel appear as archangels in many religious traditions, including Judaism, Islam and Christianity ...but where did they come from? It is widely speculated that the Hebrews brought the idea and the names of angels with them out of the Babylonian captivity.

Angels in religious tradition began with the Zoroastrian *Amesha Spenta* (the Bountiful Immortals) - six divine sparks created by Ahura Mazda, the Creator god of Zoroastrianism. It is not known exactly when Zoroaster or Zarathrustra lived. Scholarly guess-timates place Zoroaster as having lived anywhere from 1200 BCE to 600 BCE. The Amesha Spenta were also considered the foundation upon which the world is governed. They are:

Name (Avesta)	Meaning	Domain
Vohu Manu	Benevolent Mind	Animal Life
Asha Vahishta	Righteousness	Luminaries/Fire
Vohu Kshatra	Authority & Power	Metals & Minerals
Armaiti	(Intuitive) Wisdom	Earth
Haurvatat	Perfection/Plenty	Water
Ameratat	Immortality	Plant Life

Ahura Mazda, is implicitly counted amongst the Amesha Spenta as *Spenta Mainyu*, making a seventh archangel. Spenta Mainyu's relationship to Ahura Mazda is similar to the relationship between *Ruach haqodesh* (or the Shekinah) and Yahweh of Judaism, and between Jehovah and the Holy Spirit of Christianity. As such, Spenta

Mainyu was thought to have created mankind. During the reign of Ardashir I, the first Sassanid emperor (circa 226 CE), the Amesha Spenta transform from abstract concepts to personified archangels in the *Ormazd Yasht*. In this text, they are described as being 'names' or personifications of Ahura Mazda. Other angels, called *yazata* or *yazads* (also *izeds*) are subordinate to the Amesha Spenta. Their chief is Mithras. They are not specifically mentioned in the *Gathas* of Zoroaster, but existed as divine entities or concepts in pre-Zoroastrian (pagan) religions – i.e. of proto Indo-Iranian origin. It is interesting to note that Vohu Kshatra's (Authority & Power) name is quite similar to the Hindu caste of kings and warriors, the *kshatraya*.

We find a very similar concept to the Zoroastrian hierarchy of heaven in the *Meshaf Resh* – the Black Book of the Yezidi, who are worshipers of angels or *yezeds*:

> In the beginning God created the White Pearl out of His most precious Essence; and He created a bird named Anfar. And He placed the pearl upon its back, and dwelt thereon forty thousand years.
>
> On the first day, Sunday, He created an angel named 'Azazil, which is Ta'us Melek ("the Peacock Angel"), the chief of all.
>
> On Monday He created Darda'il, which is Sheikh Hasan.
>
> On Tuesday he created Israfil (Raphael), who is Sheikh Shams.
>
> On Wednesday He created Jibra'il (Gabriel), who is Sheikh Abu Bekr.
>
> On Thursday He created 'Azra'il (Azrael), who is Sajadin.
>
> On Friday He created the angel Shemna'il, who is Nasiru'd-Din.
>
> On Saturday He created the angel Nura'il, who is [...]
>
> He made Melek Ta'us chief over them.

Here, Melek Ta'us or Azazil functions in the same capacity as Spenta Mainyu, being the chief of the first created angels. No one knows for certain when the *Meshaf Resh* came to exist. It is said that it originated in ancient times as oral tradition and was finally committed to writing in about 1200 CE. The Yezidi consider themselves as the Children of Azazil. They are primarily ethnic Kurds, who live in what is now eastern Turkey (Anatolia), and the northern reaches of Iraq and Iran in the lands that were once the province of the Medes.

The Medes are credited with the foundation of Iran as a nation and empire, and established the first Iranian empire, the largest of its day until Cyrus the Great established a unified empire of the Medes and Persians. The Magi were said to be one of the six original Medean tribes. The Medes may have been the *Manda*, who lived at one time on the southern shores of the Caspian Sea mentioned by the Assyrian king Sargon.

According to Herodotus, the Medean dynasty began with one Daiukku or Deioces who was a chieftain in the Zagros mountains. Daiukku, his kinsmen and members of his tribe were transported by Sargon to Haniah (Hamath) in Syria in about 715 BCE in one of many Assyro-Babylonian forced 'foreign-exchange' programs. Sargon was evidently borrowing a page from one of his predecessors, Shalmaneser V's playbooks of conquest and socio-religious cultural re-programming. Previously, in about 770 BCE Shalmaneser V took Hebrews from Samaria (Israel) and placed them in Assyria. He then re-located some Assyrians, putting them in Samaria. This is told in II Kings, Chapter 17. There was also the (in)famous Babylonian captivity of the Hebrews, during the reign of Nebuchadneezer in about 597 BCE. It is probable that during all of these culture-swaps, elements of all the religious traditions involved were absorbed into one another to some degree or another. Thus, we find Zoroastrian angels, Assyro-Babylonian imagery, and heavenly hierarchies turning up in Hebrew literature.

Figure 4: A *karibu* gate guardian. Two of these huge Creatures flanked one of the entrances to the royal palace of Sargon, facing one another

By the time the Hebrews returned to the Holy Land from Babylon, angels were beyond a doubt a well-developed idea. However, that may not have been their first exposure to these beings, as shown above. They were certainly exposed to the images of divinities with wings during their sojourn in Egypt – i.e. Isis, Horus, Uatchit, Nekhbet and Maat, as well as the bird-like *ka* and *ba* elements of the soul depicted in tomb and temple art. While in Assyria and Babylonia, they were also beyond a doubt exposed to the images of the great guardians of the gateways and doors, the *karibu* or the formidable looking man-lion or man-bull winged beasts who may have later become the chora of cherubim.

Another figure that may have given rise to the appearance of and the idea of the seven archangels were the so-called 'gryphon demons' or *apkallu* that were quite popular in both the Middle- and Neo-Assyrian kingdoms. These were often depicted on cylinder seals. During Neo-Assyrian times, these bird-headed winged beings with human bodies were explained as the Seven Sages, who were credited with building the walls of Uruk in the *Epic of Gilgamesh*. They were also sometimes depicted as human figures with fish-heads. There were plenty of winged divinities present as well, depicted on cylinder seals, vases (*kudurrus*) and other art-forms - such as various genii, Ninurta, Anzu (Zu), Pazuzu, Inanna/Ishtar, Imdugud, and Shamash the sun god, who seems to be a prototype of Ahura Mazda – the human figure appearing in the winged solar disk.

Figure 5: Neo-Assyrian cylinder seal. The king is shown twice on either side of a stylized tree, flanked by two *apkallu*, while the sun god Shamash appears overhead in his winged sun-disk.

To return to the text of Chapter 9, we find the archangels having a bit of a dig at God, saying:

"...Thou knowest all things before they come to pass, and Thou seest these things and Thou dost suffer them, and Thou dost not say to us what we are to do to them in regard to these."

In effect, they're saying, "You knew all of this was going to happen, and yet You allowed it, and haven't told us what we're supposed to do about it." Again, this seems a bit odd and cheeky. Could we be seeing another hint of it's Gnostic origins here? The Gnostics believed Yahweh or IAO to be the Demiurge – not the true God but one who declared himself God. Chapters 1 through 5 certainly seem to be an orthodox Hebrew text praising God and his works, but one has to wonder upon reading this passage if it is so...especially coming from the mouths of his own archangels. It is as if they are thinking that if they hadn't come before him with the news, he might not have done anything at all about it. On the flip-side, this could be pointing to the idea that angels are quite important as intercessors between God and man. It would certainly be an arguing point for those who believe the *Books of Enoch* to have been of Christian authorship, along with the several references to the Son of Man later in the text - for out of all the possibilities, it is the Christians who believe in angels as divine intercessors or the carriers of mans' prayers to God. Yet, it may again point to Gnostic authorship, for the Gnostics believed that only those who had attained enlightenment or become aware of their own divinity in life were capable of teaching others the Way to reach their own divinity and by doing so, become one with the One.

Chapter 10

Due to the length and complexity of this chapter, with the various events going on in it, it seems it would be best to investigate it in relation to each event, rather than as a whole.

[Chapter 10] 1 Then said the Most High, the Holy and Great One spake, and sent Uriel to the son of Lamech, 2 and said to him: 'Go to Noah and tell him in my name "Hide thyself!" and reveal to him the end that is approaching: that the whole earth will be destroyed, and a deluge is about to come 3 upon the whole earth, and will destroy all that is on it. And now instruct him that he may escape 4 and his seed may be preserved for all the generations of the world.'

God wastes no time marshalling the troops and handing out instructions, once the situation has been brought to his attention. Here we have the annunciation of the Flood. God sends Uriel to announce to Noah, the son of Lamech (*and* a descendent of Enoch, depending upon which genealogy you care to follow) to prepare for the coming deluge.

It has been previously mentioned that the story of the Flood comes from the Old Babylonian text called *Atrahasis*. That is to say, this is the oldest currently known full story of the Flood that is written down. There are many parallels between the 'song' of *Atrahasis* and this portion of the *Books of Enoch* that might not be immediately obvious. Once it is taken into account that the *Book of the Watchers* is built around the core of the elusive *Book of Noah*, and that there is a transference in the story between the old Babylonian deities and beliefs to the beliefs of the Gnostic Hebrews, one could even say that *Atrahasis* serves as a sort of template for the *Book of the Watchers*. It seems more likely in this regard that the *Book of Watchers* is in fact the portion of the *Books of Enoch* that contains the lost *Book of Noah*, and that what is purported to be the *Book of Noah* in Chapter 60 of the *Book of Parables* is in fact a later day sort of *midrash* or interpretation on what was thought to be a 'similitude' of *Atrahasis*.

Atrahasis begins with the lines:

> When the gods instead of man, did the work, bore the loads, the gods' load was too great, the work too hard, the trouble too much, the great Anunnaki made the Igigi carry the workload sevenfold.

The tale of the Igigi is told – how they dug out the rivers and heaped up the mountains for 3,600 years. Eventually, the Igigi revolt, burning their tools and carry their complaints to the counselor of the gods, Ellil/Enlil. The Igigi are lesser gods (angels), while the Anunnaki are the greater gods, such as Ellil, Enki, Ishtar, etc. Anyone familiar with Watcher lore will recognize that 'Igigi' is another term for Watcher. The Igigi were considered the assistants or warriors of Anu, who appear in the heavens as the stars, looking down upon mankind and his doings. It is important to note that *only* in the literature of this period, during the Greek and Roman occupation of the Holy Land, that the angels are referred to as Watchers, or Grigori.

As a result of having their righteous complaints heard, the Anunna decide to make man in order to bear the work of the Igigi. The task of making man is given to Ea/Enki and Nintu/Belet-ili. In order to fashion a *lulu* or a worker, one of the Igigi (Ilawela) is slaughtered for his flesh and blood to mix with the purified clay that will constitute the body of the new being. There were seven females and seven males created from the clay. Here, we have the idea of humans created from the essence of one of the Igigi – the sons and daughters of the Watchers made in a matrix of clay. This too, as we have seen above is very much a Gnostic idea from the Ophites – that the divine spark was encapsulated within the vessel of clay (the body).

When the gods created the first human beings, they did not set a life-span on them. They lived a very long time, as is echoed in the 'begats' of *Genesis*, where we see Adam and his descendants living very long lives up until the advent of the Flood. Because of this, man multiplied upon the earth, filling it until the earth was over-crowded. In the story of *Atrahasis*, the noise of the humans becomes too much for Ellil, who cannot sleep because of it. We are told:

> *And the country became too wide, the people too numerous. The country was as noisy as a bellowing bull. The God grew restless at their racket, Ellil had to listen to their noise. He addressed the great gods, 'The noise of mankind has become too much, I am losing sleep over their racket. Give the order that the shuruppu disease shall break out.... (Atrahasis I, vii)*

Ellil's solution to the problem was to decimate the population by disease. Enki tells his lamenting faithful servant Atrahasis (Noah) to tell the people of his town to leave off worshipping their (personal) gods and make offerings to Namtara, the god or demon of plagues, that he might be shamed by such gifts and "wipe away his hand". This works. But again and again and again, the humans rebound only to be beset with a drought, famine and another plague. Finally, having his fill of humankind's noise, Ellil and the other Anunna make a pact or an oath to wipe away this plague of humans with a flood. As the Lord of the Abzu, or the abyssal waters, Enki is instructed to unfasten the locks of the rivers and the deeps. But Enki was the one who created mankind and he cannot find it in his heart to do such a thing. Enki loves humans as much as Ellil dislikes them. The Anunna accuse Enki of providing too much for the people, allowing them to flourish. He was supposed to dole out provisions, maintaining a balance. Enki and Ellil become furious with one another and Ellil makes Enki swear before them that he will not tell the humans of this plan that is sanctioned in full by Anu, the Great God.

In Chapter 9 of the *Book of the Watchers*, we see the 'noise' of the people has become their lamentations to heaven:

And now, behold, the souls of those who have died are crying and making their suit to the gates of heaven, and their lamentations have ascended: and cannot cease because of the lawless deeds which are 11 wrought on the earth.

God seems not to hear them – or at least is not concerned with all the noise, now. The situation has to be brought to his attention by his 'viziers' the archangels. It is only then that he takes action, like Ellil, to relieve the earth of the plague of the offspring of the Watchers *and* corrupted humanity. It may be significant that in *Enoch*, it is Ur-iel that Yahweh sends to warn Noah. Ur was one of the premier cities of Sumer, a city-port on the Euphrates on the coast of the Arabian Gulf that was eventually inundated by the rising waters of the gulf. However, it is the clever, all-seeing, all-knowing Enki who warns Atrahasis in the original story, and instructs him in the building of the ark, to collect birds, fish, etc. Enki does this by speaking to Atrahasis through the walls of his reed hut in the night, as if it is a dream. It is also of significance to note that Enki himself was said to have mated with human women (including Hawah or Eve) and was by some later accounts the sire of Cain.

Another parallel we see between *Atrahasis* and the *Book of the Watchers* is the oath. In Chapter 6, we see the Watchers who have come down upon Mount Hermon swearing an oath at the behest of their leader Shemyaza to share the responsibility of their decision to leave heaven and take themselves wives from amongst the daughters of men. Once the waters of the deluge have subsided and the gods discover a few humans still live, we read:

> *The warrior Ellil spotted the boat and was furious with the Igigi. 'We, the great Anunna, all of us, agreed together on an oath! No form of life should have escaped! How did any man survive the catastrophe?' Anu made his voice heard and spoke to the warrior Ellil, 'Who but Enki would do this? He made sure that the [reed hut] disclosed the order.' Enki made his voice heard and spoke to the great gods, 'I did it, in defiance of you! I made sure life was preserved...'. (Atrahasis III, vi).*

Here, we see Enki as the Rebel of Heaven, a role that later becomes the one taken by Shemyaza, and subsequently Samael/Satan or Lucifer. Enki, too is made to swear an oath – that he will not disclose the secret of the gods. Revealing the secrets of heaven is one of the crimes of the Watchers. En-ki, whose name translates as "Lord of the

Earth" was the Sumerian god of wisdom and incantations. He sent the Seven Sages to teach men the arts and skills of civilization. He was the Keeper of the Me, or the laws of proper conduct and civilization. He is also known as Ushumgal, meaning 'great serpent' and is thought by many scholars to be the prototype of the Serpent of Eden. The fight between Ellil and Enki over the Flood may have also served as the basis for the disagreement between Samael and Yahweh, wherein Samael became Satan. But contrary to the idea that Satan hated mankind (also ascribed to Azazel in the Quran), Enki was quite fond of his creations.

And again the Lord said to Raphael: 'Bind Azazel hand and foot, and cast him into the darkness: and make an opening 5 in the desert, which is in Dudael, and cast him therein. And place upon him rough and jagged rocks, and cover him with darkness, and let him abide there for ever, and cover his face that he may 6,7 not see light. And on the day of the great judgment he shall be cast into the fire. And heal the earth which the angels have corrupted, and proclaim the healing of the earth, that they may heal the plague, and that all the children of men may not perish through all the secret things that the 8 Watchers have disclosed and have taught their sons. And the whole earth has been corrupted 9 through the works that were taught by Azazel: to him ascribe all sin.'

Raphael is assigned the task of binding Azazel. This appears to be another pun on the root of Raphael's name, *rapha*, which means 'to bind' or to 'make fast'. According to some sources, it is Raphael who delivers a ring to King Solomon and teaches him how to bind demons to help him build the Temple. This bit of information is from *The Testament of Solomon,* another pseudepigraphical work that is generally thought to have been written in the first century CE. However in the translation by F.C. Conybeare, it is the archangel Michael who delivers the ring to Solomon and teaches him the methods of binding demons. It is possible that like *Enoch* and other pseudepigraphical texts, there is more than one version. Said ring is a stone engraved with a pentalpha or pentagram.

The name Dudael is said to mean something like 'God's crucible' or 'God's boiling pot', which conjures up visions of sulfurous springs bubbling up from the desert in some active geothermal area, much like what is found in the area of the Dead Sea. The reference to casting Azazel into 'an opening in the desert' and placing rocks upon him may allude to the ritual of the Day of Atonement (Yom Kippur), wherein two goats are chosen – one for Yahweh and one for Azazel. The Ritual of the Scapegoat will be dealt with in more depth in the section on the individual Watchers. This reference is made clear by a sort of pun in the last line:

> '...And the whole earth has been corrupted 9 through the works that were taught by Azazel: to him ascribe all sin.'

We can also see a similarity here with Azazel and the Greek Titan (giant) Prometheus. Prometheus is said to be the inventor of architecture, writing, astronomy, medicine and metal-work. We see all of these disciplines echoed in the knowledge of the individual Watchers. In one version of this story, Prometheus was the creator of mankind. His brother Epimetheus was the creator of beasts and birds. They were both given gifts to give to their creations, but it took Prometheus so long to make man, that by the time he'd finished, his brother had given all the gifts to the beasts and the birds. At a loss as to what gift he might give his creations, Prometheus decided to steal the fire from Heaven and give it to mankind. When Zeus discovered what Prometheus had done, he became furious. Fire was intended only for the gods, and not for mankind. As a punishment, Zeus had Prometheus chained to a cliff on a mountain top, where an eagle would come and tear out his liver daily. His liver regenerated, and so he endured this punishment for many long years – until the god-man and hero Hercules came and killed the eagle and rescued him. The son of Prometheus was Deucalion, who is the Greek hero of the Flood myth. Deucalion is the Greek version of Noah/Ziusudra/Utnapishtim.

Some versions of Deucalion's story give his mother as Pandora. The story of Pandora's Box is well known, but will be recalled here. Pandora was the first woman. Zeus ordered her created by Hephaestus, the god of fire, and made so perfectly that her beauty would cause strife amongst men – rather like Helen of Troy. She was given many gifts by the gods: beauty, eloquence, charm, the ability to heal and sing enchantingly. Zeus also gave her a box and told her not to open it, but her curiosity got the better of her and she did this. All the ills and plagues of the flesh were contained in the box, and when she opened it, she unleashed them on the world. Only Hope was left in the box.

Azazel and the Watchers, like Prometheus and Pandora, give the secrets of the sciences and civilization to mankind, unleashing all the ills of the world upon humanity. As Azazel is the Scapegoat, the fallen Watchers became the scapegoats for what was wrong with mankind, shifting the blame from humans to the Watchers.

And to Gabriel said the Lord: 'Proceed against the bastards and the reprobates, and against the children of fornication: and destroy [the children of fornication and] the children of the Watchers from amongst men [and cause them to go forth]: send them one against the other that they may destroy each other in 10 battle: for length of days shall they not have. And no request that they (i.e. their fathers) make of thee shall be granted unto their fathers on their behalf; for they hope to live

an eternal life, and 11 that each one of them will live five hundred years.'

Gabriel is the archangel given the task of destroying the children of the Watchers by setting them against one another, and destroy each other in battle. While Gabriel is more commonly known as the Angel of the Annunciation in Christianity, as well as an angel of resurrection and mercy, he is also a dealer of death, vengeance and destruction. Jewish legend has it that Gabriel was the one who rained death and destruction upon Sodom and Gomorrah, as well as he who destroyed Sennacherib's army. Certainly, the author of *Watchers* saw the times in which he lived as rivaling the depravity of the days of Sodom and Gomorrah – just in a different context. It is a well known fact that there was a constant in-fighting between the Seleucid kings who inherited the remnants of Alexander's empire. They were constantly at war with one another, attempting to usurp more territory than was allotted to them. They poisoned and killed one another in order to assume a kingship that was slow in coming or was simply not theirs to take in the first place. Of course, this was also the case with the Hebrew kings, as evidenced in the stories told in the two books of *Kings* in the Old Testament. Is it possible that the author of the *Book of Watchers* was alluding to this?

Here, we also find a reference to eternal life or, at least, longevity of years. God warns Gabriel not to listen to any request from the Watchers regarding the lives of their sons, exactly because Gabriel *is* the angel of mercy and resurrection. There is a similar bit in *Genesis*, where Yahweh sets a limit upon the lifetime of man:

> *And the Lord said, My spirit shall not always strive with man, for that he also is flesh: yet his days shall be an hundred and twenty years (Genesis 6:3)*

This harkens back to the story of *Atrahasis*, where the original humans created by Enki and Nintu were not given a finite life-span and lived to be quite old, until the gods visited them with various diseases and droughts. It also coincides with the idea of the heroic or divine Hellenic and Egyptian kings, who nonetheless proved over and over again to be quite mortal.

And the Lord said unto Michael: 'Go, bind Semjaza and his associates who have united themselves with women so as to have defiled themselves 12 with them in all their uncleanness. And when their sons have slain one another, and they have seen the destruction of their beloved ones, bind them fast for seventy generations in the valleys of the earth, till the day of their judgment and of their consummation, till the judgment that is 13 for ever and ever is consummated. In those days they shall be led off to the abyss of fire: and 14 to the torment and the prison in which they shall be confined for ever. And

whosoever shall be condemned and destroyed will from thenceforth be bound together with them to the end of all 15 generations. And destroy all the spirits of the reprobate and the children of the Watchers, because 16 they have wronged mankind.

As previously mentioned, it was Michael who delivered the ring of binding to Solomon, so it seems altogether fitting here that it is Michael who is set to the task of binding "Shemyaza and his associates". At the time the *Book of the Watchers* was written it was thought that Armageddon was not far off. Apparently, the author was of the opinion that it was 'seventy generations' away. However, in biblical times, a generation was 40 years. According to this calculation, we still have about 650 years before the Final Judgement. This is a strange comment, regarding 'seventy generations', seeing as how the Yahad was plotting their own version of Armageddon.

The 'abyss of fire' and all that follows mentioned here was most likely a reference to the Valley of Gehinnom or Hinnom Valley, which sits below the steep southern wall of Jerusalem. In the days before the Babylonian Exile, pagans used the valley to perform their rituals to their gods (probably Chemosh and others), which included burning children alive. After the Exile, because of its past associations, the Hinnom Valley was a virtual dumping ground for refuse and the carcasses of dead animals. It was also where the bodies of people considered unclean or impure (pagans, criminals and apostates) were cremated. The fires burned there night and day, the putrid smoke rising into the sky. One portion of the Valley is called Tophet, which means *inferno*. Often referred to as 'The Pit', it is beyond a doubt one of the archetypal images of Hell. The Greeks called it *Gehenna*. Because of this reference to the 'abyss of fire' it seems more likely that Enoch was written *after* the Babylonian Exile and not before.

Destroy all wrong from the face of the earth and let every evil work come to an end: and let the plant of righteousness and truth appear: and it shall prove a blessing; the works of righteousness and truth shall be planted in truth and joy for evermore. 17 And then shall all the righteous escape, And shall live till they beget thousands of children, And all the days of their youth and their old age Shall they complete in peace. 18 And then shall the whole earth be tilled in righteousness, and shall all be planted with trees and 19 be full of blessing. And all desirable trees shall be planted on it, and they shall plant vines on it: and the vine which they plant thereon shall yield wine in abundance, and as for all the seed which is sown thereon each measure (of it) shall bear a thousand, and each measure of olives shall yield 20 ten presses of oil. And cleanse thou the earth from all oppression, and from all unrighteousness, and from all sin, and from all godlessness: and all the uncleanness that is wrought upon the earth 21 destroy from

off the earth. And all the children of men shall become righteous, and all nations 22 shall offer adoration and shall praise Me, and all shall worship Me. And the earth shall be cleansed from all defilement, and from all sin, and from all punishment, and from all torment, and I will never again send (them) upon it from generation to generation and for ever.

This section seems a bit of wishful thinking on the part of the author, when all sin, oppression and unrighteousness shall be cleansed from the earth...a hope for a new day when everything is harmonious and good. Such platitudes are born of years of foreign domination, political intrigues, rampant sin, usury and deception – which was precisely the climate of the times during the rule of Antiochus Epiphanes IV and the later Roman occupation of Jerusalem and the Holy Land.

Chapter 11

[Chapter 11] 1 And in those days I will open the store chambers of blessing which are in the heaven, so as to send 2 them down upon the earth over the work and labour of the children of men. And truth and peace shall be associated together throughout all the days of the world and throughout all the generations of men.'

This seems to be a continuation of the later portion of Chapter 10.

Chapter 12

[Chapter 12] 1 Before these things Enoch was hidden, and no one of the children of men knew where he was 2 hidden, and where he abode, and what had become of him. And his activities had to do with the Watchers, and his days were with the holy ones. 3 And I Enoch was blessing the Lord of majesty and the King of the ages, and lo! the Watchers 4 called me - Enoch the scribe- and said to me: 'Enoch, thou scribe of righteousness, go, declare to the Watchers of the heaven who have left the high heaven, the holy eternal place, and have defiled themselves with women, and have done as the children of earth do, and have taken unto themselves 5 wives: "Ye have wrought great destruction on the earth: And ye shall have no peace nor forgiveness 6 of sin: and inasmuch as they delight themselves in their children, The murder of their beloved ones shall they see, and over the destruction of their children shall they lament, and shall make supplication unto eternity, but mercy and peace shall ye not attain."'

We are told that Enoch – now called "the scribe" - had disappeared from the eyes of men and now spent his days with the Watchers. By this is meant the Watchers who had not fallen and remained in heaven, for "his days were with the holy ones". They instruct him to go and deliver the pronouncements of doom to the fallen Watchers that have been leveled against them in heaven.

What is most notable here is that there is no forgiveness for them. This seems quite a harsh edict, all things considered. Similarly, in *Atrahasis*, Ellil and Anu will not relent upon their decision to send the Deluge, in spite of Enki's protestations. Logically, there can be no taking back this decision, for the Flood was a fact of history – long since passed at the time this was written, but kept alive through myth and legend. The fact is, Anu severely regrets his decision to send the Flood in the story of *Atrahasis*:

> *Anu went berserk, the gods [...] his sons [...] before him.... However could I, in the assembly of gods, have ordered such destruction with them? Ellil was strong enough to give a wicked order. Like Tiruru he ought to have cancelled that wicked order! I heard their cry leveled at me, against myself, against my person. Beyond my control my offspring have become like white sheep. As for me, how am I to live in a house of bereavement? My noise has turned to silence. (Atrahasis III, iii)*

The reference to Tiruru remains a mystery, but was most likely understood in the time *Atrahasis* was written. The allusion to his offspring becoming like "white sheep" is probably intended to mean 'sacrificial sheep'. It is well to keep in mind that the cities of Sumer, Akkad and Babylonia were referred to as 'sheepfolds' and the people in them were the flock of the shepherd kings. The shepherd's crook was symbolic of the king's authority and rule. The crook and flail are also symbolic of the Egyptian pharaohs' authority, and have come down to us today in Christianity in the form of the Bishops' crozier.

This brings us to another pseudepigraphical text found amongst the *Dead Sea Scrolls* in Caves 4 and 5, known as the *Damascus Document*. This is considered an important document in relation to the sect at Qumran, their beliefs and rules. In a section known as the *Homily on a Willful Heart* we find this:

> *So now my children, listen to me that I may uncover your eyes to see and to understand the deeds of God, choosing what pleases Him and hating what He rejects, living perfectly in all His ways, not turning away through thoughts caused by the sinful urge and lecherous eyes.*
>
> *For many have gone astray by such thoughts, even strong and doughty men of old faltered through them, and still do.*
>
> *When they went about in their willful heart, the Guardian Angels of Heaven fell and were ensnared by it, for they did not observe the commandments of God. Their sons, who were as tall as cedars, and whose bodies were as big as mountains fell by it.*
>
> *Everything mortal on dry land expired and became as if they had never existed, because they did their own will, and did not keep the commandments of their Maker, until finally His anger was aroused against them.*
>
> *By it the sons of Noah and their families went astray, and by it they were exterminated....*
>
> *But the sons of Jacob went astray by them and were punished for their errors. In Egypt their descendants lived by their willful heart, too obstinate to consult the commandments of God, each one doing what was right in his own eyes. They even ate blood; and the men were exterminated in the wilderness.*

This text has also been dated to the first century BCE and was first published by the Jewish historian Solomon Schecter in 1910 as the Zadokite Fragments from the Cairo Geniza manuscripts. Another portion of this text relates the following:

> So it is with all the men who entered the new covenant in the land of Damascus, but then turned back and traitorously turned away from the fountain of living water. They shall not be reckoned among the council of the people, and their names shall not be written in their book from the day the Beloved Teacher dies until the Messiah from Aaron and from Israel appears. Such is the fate for all who join the company of the men of holy perfection and then become sick of obeying virtuous rules. This is the type of person who "melts in the crucible". (Geniza B document, verses 19-20)

We see in these passages written during the time of Antiochus Epiphanes IV that the members of the sect at Qumran had some very definite ideas about their own righteousness, as well as the fall of the "Guardian Angels of Heaven" being a subject that was held up as an admonition that even the strong may fall to lecherousness and defilement. This was a common element of their teachings. We also see that there seems to have been a community of this same sect located in the land of Damascus, who succumbed to the evils of the flesh and turned away from the covenant with God. This is mentioned, because the city of Damascus itself lies approximately 30 miles to the east of Mount Hermon.

The line "This is the type of person who melts in the crucible" recalls the fate of Azazel, who was thrown into Dudael, i.e. 'God's crucible'. This line also refers to a chapter of *Ezekiel* describing the catalogue of sins in Jerusalem, and the general corruption of the prophets, priests, princes and people:

> Yea, I will gather you, and blow upon you in the fire of my wrath, and ye shall be melted in the midst thereof. 22 As silver is melted in the midst of the furnace, so shall ye be melted in the midst thereof; and ye shall know that I the Lord have poured out my fury upon you. (Ezekiel 22: 21-22)

Keeping these facts in mind, let us proceed to the following chapter.

Chapter 13

[Chapter 13] 1 And Enoch went and said: 'Azazel, thou shalt have no peace: a severe sentence has gone forth 2 against thee to put thee in bonds: And thou shalt not have toleration nor request granted to thee, because of the unrighteousness which thou hast taught, and because of all the works of godlessness 3 and unrighteousness and sin which thou hast shown to men.' Then I went and spoke to them all 4 together, and they were all afraid, and fear and trembling seized them. And they besought me to draw up a petition for them that they might find forgiveness, and to read their petition in the presence 5 of the Lord of heaven. For from thenceforward they could not speak (with Him) nor lift up their 6 eyes to heaven for shame of their sins for which they had been condemned. Then I wrote out their petition, and the prayer in regard to their spirits and their deeds individually and in regard to their 7 requests that they should have forgiveness and length. And I went off and sat down at the waters of Dan, in the land of Dan, to the south of the west of Hermon: I read their petition till I fell 8 asleep. And behold a dream came to me, and visions fell down upon me, and I saw visions of chastisement, and a voice came bidding (me) I to tell it to the sons of heaven, and reprimand them. 9 And when I awaked, I came unto them, and they were all sitting gathered together, weeping in 10 'Abelsjail, which is between Lebanon and Seneser, with their faces covered. And I recounted before them all the visions which I had seen in sleep, and I began to speak the words of righteousness, and to reprimand the heavenly Watchers.

Enoch first goes to Azazel, and then to the other Watchers. This seems a bit odd, but not in light of the fact that Azazel is not named amongst the chiefs of tens in Chapter 6. He is not named until Chapter 8. Azazel appears to be a sort of free-agent, who is working in his own time and ways, apart from the others. This isn't the only place where this happens. It also occurs in the text of the *Book of Giants*:

> 4Q530 Frag. 7 ...Thereupon Ohya said to Hahya [...] Then he answered, It is not for us, but for Azazel, for he did [...the children of] angels are the giants, and they would not let all their loved ones be neglected [...we have] not been cast down; you have strength [...]

Ohya and Hahya are the sons of Shemyaza, according to the *Book of Giants*. Although the text is (again) terribly fragmented, whichever of Shemyaza's sons is speaking seems to be of the opinion that whatever 'it' is has nothing to do with them, but everything to do with Azazel. The *Book of Giants* is a curious work because it presents the giants in a rather sympathetic light. They're very human and very disturbed by their dream-visions of disaster. It also mentions Gilgamesh, the hero of Uruk and slayer of Humbaba. Here Ohya seems to relate that the impending destruction is only for the earthly kings:

> 4Q530 Col.2:...concerns the death of our souls [...] and all his comrades, and Ohya told them what Gilgamesh said to him [...] and it was said [...] concerning [...] the leader has cursed the potentates and the giants were glad at his words. Then he turned and left [...]

Here too, in this chapter of Enoch, the Watchers are portrayed somewhat sympathetically. They ask Enoch to write up a petition for them to take before God. Enoch does this, for Enoch is aware of his position as a go-between. Enoch is a man, who has found his divinity, whilst the Watchers are divinity, who have opted for humanity.

After writing the petition, Enoch goes off to sit by the waters of the river Dan, which lies to the south and west of Mount Hermon – again, a location near Damascus. The word 'dan' means 'judgment' and so we must be left wondering if this is simply another pun or a clue to the reality of there having been problems in the land of Damascus for the sect of the Yahad.

When he awakens from his vision, he goes to the Watchers and finds them "sitting gathered together, weeping in Abelsjail, which is between Lebanon and Seneser, with their faces covered". In the original Ethiopic text, Abelsjail is written as Ublesjael and is sometimes transliterated as Oubelseyael. According to John Dyneley Prince, a professor of Semitic language at New York University, Ublesjael is synonymous with Abel-Beth-Maachah, a city in northern Israel that is mentioned in both *I Kings* (Chapter 15) and *II Kings* (Chapter 15). Abel-Beth-Maachah, also known as Abel-maim, lies directly east of Tyre on the other side of the Lebanon. Abel-Beth-Maachah means 'meadow of the house of Maachah'. The story told in *I Kings*, Chapter 15 relates how there reigned a wicked king over Judah (the southern kingdom) named Abijam. It is said that Abijam's mother is Maachah. When Abijam dies, Judah is ruled by his son Asa. It is also said that Asa's mother is Maachah:

> And he took away the sodomites out of the land, and removed all the idols that his fathers had made. 13 And also Maachah his mother, even her he removed from being queen, because she had made an idol in a grove; and Asa destroyed her idol and burnt it by the brook of Kidron. 14 But the high places were not removed: nevertheless Asa's heart was perfect with the Lord all his days.(I Ki. 15:12-14)

The "high places" refers to the sacred groves and woodland temples of the pagans, generally found on the tops of hills and mountains. We have here an indication that the peoples in this area tended to worship idols – that is, they were pagans. The Maachathites were evidently an indigenous people of the region, for in *Joshua*, we are told:

> *And Gilead, and the border of the Geshurites and Maachathites, and all of Mt. Hermon, and all Bashan unto Saleah; 12 All the kingdom of Og in Bashan, which reigneth in Ashtaroth and in Edrei, who remained of the remnant of the giants; for these did Moses smite, and cast them out. 13 Nevertheless, the children of Israel expelled not the Geshurites, not the Maachathites: but the Geshurites and the Maachathites dwell among the Israelites until this day. (Josh. 13:11-13)*

Evidently, Abijam and Asa were of the tribe of the Maachathites, who lived in the northern land of Israel, but were kings of the southern land of Judah. Were the Maachathites also 'giants'? The word "nevertheless" at the beginning of verse 13 gives one pause to wonder. Whether or not they were, Abel-Beth-Maachah is in the land of the giants and near to Mt. Hermon. The word *maakh* means 'squashed' or 'crushed', which may refer to the subjugation of the peoples of this area. It also means 'depression', as a geographical inference of lowlands.

Chapter 15 of *I Kings* goes on to tell how there was war between Asa and Baasha the king of Israel all their days. Asa seeks an ally in his wars against Baasha (whose name sounds rather like Bashan), in the person of one Ben-Hadad, the king of Syria who dwelled in Damascus. Asa basically bribes Ben-Hadad with silver and gold to forget his alliance with Baasha and come over to their side. Ben-Hadad breaks his alliance with Baasha and sends his troops to attack the lands of the tribes of Naphtali and Dan, including the towns of Ijon, Dan and Abel-Beth-Maachah – Asa's homeland. Asa is said to have died because he had a disease in his feet, probably leprosy. Ben-Hadad also contracts the dreaded disease. More can be read about Ben-Hadad in the article TWO PROPHETS AND A KING NAMED HAZAEL.

The word *abel* which originally meant 'meadow', later comes to mean 'mourning'. Is this another play on words, that we find the Watchers in this place weeping for their fate and the fate of their sons?

Ijon, Dan and Abel-Beth-Maachah are again attacked in *II Kings*, Chapter 15 by Tiglath-pileser III, the king of Assyria. Tiglath-pileser III carried many of the inhabitants of this area away into captivity in Assyria, including the tribes of Dan and Naphtali. Damascus fell to Tiglath-pileser III in about 732 BCE. While the location of Abelsjail is a small thing, which might go unnoticed by most, it is a key to understanding some of the inferences of the history of these peoples related to what is said in Enoch. Abel-Beth-Maachah lies within a short distance of the old city of Laish, which became the city of Dan. This is important for several reasons, which are discussed in articles found in the articles THE SONS OF DAN and THE STORY OF SAMSON.

By the waters of the Dan, the first dream-vision of Enoch is experienced. Upon waking, he goes to the Watchers and relates what he has seen in his dream....

Chapter 14

[Chapter 14] 1 The book of the words of righteousness, and of the reprimand of the eternal Watchers in accordance 2 with the command of the Holy Great One in that vision. I saw in my sleep what I will now say with a tongue of flesh and with the breath of my mouth: which the Great One has given to men to 3 converse therewith and understand with the heart. As He has created and given to man the power of understanding the word of wisdom, so hath He created me also and given me the power of reprimanding 4 the Watchers, the children of heaven. I wrote out your petition, and in my vision it appeared thus, that your petition will not be granted unto you throughout all the days of eternity, and that judgment 5 has been finally passed upon you: yea (your petition) will not be granted unto you. And from henceforth you shall not ascend into heaven unto all eternity, and in bonds of the earth the decree 6 has gone forth to bind you for all the days of the world. And (that) previously you shall have seen the destruction of your beloved sons and ye shall have no pleasure in them, but they shall fall before 7 you by the sword. And your petition on their behalf shall not be granted, nor yet on your own: even though you weep and pray and speak all the words contained in the writing which I have 8 written.

Here, Enoch breaks the bad news that nothing they can say will absolve the Watchers or their sons of their sins against the people. God forgives David for his indiscretion with Bathsheba the wife of Uriah, and his subsequent betrayal of Uriah – sending him to the front lines of battle to be killed. He evidently forgave Solomon of his sins...which included taking pagan women as his concubines and wives, and even engaging in their idolatrous worship. God could be forgiving, but here it is portrayed that He is not in the least inclined to be so. In all actuality, this sounds more like the strict policy of the Yahad against lecherers and backsliders:

> *The operations of the spirit of falsehood result in greed, neglect of righteous deeds, wickedness, lying, pride and haughtiness, cruel deceit and fraud, massive hypocrisy, a want of self-control and abundant foolishness, a zeal for arrogance, abominable deeds fashioned by whorish desire, lechery in its filthy manifestation, a reviling tongue, blind eyes, deaf ears, stiff neck, and hard heart – to the end of walking in all the ways of darkness and evil cunning.*
> *The judgment of all who walk in such ways will be multiple afflictions at the hand of the angels of perdition, everlasting damnation in the wrath of God's furious vengeance, never-ending terror and reproach for all eternity, with shameful extinction in the fire of Hell's outer darkness. For all their*

> eras, generation by generation, the will know doleful sorrow, bitter evil, and dark happenstance, until their utter destruction with neither remnant nor rescue. (Charter of a Jewish Sectarian Association).

Quite a list of sins there, with punishments to match. There is another key passage in this same document that seems to apply to the fate of the Watchers:

> Any man who, having been in the society of the Yahad for ten full years, backslides spiritually so that he forsakes the Yahad and leaves the general membership, walking in his willful heart, may never again return to the society of the Yahad.

> Also, any man belonging to the Yahad who shares with him his own pure food, his own wealth or that of the Yahad, is to suffer the same verdict: he is to be expelled.

These people brook nothing that they consider sinful or shameful in the eyes of the Lord. They have several other punishments listed in the documents for cursing, harboring a grudge against one's brother, spitting, gesturing with the left hand, speaking foolishness, sleeping in the assembly, gossiping, appearing naked in front of others, and other such 'minor' transgressions. According to their own words, backsliding is *the* worst sin of all and never to be forgiven. Yet, backsliding is the sin of Solomon, as well as the sin of Samson and others in the Old Testament. Note the wording "...so that he forsakes the Yahad and leaves the general membership, walking in his willful heart..." This is exactly what Shemyaza does. Could Shemyaza have been a member of the Yahad, who walked out and took two hundred members and nineteen chiefs of tens with him? The idea is certainly compelling in the face of what is revealed about the Yahad in this document. However, there is other evidence – some of which has already been discussed – that this is only an exoteric interpretation of what is going on in Enoch.

And the vision was shown to me thus: Behold, in the vision clouds invited me and a mist summoned me, and the course of the stars and the lightnings sped and hastened me, and the winds in 9 the vision caused me to fly and lifted me upward, and bore me into heaven. And I went in till I drew nigh to a wall which is built of crystals and surrounded by tongues of fire: and it began to affright 10 me. And I went into the tongues of fire and drew nigh to a large house which was built of crystals: and the walls of the house were like a tesselated floor (made) of crystals, and its groundwork was 11 of crystal. Its ceiling was like the path of the stars and the lightnings, and between them were 12 fiery cherubim, and their heaven was (clear as) water. A flaming fire surrounded the walls, and its 13 portals blazed with fire. And I entered into that house,

and it was hot as fire and cold as ice: there 14 were no delights of life therein: fear covered me, and trembling got hold upon me. And as I quaked 15 and trembled, I fell upon my face. And I beheld a vision, And lo! there was a second house, greater 16 than the former, and the entire portal stood open before me, and it was built of flames of fire. And in every respect it so excelled in splendour and magnificence and extent that I cannot describe to 17 you its splendour and its extent. And its floor was of fire, and above it were lightnings and the path 18 of the stars, and its ceiling also was flaming fire. And I looked and saw therein a lofty throne: its appearance was as crystal, and the wheels thereof as the shining sun, and there was the vision of 19 cherubim. And from underneath the throne came streams of flaming fire so that I could not look 20 thereon. And the Great Glory sat thereon, and His raiment shone more brightly than the sun and 21 was whiter than any snow. None of the angels could enter and could behold His face by reason 22 of the magnificence and glory and no flesh could behold Him. The flaming fire was round about Him, and a great fire stood before Him, and none around could draw nigh Him: ten thousand times 23 ten thousand (stood) before Him, yet He needed no counselor. And the most holy ones who were 24 nigh to Him did not leave by night nor depart from Him. And until then I had been prostrate on my face, trembling: and the Lord called me with His own mouth, and said to me: 'Come hither, 25 Enoch, and hear my word.' And one of the holy ones came to me and waked me, and He made me rise up and approach the door: and I bowed my face downwards.

In this chapter, Enoch is conveyed by the wind, the course of the stars and lightning to Heaven, which is a 'house' made of crystal and fire. Its ceiling is said to be "like the path of the stars and the lightnings" several times, perhaps an allusion to the heavens we can see – or something like it on a parallel plane. We are then told "and between them were fiery cherubim". Some of this is quite reminiscent of Tablet IX of the *Epic of Gilgamesh*, which unfortunately has a lot of missing pieces. However, you will get the idea from these snippets from the tablet. Three stars (***) indicate where sections of the text are not shown here:

> He was sleeping in the night, but awoke with a start with a dream...
>
> ***
>
> The Scorpion-Beings
> The mountain is called Mashu.
> Then he reached Mount Mashu,
> which daily guards the rising and setting of the Sun,

*above which only the dome of the heavens reaches,
and whose flank reaches as far as the Netherworld below,
there were Scorpion-beings watching over its gate.
Trembling terror they inspire, the sight of them is death,
their frightening aura sweeps over the mountains.
At the rising and setting they watch over the Sun.
When Gilgamesh saw them, trembling terror blanketed his face,
but he pulled himself together and drew near to them.
The scorpion-being called out to his female:
"He who comes to us, his body is the flesh of gods!"
The scorpion-being, his female, answered him:
"(Only) two-thirds of him is a god, one-third is human."
The male scorpion-being called out,
saying to the offspring of the gods:
"Why have you traveled so distant a journey?
Why have you come here to me,
over rivers whose crossing is treacherous!
I want to learn your ...
I want to learn ..."*

[16 lines are missing here. When the text resumes Gilgamesh is speaking.]

*"I have come on account of my ancestor Utnapishtim,
who joined the Assembly of the Gods, and was given eternal life.
About Death and Life I must ask him!"
The scorpion-being spoke to Gilgamesh ..., saying:
"Never has there been, Gilgamesh, a mortal man who could do that.
No one has crossed through the mountains,
for twelve leagues it is darkness throughout--
dense is the darkness, and light there is none.
To the rising of the sun ...
To the setting of the sun ...
To the setting of the sun ...
They caused to go out..."*

***

*It was impossible for him to see ahead or behind.
When he had achieved ten leagues...
Eleven leagues he traveled and came out before the sun(rise).
Twelve leagues he traveled and it grew brilliant.
...He came out in front of the sun.
...brightness was everywhere.
All kinds of thorny, prickly, spiky bushes were visible,
blossoming with gemstones.
Carnelian bore fruit*

> Hanging in clusters, lovely to look at,
> Lapis lazuli bore foliage,
> Bore fruit, and was delightful to view.
>
> (about 24 lines are missing here, describing the garden in detail.]
>
> ... cedar
> Its fronds of banded agate...
> ... of the sea ... lapis lazuli,
> like brambles and thorn bushes of carnelian-stone,
> Carob trees...of green emerald stone,
> rubies, hematite,...
> Riches and wealth...
> Like turquoise...
> ... of the sea,
> Gilgamesh walking about...
> He raised his eyes and saw ...

As we've seen in the fragments from the *Book of Giants*, these people were familiar with the legend of Gilgamesh and appear to number him amongst the giants. At the beginning of his journey, as he is wandering in the open spaces, he sees lions and is afraid. Gilgamesh prays to Sin, the moon god, and takes courage. Implausibly, he goes to sleep and awakes from his dream glad to be alive. He then takes up his axe and his sword and falls among the lions "like an arrow". Like Samson and Heracles, Gilgamesh is a slayer of lions and we are told in Tablet X that he is wearing a lion's hide. In the *MUL.APIN* a group of Babylonian astrological texts that now reside in the British Museum, we are told that the constellation of Orion (the giant of the winter night sky) is in fact Gilgamesh. He is known as SIPA.ZI.AN.NA here and appears in the Way of Anu. SIPA.ZI.AN.NA can be roughly translated as 'the eternal spirit of heaven'. Above Orion is the constellation of Perseus, whose Sumero-Babylonian equivalent is Enkidu, and possibly some aspects of Dumuzi or Tammuz. This constellation is called LU.CHUN.GA which is translated 'king of the fields'. The garden of gemstones is described as being "like brambles and thorn-bushes" which would be of a spiky appearance, not unlike something composed of crystals.

It isn't too far-fetched to associate this portion of the *Book of Watchers* with this particular portion of the *Epic of Gilgamesh*, for it is in this section that Gilgamesh is struggling to find his ancestor Ziusudra or Utnapishtim (Noah), to find the secret of eternal life. The 'bright place' to which Gilgamesh comes is an eternal land where the immortal Utnapishtim lives. Keep in mind that in the time that Gilgamesh was written, it was not believed that any soul – immortal or not – went to heaven to abide eternally. Most souls journeyed to the Underworld, Kurnugi...the Land of No Return. This 'bright place' is the mythical Dilmun – a different and special place where Utnapishtim and his wife were sent to live in their immortality.

Here, in *Enoch*, it has become an abode of the Supreme God in Heaven, yet there are many things about it which 'speak' of the Underworld – a place of fire and crystals. The Scorpion-beings have been replaced by "fiery cherubim". When God speaks to Enoch to approach, he says that "one of the holy ones" comes and awakens him, as Gilgamesh awakens from his sleep.

Chapter 15

[Chapter 15] 1 And He answered and said to me, and I heard His voice: 'Fear not, Enoch, thou righteous 2 man and scribe of righteousness: approach hither and hear my voice. And go, say to the Watchers of heaven, who have sent thee to intercede for them: "You should intercede for men, and not men 3 for you:

God tells Enoch here that the Watchers should intercede for men. The idea of the intercession of 'lesser' deities – including kings - to the Higher Power of the supreme god of any pantheon is not a new idea presented in Enoch. When Enkidu, the pure and strong wild-man who is tamed and civilized by the hierodule/harlot Shamhat, is swallowed by the Earth, Gilgamesh attempts to intercede to have him released by going first to speak to Ellil, then to Sin, and then to Ea. It is Ea that answers him, at last. In *Atrahasis* Ea intercedes with his brother Ellil (who is favored by Anu over Ea) on behalf of the striking Igigi who are weary from their work. Athirat and Anat intercede on behalf of Baal with his father El, that he may have a palace of his own. The Sumero-Babylonian kings 'interceded' on behalf of their land and people by laying with the High Priestess of Inanna/Ishtar once a year so that the land, the animals and the people would be fruitful. Any male issue born of this union stood as heir to become the next *lugal* or king. Any female child born would assume her mother's place as the High Priestess. The kings, priest-kings and priests were all seen as intercessors, as were the lesser deities to the most high gods.

Wherefore have ye left the high, holy, and eternal heaven, and lain with women, and defiled yourselves with the daughters of men and taken to yourselves wives, and done like the children 4 of earth, and begotten giants (as your) sons?

While this pronouncement is aimed at the Watchers, it may just as well be an indictment against the lecherous escapades of Zeus, the supreme god of the Greek pantheon. Zeus often left the high, holy and eternal halls of Olympus to visit earth. More than once or twice, he saw a human woman who caught his eye and he would not rest until he possessed her. Zeus often disguised himself in various ways, when approaching his 'quarry', be it human or divine. He disguised himself as Amphitryon, the dead husband of Alcmene. From her was born the hero Heracles. He comes into the imprisoned Danae as a shower of gold falling from heaven, and begets Perseus. He carries off Europa, disguised as a white bull, and fathers Minos, Rhadamanthus, and Sarpedon. He turns Io into a pretty little heifer to allay the suspicions of the jealous Hera, and Io bears Epaphus. He seduces Leda, transforming himself into a swan, and Leda bears the twins Castor and Pollux, and their sister Helen. He is also the father of Arcas by Callisto – the daughter of Lycaon. While on the surface Zeus seems a randy sort of fellow, this is comparable to the story of Jacob, his wives Leah and Rachel and their handmaids, Zilpah and Bilhah in *Genesis*. By these four women were the original 'twelve tribes' of Israel born. Leah and Rachel were the daughters of the Syrian, Laban. Bilhah was a slave, whose name may be a feminine form of Baal – Baalah. From her came Dan and Naphtali. Zilpah, another slave, is the mother of Gad and Asher.

This comparison can be made because the male offspring of Zeus are either heroes – mighty men of old – Heracles and Perseus, or the patriarchs and kings of various nations...all god-men. Perseus has the distinction of being both a hero and the first king of the Mycenaean Greeks. Minos and Rhadamanthus are the kings of Crete. Sarpedon, their brother, was the king of Lycia. Epaphus became the king of Egypt, who founded the city of Memphis. His mother, Io, was sometimes equated with Isis by the Greeks. Arcas, the son of Callisto becomes the king of Arcadia. These genealogies are of particular interest, as we shall see later.

The story of the Watchers also echoes the story of Enkidu and Gilgamesh. Enkidu was 'made' as a companion to Gilgamesh – one who could match his strength and teach the proud and willful king some humanity. In Tablet I of *Gilgamesh* we are told.

> *Gilgamesh will not leave any son alone for his father. Day and night his behaviour is overbearing. He is the shepherd of Uruk the Sheepfold, He is their shepherd, yet... Powerful, superb, knowledgeable and expert, Gilgamesh will not leave young girls alone, the daughters of warriors, the brides of young men. Anu often hears their complaints. They called upon great Aruru: 'You Aruru, you created mankind! Now create someone for him, to match the ardour of his energies! Let them be regular rivals, and let Uruk be allowed peace!' When Aruru heard this, she created inside herself the word of Anu. Aruru washed her hands, pinched off a piece of clay, cast it out into open country. She created a primitive man, Enkidu the warrior: offspring of silence (?) sky bolt of Ninurta. His whole body was shaggy with hair, he was furnished with tresses like a woman, his locks of hair grew luxuriant like grain.*

A hunter, accustomed to trapping in the woods and fields there sees Enkidu and is dumbstruck and afraid of him. Enkidu will not allow him to hunt amongst 'his brothers' the wild beasts of the field. Frustrated and afraid, the hunter tells his father about this wildman, and then relays the news to Gilgamesh. Gilgamesh's solution is to send the harlot Shamhat out to 'tame' Enkidu. For six days and seven nights, Enkidu and Shamhat make love. After this, Enkidu returns to the fields, but his previous friends, the gazelles and cattle want nothing to do with him. He has become a man. His legs are weakened and he cannot keep up with the wild beasts as he once did. Shamhat tells him in so many words that it's *quid pro quo* - he's gained wisdom and judgment in place of his superior strength.

Shamhat takes Enkidu to Uruk, where there is a wedding ceremony taking place. As usual, Gilgamesh has decided it's his right to take the bride before her husband has her. Enkidu hears of this and isn't about to let it happen. He bars the way into the house where the bride is staying and will not let Gilgamesh pass. We are told:

> *Enkidu blocked his access at the door of the father-in-law's house, He would not allow Gilgamesh to enter. They grappled at the door of the father-in-law's house, wrestled in the street, in the public square. Doorframes shook, walls quaked. (Gilgamesh, Tab. II)*

They end up being friends, because that's what they were meant to be. There are a few elements here to consider in relation to the stories of Samson, and of Jacob and at least one of his offspring.

Like Samson, Enkidu has luxuriant hair. Like Samson, Enkidu is weakened by a harlot. Unlike Delilah, Shamhat has no evil intent in her seduction of Enkidu. She is simply doing the will of her king. Delilah was a temple harlot of Dagon, the god of the sea, whereas Shamhat appears to be a temple harlot of Utu-Shamash, the sun god. She 'enlightens' Enkidu, but also weakens him. Still, he is equal to fighting with the mighty Gilgamesh.

When Jacob is trying to avoid the meet with his 'hairy' brother Esau, he sends his wives, children and his 'gift' to Esau across the ford of the brook of Jabbock. Jacob has the right to be concerned about this meeting, for earlier in life, he stole away Esau's inheritance as the first-born twin for a bowl of lentil soup, taking advantage of Esau's hunger. Esau was the hunter, the man of the fields. Once he's sent his family across the brook, Jacob is left alone. There in the night, he wrestles with 'a man'. It is this 'man' (also cast as an angel in some versions) who bestows the name Israel upon Jacob. We read here:

> *24 And Jacob was left alone; and there wrestled a man with him until the breaking of day. 25 And when he saw that he prevailed not against him, he touched the hollow of his thigh; and the hollow of Jacob's thigh was out of joint, as he wrestled with him. 26 And he said, Let me go, for the day breaketh. And he said, I will not let thee go, except thou bless me. (Genesis 32)*

It is of interest to note that the man asks Jacob to let him go "for the day breaketh". The day, when the sun blots out the stars of the night and the figures of Enkidu (Perseus) and Gilgamesh (Orion) are blotted out from the sky. While there has been much written analyzing if

Jacob was wrestling with his own conscience, or with one of God's angels, but comparing the stories from this angle, it seems to reflect the story of the two mighty men of old, Enkidu and Gilgamesh.

These bouts of wrestling lead to yet another bout of wrestling. When the fifth child of Jacob is born, we are told:

> 5 And Bilhah conceived, and bare Jacob a son. 6 And Rachel said, God hath judged me, and hath also heard my voice, and given me a son: therefore, she called his name Dan.

When the sixth child of Jacob is born, Rachel makes the declaration:

> 7 And Bilhah, Rachel's maid conceived again, and bare Jacob a second son. 8 And Rachel said, With great wrestlings have I wrestled with my sister, and I have prevailed; and she called his name Naphtali (Genesis 30)

Samson of the long-hair, the son of Dan was a judge of Israel. We are told that the name Naphtali literally means 'my wrestling'. These and other little bits of information seem to link these later biblical tales to the old Sumero-Babylonian stories of Enkidu and Gilgamesh. The battle between Rachel and Leah for the attentions of Jacob is also somewhat reminiscent of the feud between Inanna and her sister Ereshkigal, but that is a story for another time. We know for a fact that the story of Noah and the Flood is from *Atrahasis*. It only follows that other stories, and in particular the popular *Epic of Gilgamesh*, were also 'borrowed' and converted into the tales of the patriarchs.

And though ye were holy, spiritual, living the eternal life, you have defiled yourselves with the blood of women, and have begotten (children) with the blood of flesh, and, as the children of men, have lusted after flesh and blood as those also do who die 5 and perish. Therefore have I given them wives also that they might impregnate them, and beget 6 children by them, that thus nothing might be wanting to them on earth. But you were formerly 7 spiritual, living the eternal life, and immortal for all generations of the world. And therefore I have not appointed wives for you; for as for the spiritual ones of the heaven, in heaven is their dwelling.

Much has been said and made of "the blood of women" by certain authors writing on this and related subjects. Unfortunately, it is often the lunatic ravings of conspiracy theorists about the unquenchable thirst of the 'reptilian overlords' of the Niburian or Martian Anunnaki for human blood or the slightly less sensationalized Anunnaki Star Fire secret of the gods. While there is some bit of truth to the idea, it's a little more down to earth than this.

Let us first address the issue of blood, overall. As has been previously mentioned, blood was considered the vehicle of the spirit or soul. The Jews believed that the life was in the blood and the blood was the life. It is quite easy to see this connection, for both humans and animals deprived of their blood no longer live. The Romans and Arabs are said to have held the same belief. Other peoples believed that any ground upon which blood is spilt becomes cursed – particularly if the blood is royal. On the opposite side of the coin, there were groups of people who believed that blood mixed with the corn or sprinkled over the fields encouraged a fruitful harvest. To this end, some peoples including certain Amerind tribes and Hindu tribes sacrificed young men and women – often in rather horrible ways – collecting their blood as their shredded bodies bled out their lives, and sprinkling it in the planted furrows of their fields. These sacrifices were called 'meriahs', among other names. Others, such as the Greeks, reportedly mixed the menstruum of virgin priestesses with the corn and seeds before they were planted in the ground. This seems a bit more pro-life than the previous method. One man's taboo is another man's sanction.

The 'ambrosia' of the Greek gods was said to be the moon-blood of Aphrodite or Hera, mixed with honey. In imitation of this idea, a more mundane sort of ambrosia was served as part of the Greek mystery rites, using the moon-blood of the virgin priestesses. Similarly, in Egypt, the moon-blood of the priestesses of Isis was ritually collected and used in various concoctions of wine, and/or honey and other substances for sundry purposes. Reportedly, this same ritual also existed in the temples of Inanna/Ishtar, in Sumer and Babylonia with the blood collected from the priestesses. These women were known as Scarlet Women or Sacred Women for this reason. These concoctions were said to increase spiritual powers, prevent certain diseases and increase longevity.

While this is something of sympathetic magic, it has a certain basis in scientific fact, for the menstruum contains important endocrinal secretions of the pineal and pituitary glands. It also contains nutrients for the possible conception and growth of a fetus. The urine of pregnant mares is used today to manufacture the drug Premarin, which is commonly used in estrogen replacement therapy (ERT) for menopausal and post-menopausal women. Progesterone, which is a steroid involved with the female menstrual cycle, pregnancy and embryogenesis is not only an important female hormone, but one produced in tandem with testosterone in men. Progesterone regulates the deterioration of tissues in the body. In later years, when the levels of progesterone drop, symptoms of aging begin to manifest. It plays a role in the elasticity of the skin, bone density, and various organic and nerve tissues. The claim that this bloody cocktail prevents certain diseases and increases longevity is not so far-fetched. After all, it's what 'grew you' in your mother's womb.

8 And now, the giants, who are produced from the spirits and flesh, shall be called evil spirits upon 9 the earth, and on the earth shall be their dwelling. Evil spirits have proceeded from their bodies; because they are born from men and from the holy Watchers is their beginning and primal origin; 10 they shall be evil spirits on earth, and evil spirits shall they be called. [As for the spirits of heaven, in heaven shall be their dwelling, but as for the spirits of the earth which were born upon the earth, on the earth shall be their dwelling.] And the spirits of the giants afflict, oppress, destroy, attack, do battle, and work destruction on the earth, and cause trouble: they take no food, but nevertheless 12 hunger and thirst, and cause offences. And these spirits shall rise up against the children of men and against the women, because they have proceeded from them.

The author of this bit of text seems to really want to get the point across that these 'giants' are evil, evil, evil. We see something similar in Chapter 10 of the *Book of Jubilees* that might explain this a little better:

> *1And in the third week of this jubilee the unclean demons began to lead astray the children of 2 the sons of Noah, and to make to err and destroy them. And the sons of Noah came to Noah their father, and they told him concerning the demons which were leading astray and blinding and 3 slaying his sons' sons. And he prayed before the Lord his God, and said: 'God of the spirits of all flesh, who hast shown mercy unto me And hast saved me and my sons from the waters of the flood, And hast not caused me to perish as Thou didst the sons of perdition; For Thy grace has been great towards me, And great has been Thy mercy to my soul; Let Thy grace be lift up upon my sons, And let not wicked spirits rule over them Lest they should destroy them from the earth. 4 But do Thou bless me and my sons, that we may increase and Multiply and replenish the earth. 5 And Thou knowest how Thy Watchers, the fathers of these spirits, acted in my day: and as for these spirits which are living, imprison them and hold them fast in the place of condemnation, and let them not bring destruction on the sons of thy servant, my God; for these are malignant, and 6 created in order to destroy. And let them not rule over the spirits of the living; for Thou alone canst exercise dominion over them. And let them not have power over the sons of the righteous 7,8 from henceforth and for evermore.' And the Lord our God bade us to bind all. And the chief of the spirits, Mastema, came and said: 'Lord, Creator, let some of them remain before me, and let them harken to my voice, and do all that I shall say unto them; for if some of them are not left to me, I shall not be able to execute the power of my will on the sons of men; for these are for corruption and*

> *leading astray before my judgment, for great is the wickedness of the sons of men.' 9 And He said: Let the tenth part of them remain before him, and let nine parts descend into the 10 place of condemnation.' And one of us He commanded that we should teach Noah all their 11 medicines; for He knew that they would not walk in uprightness, nor strive in righteousness. And we did according to all His words: all the malignant evil ones we bound in the place of condemna- 12 tion and a tenth part of them we left that they might be subject before Satan on the earth. And we explained to Noah all the medicines of their diseases, together with their seductions, how he 13 might heal them with herbs of the earth. And Noah wrote down all things in a book as we instructed him concerning every kind of medicine. Thus the evil spirits were precluded from 14 (hurting) the sons of Noah. And he gave all that he had written to Shem, his eldest son; for he 15 loved him exceedingly above all his sons.*

If you read this closely, you will notice that this is happening *after* the flood. 'And he prayed before the Lord his God, and said: 'God of the spirits of all flesh, who hast shown mercy unto me *And hast saved me and my sons from the waters of the flood*, And hast not caused me to perish as Thou didst the sons of perdition….' This is another telling point. The 'sons of perdition' evidently did not all perish in the flood, and continued to exist. We have evidence of this, in the appearance of the Anakim, the Rephaim, the giant kings Og and Sihon, and the giant Goliath *after* the Flood in the Old Testament. Logic would dictate that being the all-powerful and mighty god that he is, Yahweh would not have left any survivors, had it been his intention to wipe them all off the face of the earth.

It is of interest here to note that Noah gives his book in which the Watchers of heaven instructed him on healing 'with the herbs of the earth' to his son *Shem*. It is the fallen angel Shemyaza who is the teacher of 'enchantments and root-cuttings'. This also reminds us that in the original story of Gilgamesh going to visit his ancestor, Utnapishtim, Gilgamesh obtains the 'plant of life', which is then stolen from him by a serpent as he is bathing.

This bit in *Jubilees* appears to be an explanation for 'why' they didn't all disappear. It is difficult as answering "Which came first, the chicken or the egg?" at this point to discern if *Jubilees* was written before or after *Enoch*. In light of the fact that *Jubilees* appears to have been written as either a pre-cursor to or a re-writing of the *Torah*, one might reflect on the 'bare-bones' nature of what we are left with in the canonical texts of today in comparison to what is laid out in *Jubilees*. *Jubilees* is extremely detailed when held up to *Genesis*, *Exodus* and *Enoch*. It's almost as if someone said, "The less said, the better…let's leave a few things in the air. We don't want to pin ourselves down *too much*." *Genesis*, *Exodus* and *Enoch* then appear to be highly editorialized versions of *Jubilees*. *Jubilees* is a valuable text, exactly for the reason that it does go into so much detail. However, all of this detail sometimes conflicts with other things that are later said.

Even the text of *Jubilees* has its internal conflicts, as we see in this passage that immediately precedes what is written above:

> 14...And thus the sons of Noah divided unto their sons in the presence of Noah their father, and he bound them all by an oath, imprecating 15 a curse on every one that sought to seize the portion which had not fallen (to him) by his lot. And they all said, 'So be it; so be it ' for themselves and their sons for ever throughout their generations till the day of judgment, on which the Lord God shall judge them with a sword and with fire for all the unclean wickedness of their errors, wherewith they have filled the earth with transgression and uncleanness and fornication and sin. (Jubilees, Chapter 9)

This is talking about when the Lord God shall judge *the sons of the sons of Noah* "with a sword and with fire for all the unclean wickedness of their errors, wherewith they have filled the earth with transgression and uncleanness and fornication and sin". We're not about the Watchers and the giants and the demons here. We're talking about the sons of the sons of Noah...men. Who are these sons of Noah?

THE SONS OF SHEM:

- **Elam**: The Elamites – a people who lived in an area east of the Tigris Euphrates Rivers. Their ancient capital was Shushan (Susa). Darius I transferred the capitol of Persia to Susa in about 520 BCE. When Tiglath-pilesar III, the Assyrian king, captured the northern kingdom of Israel (Samaria) in about 722 BCE, the Elamites were one of the national groups that were deported to Samaria. A group of Samaritans in turn were deported to Elam.
- **Asshur**: The Assyrians – the name Asher figures as one of the sons of Jacob in *Genesis*...one of the original twelve tribes. The Assyrians themselves traced their heritage to their god/ancestor Ashshur, whose attributes are said to have been borrowed from the Sumerian gods Enlil and Marduk-Bel. His emblem is the winged-disk – the emblem of Ahura Mazda and Shamash. Ashshur is said to be a god of four faces: the bull, the eagle, the lion and the man. You might recognize this symbology from *Ezekiel* 1:10: "As for the likeness of their faces, they four had the face of a man, and the face of a lion, on the right side: and

they four had the face of an ox on the left side; they four also had the face of an eagle."

- **Aram**: the Aramaeans were an ancient desert people who settled in the lands of northern Israel in about 2250 BCE. Their lands were bordered on the west by the Lebanon mountains to the Euphrates River on the east, as far as the Taurus Mountains in the north and southward to Damascus. This was also inclusive of the 'lands of Sihon and Og', and the Aramaeans were 'native' to the area at the time of the Exodus. They might be called the Syrians, today. Damascus was the seat of their power. The Aramaeans were often aligned with either Israel or Judea, one against the other. At one point, the Judeans aligned with Assyria against Israel and Aram. The Aramaeans are also known as the Amorites – the Westerners. The Canaanites or general inhabitants of Canaan were also known as Amorites, Ammorites or Amurru. Amram, the 'father' of Moses may be a reference to Moses having been born of Aramaean stock. Most of the information we now have concerning the Amurru is from tablets found at the ruin of Mari, an ancient city near the Euphrates.
- **Arpachxad**: this son of Noah is credited with having founded the city of Ur of the Chaldees on the banks of the Euphrates river. He is considered to be the ancestor of the Hebrews and Arabs. It is from this city that the patriarch Abraham was said to have come. This may also include the Sumerians and Babylonians, from whom come Gilgamesh and Enkidu.
- **Lud**: the Lydians, a group of people from Anatolia related to the Hittites or Hatti. Lydia is a large territory in Asia Minor (Turkey) that is rich in resources such as figs, grain, grapes and olives. The Lydians were called 'men of war' by the prophet Ezekiel. They were expert bowmen and often served as mercenaries defending Tyre. They also fought with the Egyptians at the battle of Carchemesh. In Greek mythology Hercules visited Lydia. It is said that the queen Omphale made Hercules her slave for three years. They had three sons, Agelaos, Alceus and Lamus. Lydia was also the home of Tantalus, the king who offended the gods by serving his infant son Pelops by cutting him up into pieces and serving him at a banquet for the gods. He was punished by being placed in Tartarus, with a raging thirst that would last for eternity.

THE SONS OF HAM

- **Cush**: it is unclear if Cush is the ancestor of the Ethiopians (Kush), the Kassites, who lived in the Zagros Mountains of Mesopotamia, or the Sumerian city of Kish. The deified hero/king Nimrod of Babel was said to be 'a son of Cush'. He was also said to have been the instigator of building the infamous Tower of Babel. Like Gilgamesh and Shemyaza, Nimrod is associated with the constellation of Orion – 'the mighty hunter before Jehovah'.
- **Mizraim**: the Egyptians. Egypt is referred to as Mizraim several times in the Bible. The name is inclusive of both Upper and Lower Egypt.
- **Phut**: (also Put) Phut appears to refer to the Libyans. Most of the references in the Bible point to them as allies of Egypt and the men of Lubim or Put were known as fierce warriors. It is questionable if there is not some confusion amongst scholars between the Lubim and the Ludim (the Lydians) as having been the mercenaries hired by the King of Tyre. As these mercenaries refer to 'skilled bowmen' it is more likely that they were the Lydians.
- **Canaan**: the Jebusites, Zemarites, Edomites, Midianites, Moabites, Rephaim, and Philistines. While the Aramaeans is a general term for the inhabitants of Canaan, Ham's son Canaan's people seem to encompass whatever is left of the peoples of Canaan that do not fall under the Amorite peoples – the southern peoples as opposed to the northern.

THE SONS OF JAPHETH

- **Gomer**: a people known as the Gimirri or Khumri. They were a nomadic race of equestrian warriors who lived in what is now Azerbaijan on the eastern coast of the Black Sea. This first mention of them is from 714 BCE and says that they joined Sargon II in defeating the kingdom of Urartu. They are mentioned in Book 11 of Homer's *Odyssey*. Herodotus says that they were displaced from the steppes of southern Russia by the Scythians. Sargon II died in battle against them in 705 BCE. They conquered Phrygia in about 695 BCE. In about 653 BCE, they attacked the kingdom of Lydia and killed Gyges, the king, then wreaked destruction upon the capitol, Sardis. They are said to have become the Sicambrians, the proto-Frankish people from whom the Merovingian kings descended. The Cimmerians are also thought by some

scholars to be the ancestors of the Welsh and Cumbrian peoples – the Cymru and Cwmry.
- **Madai**: the Medes. As the 'Amadai' the Medes first show up in Assyrian annals around 844 BCE. They were an ancient Iranian people who lived in the north, west and northwestern portions of what is Iran today – or the eastern portions of what is Kurdistan. The Medes established an empire that stretched from the modern-day Azerbaijan to Afghanistan on the east and included Persia. The Achaemenid kings of Persia, Cyrus the Great, Darius I and Xerxes I defeated the Medes and established the great Medeo-Persian empire. Herodotus names the six tribes of the Medes as the Busae, the Parataceni, the Struchates, the Arizanti, the Budii, and the Magi.
- **Javan**: the Ionian Greeks. The Assyrians called them the Yamanni and the people of Asia Minor commonly referred to all Greeks as Ionians. However, this is incorrect. The Greeks were separated into four groups according to the dialect they spoke. These four dialects were: Ionian, Doric, Achaean and Aeolian. The western coast of Asia Minor (Anatolia) was called Ionia. Most of the islands of the Aegean Sea were inhabited by Ionians. The Ionians also established the coastal city of Marseille in southern France in the Gulf of Lions.
- **Tubal**: a people of Cappadocia, an Anatolian tribe known as the Tabali. Tubal is also said to be the 'father' of the Iberians of the Caucasus (a region between the Black and Caspian Seas in Russia), and those of the Iberian peninsula which includes Spain and Portugal, as well as the Italians. Tubal is not to be confused with Tubal-Cain, who is the son of Lamech and Zillah – the 'father' of all workers in metal.
- **Meshech**: the Phrygian peoples known as the Mushki, who lived in Anatolia along with the Tabali. The Mushki may be the ancestors of the Russian Georgian peoples. The Tabali and the Mushki helped to overthrow the Hittites in about 1200 BCE.
- **Tiras**: the Thracians or Dacians, who lived in the region of what is now parts of Romania, Bulgaria, Greece and Turkey. The Thracians are mentioned in the *Illiad* as allies of the Trojans. Herodotus calls them a loose confederacy of nomadic, equestrian warrior-types who shared a more or less common language, but never achieved any effective cohesion as a nation. They could have been a very powerful people, had they united under a common banner. The Thracians were known to be highly skilled metal-workers in their day, specializing in items made of gold alloy. They

were mighty warriors - blue-eyed, red-haired, and tattooed - expert with the lance or javelin and the short dagger. A beautiful Thracian dagger – said to be dated from circa 3000 BCE - made from an alloy of gold and platinum and still very sharp, was found in a burial site near the village of Dubovo in Bulgaria in 2006.

- **Magog**: there has been no tribe or national entity linked with this son of Japheth. Chapter 9 of *Jubilees* says: "and in the north there came forth for Magog all the inner portions of the north until it reaches to the sea of 9 Me'at". The word *me'at* in modern Hebrew means 'little' or 'almost'. This may refer to the Baltic Sea, which while quite large for an inland sea is 'small' in comparison to 'the sea' such as might be construed to mean the Mediterranean or the Arabian seas. This would include the areas of what is today Poland, Romania and Hungary. Magog is claimed as an ancestor in both Irish and Hungarian medieval literature. Josephus states that Magog is the ancestor of the Scythians, who lived to the north of the Black Sea. Macc Óc is another name for the Celtic god of love, youth and beauty - Angus Óg amongst the Tuatha de Danann – sometimes equated with Eros or Cupid. Macc Óc or Mac Óg means 'young son'.

As you can well see, these 'sons of the sons of Noah' are various peoples, all of whom had some interaction with the Jews at some time or other – mostly as conquerors. They also number amongst their 'offspring' the 'giant' god-kings, kings and heroes Gilgamesh, Enkidu, Og, Sihon, Nimrod, Goliath, Hercules, and Samson. Also amongst them are the 'mighty men of old', the kings of Sumer, Assyria, Babylonia, Egypt, Greece, Medea and Persia...not to mention some fairly ferocious and doughty warrior tribes who were instrumental in shaping the history of the Mediterranean, Asia Minor and the Middle East. It is also apparent here that the 'sons of Shem' were the progenitors of most of the 'giants' mentioned in the myths and stories of these lands.

It also becomes clear that these descendants of Noah were never meant to mean the Hebrews exclusively. While some of these peoples may have interbred with the Hebrews, they cannot be considered Hebrews at all. In fact, the later attempt to assign the designation of the 'twelve tribes' of Israel to the various peoples inhabiting the Holy Land also falls short in this attempt, for it is still a listing of the various peoples who inhabited these lands at the time the Jews came into Canaan. We have seen that Jacob's wives were Syrian. Sarah, the wife of Abraham, was probably Hurrian or Syrian. Abraham himself was supposedly 'of Ur of the Chaldees'. He could have been a Hurrian, or as some have suggested, a Hittite. Abraham sent a servant to Padan Aram to find a bride for his son Isaac. There the servant finds Rebekkah – which means 'cow' - who is also probably of Hurrian origin. In Egypt, Joseph weds Asenath, the daughter of an Egyptian priest. One might ask, is there truly any such thing as a pure Hebrew? Like their stories and mythologies, they seem to be a combination of a little of everything. This is not said in a way that is meant to be at all derogatory, but a statement of what appears to be facts derived *from their own stories*.

Clearly, whoever wrote the Table of Nations in *Jubilees* and *Genesis* was very educated in the history and ethnic backgrounds of the peoples who inhabited the Mediterranean, Asia Minor and the Middle East. And from the dates mentioned as accords each group, these are people who flourished in and onward from the 9th and 8th centuries BCE - *not* in the time of the historical flood, around 4000 BCE. It also becomes clear that whoever wrote the *Book of the Watchers* and other books of Enoch was just as well familiar with both Sumero-Babylonian *and* Greek mythology and history.

The *War Scroll* has been mentioned a few times, but has yet to make an appearance in the quotes herein. This seems an appropriate time to bring it out. The *War Scroll* was one of the first seven scrolls discovered by the Bedouin boy in Cave 1 at Qumran. The following is from Columns 1 and 2 of the scroll:

> *Column 1 ...Then the Sons of Righteousness shall shine to all ends of the world, continuing to shine forth until end of the appointed seasons of darkness. Then at the time appointed by God, His great excellence shall shine forth for all the times of eternity; for peace and blessing, glory and joy, and long life for all Sons of Light. On the day when the Kittim fall there shall be a battle and horrible carnage before the God of Israel, for it is a day appointed by Him from ancient times as a battle of annihilation for the Sons of Darkness....*
>
> *Column 2 ...In the first year they shall fight against Mesopotamia, in the second against the sons of Lud, in the third they shall fight amongst the rest of the sons of Aram: Uz, Hul, Togar, and Mesha, who are beyond the Euphrates. In the fourth and fifth they shall fight against all the sons of Assyria and Persia and the easterners up to the Great Desert. In the eighth year they shall fight against the sons of Elam, in the ninth year they shall fight against the sons of Ishmael and Keturah, and during the following ten years the war shall be divided against all the sons of Ham according to their clans and their territories. During the remaining ten years the war shall be divided against all sons of Japheth according to their territories.*

It becomes evident while reading the contents of this scroll that the Yahad were not only laying out very detailed plans for war against 'everyone else', but were also providing an exhortation to those who followed them worthy of any president, prime minister or rebel leader rallying the troops in these modern times.

Chapter 16

[Chapter 16] 1 From the days of the slaughter and destruction and death of the giants, from the souls of whose flesh the spirits, having gone forth, shall destroy without incurring judgment - thus shall they destroy until the day of the consummation, the great judgment in which the age shall be 2 consummated, over the Watchers and the godless, yea, shall be wholly consummated." And now as to the Watchers who have sent thee to intercede for them, who had been aforetime in heaven, (say 3 to them): "You have been in heaven, but all the mysteries had not yet been revealed to you, and you knew worthless ones, and these in the hardness of your hearts you have made known to the women, and through these mysteries women and men work much evil on earth." 4 Say to them therefore: "You have no peace."

In this chapter God seems to be telling Enoch that those who have slain and will slay the giants and the godless will not incur and punishment for doing so. The wording here is rather convoluted, but it does appear that this is what is being said. If we are to go with the theory that the Watchers and their giant offspring are the Greeks and/or other peoples who have oppressed the Jews, this is a statement that gives the Jews *carte-blanche* to slaughter them without fear of divine reprisal. As we have seen, in the stories of the Maccabees, this did not seem to be a consideration at all. In fact, in *Leviticus* Chapter 24:10-16, we see the Lord command Moses to have 'the congregation' stone to death the son of a woman of the tribe of Dan. The boy's father was an Egyptian. The boy's crime? He blasphemed the name of the Lord. In *I Samuel* Chapter 15:3, the Lord orders Saul through Samuel to go and smite Amalek (the Amalekites) "*...slay both man and woman, infant and suckling, ox and sheep, camel and ass*". It was okay to kill…murder people in the name of the Lord.

This is perhaps a kind of 'back-up plan' in case the 'giants' don't all kill one another.

Much like the Christians who come after them, the Yahad consider themselves as the 'living Temple of God'. As we have witnessed above, they think of themselves as the angels of heaven – the pure and holy Sons of Light. Would it be so far-fetched then to consider for a moment that they might see themselves as residing in 'heaven'? Taking this into account, verse 3 may again refer to those who have been in their company and learned their 'mysteries', then departed, breaking their vow of silence to the rest of the world about what they learned in the company of the Yahad. The Yahad was not averse to taking Gentiles into their midst, as long as they were repentant of their evil ways and toed the line in regard to the very strict rules of this association. It has been shown previously that these 'worthless' mysteries included knowledge of the coming and going of the sun, moon, planets and stars. This knowledge is in fact revealed to Enoch in later chapters. The mysteries also included knowledge of herbs and healing, such as those revealed to Noah and transmitted to his son Shem. The groups at Lake Mareotis and at Mt. Carmel were healers. They were also apparently somewhat familiar with metal-working as evidenced by the unique *Copper Scroll*. The *War Scroll* contains instructions for making their trumpets and shields, and how their horsemen and priests shall be caparisoned:

> *Column 5… All of them shall bear shields of bronze, polished like a face mirror. The shield shall be bound with a border of plaited work and a design of loops, the work of a skillful workman; gold, silver and bronze bound together and jewels; a multicolored brocade….*

Presumably, this "skillful workman" was to be one of their own.

The *War Scroll* also describes what shall be written on their banners. This is of interest, because the Rule of the Banners sounds almost like a roll-call of the translations of angelic names…all ending in '-el' - of God. The few names in parentheses here are not part of the original text, but inserted to give you an idea of this:

> *When they set out to battle they shall write on the first banner, "The Congregation of God" (Jekabzeel), on the second banner, "The camps of God" (Gadreel), on the third, "The tribes of God" (Sheevatiel), on the fourth, "The clans of God", on the fifth, "The divisions of God", on the sixth, "The Congregation of God" (Jekuthiel), on the seventh, "Those called by God", and on the eighth, "The army of God". They shall write their names in full with all their order. When they draw near for the battle they shall write on their banners "The battle of God" (Kraviel), "The recompense of God", "The cause of God", "The reprisal of God", "The power of God", "The retribution of God", "The might of God" (Uzziel), "The annihilation by God of all the vainglorious nations." And their names in full shall they write upon them. When they return from battle they shall write on their banners, "The deliverance of God", "The victory of God", "The help of God", "The support of God", "The joy of God" (Sheemkhaliel), "The thanksgivings of God", "The praise of God" (Mahaleleel), and "The peace of God" (Shalomiel).*

To say that the Yahad would have had no sympathy for anyone who gave away their plans or secrets would be an understatement. They were planning a 'once and for all' offensive on those who had come into their midst and defiled their way of life. The great battle was to be the end-time of sin and corruption – the end of the old earth and the old heaven and the beginning of the new. We see something of this same nationalistic and condemnatory rhetoric in the Old Testament books of *Isaiah* and *Ezekiel*. We are all too well aware today of the importance of security in these matters, with the advent of World War I, World War II and 9/11. We have entire branches of government that are devoted to security and war strategies. This was a battle that was never won, for it continues today.

Like many movements there were some good things and bad things about the intentions of the Yahad. Clearly, they wished to put an end to certain practices of their pagan oppressors and apostate Jews, like sacrificing infants to idols, temple prostitution and bestiality, and establish a more moral mode of life amongst the Children of Israel. These are seen as the 'positive' aspects of their dogma. However, in some respects, their rhetoric and dogma traveled to the other end of the spectrum, preaching hatred and retribution on the Gentiles. In later history, we see this same problem echoed in the fierce dogmatic persecution of the Roman Catholic Church against those they considered heretics, and the establishment of the Inquisition. With the coming of the Romans to the Holy Land – around the time the *Book of Parables* was written, we see the Yahad develop into something not only religiously fanatical, but even more militant and seditionist – the Zealots and Sicarii.

It may be that the story of the Watchers was written not only to vent some commentary upon their Hellenic overlords, but as a warning to those within the Yahad that "You will not be forgiven if you betray us".

Chapters 17-19

[Chapter 17] 1 And they took and brought me to a place in which those who were there were like flaming fire, 2 and, when they wished, they appeared as men. And they brought me to the place of darkness, and to a mountain the point of whose summit reached to heaven. And I saw the places of the luminaries and the treasuries of the stars and of the thunder and in the uttermost depths, where were 4 a fiery bow and arrows and their quiver, and a fiery sword and all the lightnings. And they took 5 me to the living waters, and to the fire of the west, which receives every setting of the sun. And I came to a river of fire in which the fire flows like water and discharges itself into the great sea towards 6 the west. I saw the great rivers and came to the great river and to the great darkness, and went 7 to the place where no flesh walks. I saw the mountains of the darkness of winter and the place 8 whence all the waters of the deep flow. I saw the mouths of all the rivers of the earth and the mouth of the deep.

[Chapter 18] 1 I saw the treasuries of all the winds: I saw how He had furnished with them the whole creation 2 and the firm foundations of the earth. And I saw the corner-stone of the earth: I saw the four 3 winds which bear [the earth and] the firmament of the heaven. And I saw how the winds stretch out the vaults of heaven, and have their station between heaven and earth: these are the pillars 4 of the heaven. I saw the winds of heaven which turn and bring the circumference of the sun and 5 all the stars to their setting. I saw the winds on the earth carrying the clouds: I saw the paths 6 of the angels. I saw at the end of the earth the firmament of the heaven above. And I proceeded and saw a place which burns day and night, where there are seven mountains of magnificent stones, 7 three towards the east, and three towards the south. And as for those towards the east, was of coloured stone, and one of pearl, and one of jacinth, and those towards the south of red stone. 8 But the middle one reached to heaven like the throne of God, of alabaster, and the summit of the 9,10 throne was of sapphire. And I saw a flaming fire. And beyond these mountains Is a region the end of the great earth: there the heavens were completed. And I saw a deep abyss, with columns of heavenly fire, and among them I saw columns of fire fall, which were beyond measure alike towards 12 the height and towards the depth. And beyond that abyss I saw a place which had no firmament of the heaven above, and no firmly founded earth beneath it: there was no water upon it, and no 13 birds, but it was a waste and horrible place. I saw there seven stars like great burning mountains, 14 and to me, when I inquired regarding them, The angel said: 'This place is

the end of heaven and earth: this has become a prison for the stars and the host of heaven. And the stars which roll over the fire are they which have transgressed the commandment of the Lord in the beginning of 16 their rising, because they did not come forth at their appointed times. And He was wroth with them, and bound them till the time when their guilt should be consummated (even) for ten thousand years.'

In Chapter 17, Enoch describes a "river of fire in which the fire flows like water and discharges itself into the great sea towards the west". This sounds very much like a flow of volcanic magma. Was the author of this text perhaps borrowing from the Platonic tales of Atlantis, and the eruption of Thera on Crete? It has been posited by several modern authors, including Andrew Collins, that the column of fire which is said to have appeared before the Israelites in their exodus from Egypt was in fact the eruption of Thera (a.k.a. Santorini) on Crete. This was one of the greatest catastrophic events in the history of man and particularly those living in the area of the Mediterranean. Thera spewed out more ash and pyroclastic debris than any other volcanic eruption in known history – including Krakatoa, which caused a sort of 'nuclear winter' to fall over the earth for some years after.

He also states, "I saw the great rivers and came to the great river and to the great darkness, and went to the place where no flesh walks". All of this is directed toward the west. The 'great river' to the west of the Holy Land is the Nile. It may be that he is referring to the Western Lands of the Egyptians – the Tuat, where the dead go...the place where no flesh walks. In Chapter 18, he goes on to say that an angel tells him, "This place is the end of heaven and earth: this has become a prison for the stars and the host of heaven." This again points to the Tuat, which is the place in the west, "which receives every setting of the sun".

The Egyptians believed that the souls of the dead traveled to this underworld or otherworld. The Tuat was divided in to twelve sectors, each with its own perils and demons that must be overcome by the deceased in order to find eternal life like and with Osiris. It is a river that divides the Tuat into its twelve sections. At each of these sections is a gate that has guardians. The Sun must know the names of each of these demons and serpents in order to pass through the divisions of the night (hours) and make its way back to the east to come up again in the morning, or be 'reborn'. There are also seven arrets or circles within the divisions. Each arret is presided over by a doorkeeper, a *watcher* and a herald. These arrets are the planetary spheres. This whole set-up is quite similar to the Sumero-Babylonian ideas of Utu-Shamash disappearing into the Kur each night and traveling through the Underworld to again rise in the east, but a lot more complex. We see these 'gates' and 'gatekeepers' in both *Inanna's Descent* and as the Scorpion beings in the *Epic of Gilgamesh*. While ingeniously including both of these stories into the narrative of *Enoch*, the author seems to point to both the Egyptians and the Mesopotamian peoples as the 'stars' which are imprisoned there in their beliefs of the afterlife.

This part of *Enoch* is again reminiscent of the first portions of the *Epic of Gilgamesh*. In Tablet I we are introduced to the great king of Uruk with the following words:

> *Of him who found out all things, I shall tell the land, Of him who experienced everything, I shall teach the whole. He searched the lands everywhere. He who experienced the whole gained complete wisdom. He found out what was secret and uncovered what was hidden, He brought back a tale of the times before the Flood....*
>
> *...He is Gilgamesh, perfect in splendour, Who opened up passes in the mountains, Who could dig pits even in the mountainside, Who crossed the ocean, the broad seas, as far as the sunrise. Who inspected the edges of the world, kept searching for eternal life....*

Eternal Life. The search for it is the motivation of all religions, and while it is only more or less explicitly stated in the works of the Yahad, it is their wish as well. It becomes clear that they believe that by living righteous lives and exterminating the heathens from their midst, they will gain this...and it is to this end all their rules and exhortations are made. These chapters seem to be poking a bit of cynical fun at the 'heathens' for their beliefs, saying that they will not be freed by them, but bound eternally in the fire.

[Chapter 19] 1 And Uriel said to me: 'Here shall stand the angels who have connected themselves with women, and their spirits assuming many different forms are defiling mankind and shall lead them astray into sacrificing to demons as gods, (here shall they stand,) till the day of the great judgment in 2 which they shall be judged till they are made an end of. And the women also of the angels who 3 went astray shall become sirens.' And I, Enoch, alone saw the vision, the ends of all things: and no man shall see as I have seen.

Here again, we have the pronouncement of doom upon the wicked angels, who have sacrificed to demon-gods – i.e. not Yahweh – and defiled themselves with women. Here, we also have a judgment on the women of the Watchers, that they shall become "sirens". The sirens are *not* part of Hebrew or Jewish lore, but out of the body of Greek myth. The sirens were nymphs who lived on the islands off the southern coast of Italy in the Mediterranean. Their sweet songs lured sailors to their doom in the sea. The only ones to avoid their trap were Jason and the Argonauts, and Odysseus. Odysseus had his men plug their ears with wax while passing these treacherous isles, so as not to hear the sound of their voices. Only Odysseus hears them, having lashed himself to the mast of his ship and instructing his men that no matter what they see of his reactions to them, they are to keep rowing on past. While he is greatly tormented with desire for them, he accomplishes something no other man has and lived to tell about it. It is said that the sirens witnessed Persephone being raped by Hades. They were given wings by Zeus to carry out their revenge...like angels. The sirens are represented as birds with wings and the heads and breasts of women, much like the harpies of Greek lore.

In the last few lines, Enoch's statement that he has seen "the ends of all things: and no man shall see as I have seen" seems to be a direct reference to the portion of *Gilgamesh* related above.

Chapters 20-21

[Chapter 20] 1,2 And these are the names of the holy angels who watch. Uriel, one of the holy angels, who is 3 over the world and over Tartarus. Raphael, one of the holy angels, who is over the spirits of men. 4,5 Raguel, one of the holy angels who takes vengeance on the world of the luminaries. Michael, one 6 of the holy angels, to wit, he that is set over the best part of mankind and over chaos. Saraqael, 7 one of the holy angels, who is set over the spirits, who sin in the spirit. Gabriel, one of the holy 8 angels, who is over Paradise and the serpents and the Cherubim. Remiel, one of the holy angels, whom God set over those who rise.

Chapter 20 tells the names of the seven archangels, according to Jewish thought at the time. This listing has not stood the test of time, as Pope Zachary of the Holy Roman Church reprobated both Uriel and Raguel, along with other high-ranking angels in the Council at Rome in 745 CE.

This listing of seven angels could be viewed as a Jewish version of the Amesha Spenta of Zoroastrian belief. This and the inclusion of Mastema as the chief of the demon spirits in *Jubilees* (see the commentary on Chapter 15), and a later reference to Satan in Chapters 53 & 54 of *Enoch* would appear to suggest that the Jews were attempting to build their own version of the Zoroastrian belief system, with the duality of the Lord of Light, Ahura Mazda as Yahweh and the Lord of Darkness, Angira Mainyu as Satan. They would have learned of this system during their Babylonian captivity under Cyrus the Great and Darius I, for Zoroastrianism had begun to flourish at that time. It is known from inscriptions from both of these kings that they were devotees of Ahura Mazda – particularly Darius. But Darius was not averse to practicing 'religious tolerance' as many of the subjects of his great empire were pantheists or pagan. It is known that Darius the Great encouraged the Jews in rebuilding the Temple and even provided them with a generous subsidy to do so. Was this encouragement given with the understanding that the Jews would establish a 'more Zoroastrian' approach to their religious beliefs? Darius was known to have established a set of laws that were similar to the Code of Hammurabi – parts of which have often been compared with the Ten Commandments of Moses.

It is possible that the Great Assembly of post-exilic rabbis were the body who undertook this effort. Let us not forget that they claimed to have 'received the *Torah* from the prophets themselves'. Let us also not forget that *Daniel* was not written until around the same period of time that the *Book of the Watchers* was written. Daniel was purported to be one of the prophets who endured the captivity. While it is possible that his story survived in oral tradition, it seems rather odd that it was not written down by these learned men in full at the time of the Great Assembly – for Daniel was said to have returned from the captivity with Ezra, one of the founders of the Great Assembly. Instead, we have amongst the documents preserved by the Yahad *The Healing of King Nabonidus*:

> *I, Nabonidus, was smitten with a severe inflammation lasting seven years. Because I was thus changed, becoming like a beast, I prayed to the Most High, and He forgave my sins. An exorcist – a Jew, in fact, a member of the community of exiles – came to me and said, "Declare and write down this story, and so ascribe glory and greatness to the name of God Most High." Accordingly, I have myself written it down" I was smitten with a severe inflammation while in Teima, by the command of God Most High. Then for seven years I continued praying to the gods made of silver and gold, bronze, iron, wood, stone, and clay, for I used to think that they really were gods. (Q2:242, frags. 1-3)*

Like Enoch, Daniel became a hero of a whole cycle of stories, many of which are now lost. Another extremely fragmented scroll found at Qumran in cave 4 is called *The Vision of Daniel*. We also have other fragments of scrolls with such intriguing titles as *A Reworking of Genesis and Exodus*, *An Account of the Story of Samuel*, *The Last Words of Naphtali*, *A Paraphrase of Genesis and Exodus* and *The Psalms of Joshua*. Little did we know that Joshua the warrior was, like Solomon the king, a poet. It would seem, from this and other indications given throughout this narrative (and yet to come) that the Yahad may have been the 'heirs' of this tradition and it's keepers down through the centuries to follow.

We are told in this chapter that Uriel is over Tartarus, which is again a distinctly Greek concept of the underworld. It is the final resting place for the spirits of wicked *mortals*. The author here is consigning the fallen angels to their own version of Hell. Tartarus was originally a prison for the gods who had 'fallen' from the heights of Olympus as well as the Titans, who were the enemies of Zeus, the supreme god of the Greeks. Interestingly, one of those who was thrown down from Olympus by Zeus for his imperfections was Hephaestus, the smith of the gods, who could be equated with the Watcher Azazel and Tubal-Cain. One of the personifications of Tartarus was said to have been born of Chaos. In the next chapter, Enoch describes the place where he is as "chaotic and horrible".

Saraqael or Sarakiel is sometimes equated with Sariel, one of the chiefs of tens of the Watchers, but they do not seem to be one in the same.

The reference to Gabriel being over "the serpents and the Cherubim" appears to refer to the chora of angels known as the Seraphim, or the 'fiery serpents'.

[Chapter 21] 1,2 And I proceeded to where things were chaotic. And I saw there something horrible: I saw neither 3 a heaven above nor a firmly founded earth, but a place chaotic and horrible. And there I saw 4 seven stars of the heaven bound together in it, like great mountains and burning with fire. Then 5 I said: 'For what sin are they bound, and on what account have they been cast in hither?' Then said Uriel, one of the holy angels, who was with me, and was chief over them, and said: 'Enoch, why 6 dost thou ask, and why art thou eager for the truth? These are of the number of the stars of heaven, which have transgressed the commandment of the Lord, and are bound here till ten thousand years, 7 the time entailed by their sins, are consummated.' And from thence I went to another place, which was still more horrible than the former, and I saw a horrible thing: a great fire there which burnt and blazed, and the place was cleft as far as the abyss, being full of great descending columns of 8 fire: neither its extent or magnitude could I see, nor could I conjecture. Then I said: 'How 9 fearful is the place and how terrible to look upon!' Then Uriel answered me, one of the holy angels who was with me, and said unto me: 'Enoch, why hast thou such fear and affright?' And 10 I answered: 'Because of this fearful place, and because of the spectacle of the pain.' And he said unto me: 'This place is the prison of the angels, and here they will be imprisoned for ever.'

The "seven stars of the heaven" mentioned here and previously would seem to be the planets, which were worshiped as anthropomorphised deities since ancient times. As we know, this began in ancient Sumer, with the worship of the Sun (Utu-Babar), the Moon (Naram-Ŝin), Venus (Inanna), Mars (Erra-Nergal) and others. The author sees them, along with other stars as being bound in a perdition of burning fire – the place he certainly would have liked to have seen these pagan idols tossed. It was in fact a custom to burn the wooden idols of the pagans when they were found and destroyed. We are told in *I Kings* that this is exactly what king Asa did with his mother's idol (see commentary on Chapter 13).

Uriel asks Enoch why does he want to know? Why does he care what becomes of these? This and Enoch's fear of the place, and his sympathy to the pain endured there portrays Enoch as still having human feelings. By asking why he should care, Uriel seems to be telling him that he shouldn't bother wasting his sympathies on such as these. Here, at the ends of the earth, in the great abyss of fire and chaos where there is no dimension and time seems eternal, is the prison of the angels. This is quite interesting, for earlier in the text, we are told that Shemyaza and his companions shall be bound for seventy generations *in the valleys of the earth*. As the text progresses, the punishments seem to become more severe and of a longer duration.

Chapters 22-36

These chapters tell more of the travels of Enoch over the earth and heavens, and what he sees there. This again seems to be an expansion on the travels of Gilgamesh, as commented on for Chapters 17-19.

As Gilgamesh, or SIPA.ZI.AN.NA is the giant lord of the winter night sky, he too travels across the world, from the east to the west every night and sees all things from one end of the earth to the other. Enoch-Metatron, as a solar deity would seem to be the lord of the day, who also travels across the world from end to end – even unto the dark and chaotic places of the underworld, only to be reborn or re-emerge to the sight of man in the morning. Perhaps this is what is meant, when it is said at the beginning of Chapter 12 that "Before these things Enoch was hidden, and no one of the children of men knew where he was hidden, and where he abode, and what had become of him". The time before Enoch, the enlightened man who wrote the laws and ascended into heaven, was the time of darkness and Enoch's revelations are the dawning of a new day.

Thus ends the *Book of the Watchers.*

Mention of Azazel and his companions is made in Chapters 54 and 55, but they offer no new perspectives as to the Watchers or Enoch, carrying on in more of the same fashion as the previous chapters, and so they will not be commented upon. The next chapter that is of any interest in pursuing the knowledge and identity of the Watchers is Chapter 69, which in included in the *Book of Parables* and follows.

Chapter 69

[Chapter 69] 1 And after this judgment they shall terrify and make them to tremble because they have shown this to those who dwell on the earth. 2 And behold the names of those angels [and these are their names: the first of them is Samjaza, the second Artaqifa, and the third Armen, the fourth Kokabel, the fifth Turael, the sixth Rumjal, the seventh Danjal, the eighth Neqael, the ninth Baraqel, the tenth Azazel, the eleventh Armaros, the twelfth Batarjal, the thirteenth Busasejal, the fourteenth Hananel, the fifteenth Turel, and the sixteenth Simapesiel, the seventeenth Jetrel, the eighteenth Tumael, the nineteenth Turel, 3 the twentieth Rumael, the twenty-first Azazel. And these are the chiefs of their angels and their names, and their chief ones over hundreds and over fifties and over tens].

Once again, we are introduced to the chiefs of tens. Let us compare this with what we read in Chapter 6:

> And these are the names of their leaders: Samiazaz, their leader, Arakiba, Rameel, Kokabiel, Tamiel, Ramiel, Danel, Ezeqeel, Baraqijal, 8 Asael, Armaros, Batarel, Ananel, Zaqiel, Samsapeel, Satarel, Turel, Jomjael, Sariel. These are their chiefs of tens.

We seem to have gained a few and lost a few. Many of the differences can be explained by transliteration. The Hebrew of the text was not written with any vowel points. *Some* variations in spelling can be attributed to that, as in Rameel/Rumael. The fact that the *yod* can be transliterated as a J, I or Y explains others. Hananel is just Anael written in a different way. Azazel appears here in Chapter 69 twice, as the tenth and twenty-first chiefs of ten. This may be due to damaged text. In Chapter 6, we are told that there are twenty chiefs of ten, but only nineteen are named. In Chapter 6, we seem to have a duplicate in the names Rameel and Ramiel. However, in Chapter 69 they are spelled two different ways, Rumael and Ramjal. In Chapter 69, we have two Turels. Neqael, Busasejal, and Jetrel are new in Chapter 69, seeming to have replaced Ezeqeel, Zaqiel and Sariel.

What is going on here, we might well ask? Busasejal may be a name of Ethiopian derivation, much like the name Oubelseyael in Chapter 13. Their endings, in spite of the spelling differences in transliteration, are the same. Some give the alternate of this name as Bezaliel, 'the shadow of God'. Simasapiel may also be an Ethiopian rendering of the name Samsapeel. Neqael appears to be the replacement name for Ezeqeel and possibly Zaqiel. Jetrel may be a pun to cover 'the excess', for that is the meaning of *yeter* – 'the rest, excess'. In that case, he would be replacing Sariel. Why would Ezeqeel/Zaqiel or Ezekiel and Sariel need to be replaced?

The *Book of Parables* (a.k.a. the *Book of Similitudes*) is thought to have been written in the first century CE, whereas the *Book of the Watchers* was written around 165-150 BCE. There is a span of 150-200 years between them. A lot changed in that time. The Romans replaced the Greeks, and the priesthood became further and further debased, often bending to the will of the Romans' pagan kings they placed over the Jews, or at the least, seeking their favor.

The *War Scroll* is thought to have been written sometime after the mid 1st century BCE to the beginning of the 1st century CE - about the same time as the *Book of Parables*. Sariel appears in the *War Scroll* as the third of the four commanders of the 'towers' or battle divisions of the army of the Sons of Light. It would hardly do for him to appear in another, earlier text as a fallen angel.

There is also the question of Ezeqiel and Zaqiel – names which are very similar to the great prophet Ezekiel. There has been a good deal of debate amongst biblical scholars as to the authorship of the books of *Ezekiel*.

> In 1924, Gustav Hoelscher questioned the authorship of Ezekiel, challenging the conventional wisdom that the book was written by one person and expresses one train of thought and style, and arguing instead that 1,103 of the verses in Ezekiel were added at a later date.
>
> Since then, the academic community has been split into a number of different camps over the authorship of the book. W. Zimmerli, who has a rather large following, proposes that Ezekiel's original message was influenced by a later school that added a deeper understanding to the prophecies. Other groups, like the one led by M. Greenberg, still tend to see the majority of the work of the book done by Ezekiel himself. (Wikipedia – Book of Ezekiel)

If we take Hoelscher's theory into consideration and even Zimmerli's, it might be that these guardians of the scriptures, the Yahad, were in fact the group that added the later thousand plus verses, or who were the influential "later school that added a deeper understanding to the prophecies". Since Ezekiel was an highly estimed prophet of the Jews, it also would not do to have anything *sounding* like his name associated with fallen angels. The fact that the Yahad was writing their *War Scroll* in the first century CE and that the *Book of Parables* was written about the same time would give credence to the possibility. Given the time-frame of the writing of the *War Scroll*, the vehemence of its rhetoric, and the fact that the Sicarii – the last defenders of Masada were also the last employers of the 364 day solar calendar found at Qumran, it stands to reason that the members of the Yahad later became the Sicarii and the Zealots. It was in 70 CE that the Roman legions took Jerusalem. Masada was the last stronghold of the Jewish zealots and fell in 73 CE.

This re-introduction to the Watchers may have been a redaction to correct these literary *faux-pas*, as well as other 'errors' seen in the list of names in Chapter 6. As it has been shown, the *Book of Watchers* has many elements in it that point to the 'lost *Book of Noah*' which this author believes to in fact be *Atrahasis* and pertinent portions of the *Epic of Gilgamesh*. The *Book of Parables* is written in a completely different style, as if trying to mimic the old style of the Babylonian songs, where key verses were oft-repeated. There is also the fact that God is here called 'Lord of Spirits' (the name of Ellil/Enlil) in an effort to make the text seem more authentically Babylonian. Chapter 69 is part of this re-write. It was earlier mentioned that two different versions of *Jeremiah* were found at Qumran. We also see that the *Torah* is being re-written there. It is therefore, not impossible that the *Book of Parables/Similitudes* was meant to replace of the *Book of the Watchers*.

We also see an extra bit at the end of verse 3:

> *And these are the chiefs of their angels and their names, and their chief ones over hundreds and over fifties and over tens.*

This again refers to the same military terminology that is seen in *Exodus*, Chapter 18 that was quoted in the commentary on Chapter 6. It still does not explain why there are now twenty-one chiefs of tens and Azazel is mentioned twice. It can hardly be an oversight for the two instances are but a few lines apart. The explanation is that the text was damaged at one of the mentions and the translator decided to list Azazel twice.

We come now to a sort of secondary introduction, which provides us with yet another group of names, completely different than anything else we've seen so far…yet a few of them do have some relevance to the first sets of names.

4 The name of the first Jeqon: that is, the one who led astray [all] the sons of God, and brought them 5 down to the earth, and led them astray through the daughters of men.

See the WATCHER NAMES section.

And the second was named Asbeel: he imparted to the holy sons of God evil counsel, and led them astray so that they defiled 6 their bodies with the daughters of men.

See the WATCHER NAMES section.

And the third was named Gadreel: he it is who showed the children of men all the blows of death, and he led astray Eve, and showed [the weapons of death to the sons of men] the shield and the coat of mail, and the sword for battle, and all the weapons 7 of death to the children of men. And from his hand they have proceeded against those who dwell 8 on the earth from that day and for evermore.

See the WATCHER NAMES section.

And the fourth was named Penemue: he taught the 9 children of men the bitter and the sweet, and he taught them all the secrets of their wisdom. And he instructed mankind in writing with ink and paper, and thereby many sinned from eternity to 10 eternity and until this day. For men were not created for such a purpose, to give confirmation 11 to their good faith with pen and ink. For men were created exactly like the angels, to the intent that they should continue pure and righteous, and death, which destroys everything, could not have taken hold of them, but through this their knowledge they are perishing, and through this power 12 it is consuming me.

This is one of the most curious and poignant passages in *Enoch* regarding the Watchers. We are introduced here to a Watcher named Penemue, who has not appeared before this in the text. He does not match up with any of the other Watchers first listed, as to his knowledge. He seems rather to be an alter-ego of the scribe who is writing this text - or of the scribes who have written all the texts - who seems to be bemoaning the fact that he is consigned to doing it at all. His words seem to indicate a belief that men should not have to be told what to believe or how to act. They should *know* these things in their hearts and act accordingly. It should be noted that the text is damaged at the statement "it is consuming me" and so that is a translative speculation as to what is actually written there. See the WATCHER NAMES section for more about Penemue.

And the fifth was named Kasdeja: this is he who showed the children of men all the wicked smitings of spirits and demons, and the smitings of the embryo in the womb, that it may pass away, and [the smitings of the soul] the bites of the serpent, and the smitings 13 which befall through the noontide heat, the son of the serpent named Taba'et.

Here, we meet Kasdeja for the first time. Kasdeja seems to be the physician of the group and his knowledge is not related to any of the original chiefs of tens mentioned in Chapter 8 – at least none that are given. In his book *The Ethiopic Book Of Enoch*, Michael Knibb equates Kasdeja with Tamiel and gives the translation of the name Kasdeja as 'the observer of the hands' or 'knowledge of the hands'. However, Knibb inverts the spelling of the name to Kasyade, to make his translation from the Hebrew word *yedeeah*, which means 'knowledge' and yedey, which means 'hands'...completely ignoring the prefix of '*kas*-'. See WATCHER NAMES section for more on Kasdeja.

And this is the task of Kasbeel, the chief of the oath which he showed to the holy ones when he dwelt high 4 above in glory, and its name is Biqa. This (angel) requested Michael to show him the hidden name, that he might enunciate it in the oath, so that those might quake before that name and oath who revealed all that was in secret to the children of men. And this is the power of this oath, for it is powerful and strong, and he placed this oath Akae in the hand of Michael. 16 And these are the secrets of this oath . . . And they are strong through his oath: And the heaven was suspended before the world was created, And for ever. 17 And through it the earth was founded upon the water, And from the secret recesses of the mountains come beautiful waters, From the creation of the world and unto eternity. 18 And through that oath the sea was created, And as its foundation He set for it the sand against the time of (its) anger, And it dare not pass beyond it from the creation of the world unto eternity. 9 And through that oath are the depths made fast, And abide and stir not from their place from eternity to eternity. 20 And through that oath the sun and moon complete their course, And deviate not from their ordinance from eternity to eternity. 21 And through that oath the stars complete their course, And He calls them by their names, And they answer Him from eternity to eternity. 22 [And in like manner the spirits of the water, and of the winds, and of all zephyrs, and (their) paths 23 from all the quarters of the winds. And there are preserved the voices of the thunder and the light of the lightnings: and there are preserved the chambers of the hail and the chambers of the 24 hoarfrost, and the chambers of the mist, and the chambers of the rain and the dew. And all these believe and give thanks before the Lord of Spirits, and glorify (Him) with all their power, and their food is in every act of thanksgiving: they thank and glorify and extol the name of the Lord of Spirits for ever and ever.] 25 And this oath is mighty over them And through it [they are preserved and] their paths are preserved, And their course is not destroyed.

Here, we meet Kasbeel. He seems to be an alter-ego of Kasdeja. The word *hakh* which is transliterated here as 'Akae' means 'to strike or smite'. We are told that Kasdeja is a 'smiter' of demons and other maladies. This word has been interpreted by others as being an alternative for the ineffable name of God, which is capable of manifesting creation, which could be interpreted as having power over life and death, as physicians do. Physicians are sometimes seen as 'playing God' in this capacity. This oath may refer to the *logos* as world order and the self-revealing will of God. Recall that when Aruru (Belit-ili) forms Enkidu, she 'forms the word of Anu' inside herself. In other words, she is making use of the will of Anu and the template of manifest creation to create Enkidu.

According to Davidson's *Dictionary of Angels*, Biqa was the name of Kasbeel before he fell. However, the text says "and *its* name *is* Biqa", which would seem to indicate that Biqa is another name for the oath. The word *beeka*, spelled exactly like 'Biqa' in Hebrew means 'valley' but it also means 'split or cleaved'. It is also a colloquial name for the Jordan valley (*ha beekah*). There was also a western Semitic Baal, called Ba'al-Biqah, who was a weather god.

This passage would seem to be the root of the Hebrew legend of Shemyaza being tempted by the maiden Ishtahar to reveal to her the ineffable name of God. Kasbeel's name is said by some scholars to mean 'he who lies to God' or to mean 'sorcery'. Shemyaza *is* an 'enchanter' – which could refer to his power of rhetoric to convince his fellows to depart heaven. However, the name and the story appear *right after* the portion of the text referring to Kasdeja. The name Kasbeel could in fact be transliterated as Kasbaal – perhaps a punning cross-reference to him having fallen back to the worship of one of the Baals, as with the name Aŝbeel/Aŝbaal.

We are told in *I Chronicles* the genealogy of King Saul:

> *And Ner begat Kish, and Kish begat Saul, and Saul begat Jonathan, and Malchi-shua, and Abinadab, and Esh-baal. (I Chron. 8:33)*

However, in Chapter 2 of *II Samuel* this son of Saul is continuously referred to as Ish-bosheth (man of shame). We have a clue to the reason for this in *Jeremiah*:

> *For according to the number of thy cities were thy gods, O Judah; and according to the number of the streets of Jerusalem have ye set up altars to that shameful idol (la-bosheth), even altars to burn incense unto Baal (la-baal). (Jer. 11:13) [Italicized translations added.]*

It is unclear what exactly is the relationship between these two words 'bosheth' and 'baal' but Eshbaal seems to have been renamed to avoid any association with this "shameful idol". Conversely, anyone associated with Baal may have their name changed back to have a -*baal*, -*beel* or -*bel* suffix as an indicator of their 'religious preferences'.

26 And there was great joy amongst them, And they blessed and glorified and extolled Because the name of that Son of

Man had been revealed unto them. **27 And he sat on the throne of his glory, And the sum of judgment was given unto the Son of Man, And he caused the sinners to pass away and be destroyed from off the face of the earth, And those who have led the world astray. 28 With chains shall they be bound, And in their assemblage-place of destruction shall they be imprisoned, And all their works vanish from the face of the earth. 29 And from henceforth there shall be nothing corruptible; For that Son of Man has appeared, And has seated himself on the throne of his glory, And all evil shall pass away before his face, And the word of that Son of Man shall go forth And be strong before the Lord of Spirits.**

The remainder of Chapter 69 (verses 26-29) will not be commented upon, as it refers to the "Son of Man", which deserves its own commentary.

THE YAHAD

JUDGES, ASSASSINS & WATCHERS

Who were the Yahad, and where did they come from? The Old Testament is full of references to shadowy figures, assassins and others who leave more questions unanswered than not. They are perhaps clues as to the nature and identity of the Yahad.

First, let us begin with the Watchers, themselves. The Watchers are sometimes known as the *bene Elohim*. This can be translated as "sons of the Goddess" or "sons of God", for *Elohim* is a very curious word. In structure, it is both masculine and feminine; syntactically, it is both singular and plural. *Bene Elohim* could also be translated as 'sons of the gods'. This divine title then must always be considered in relation to its context within the structure of the sentence and what is being said. Sometimes, it is impossible to tell which is meant.

It seems strange for these angels to be referred to as "sons of the goddess" in a religion that is to all outward appearances dominated by the patriarchal Father god, Yahweh. Part of the mysteries of the Jewish religion include a female half of the god. She is called the *Shekinah*. She is the Mother of the material universe. Qaballistically speaking, this is the equivalent of the sephira Binah, who is the Mother in relation to the Father, Chokmah. The reference to 'sons of the gods' seems more fitting to the Watchers, but just for the sake of what is to follow, let us delve into the possibility that they are meant to be all three.

Binah controls the left side of the Tree of Life, or the Pillar of Severity, while Chokmah controls the right side of the Tree, the Pillar of Mercy. These names come from the middle sephirot on the respective left and right pillars, Geburah and Chesed. Geburah is the sephira of Judgment, while Chesed rules the sphere of Mercy. Geburah emanates directly from the Mother as the FIFTH sephira of the divine emanation. The pentagram or pentagon is the sigil of this sephira. It is no odd coincidence that the headquarters of the United States military forces is called The Pentagon. The color of Geburah is red. The sephira of Judgment is known also as "strength." A familiar word? Azazel's name is sometimes translated as "the strength of God" and Shemyaza's as "the name of the Strong." The *seraphim* or the "fiery serpents" are the angelic chora assigned to Geburah. Last but not least, the planet of Geburah is Mars, the God of War and the planetary metal, iron. Geburah and Chesed are known as the left and right hands of God. The sephirot directly beneath them are the "thighs" of God, Hod (left) and Netzach (right).

In reading the Bible and the history of Mesopotamia, it becomes obvious that war was not invented by anyone in particular. War as a concept in Jewish philosophy is the judgment of the Lord against the people for their backsliding and sins. This becomes very clear in reading both books of *Samuel* and *Kings*, and the book of *Judges*. War was said to have come upon the Hebrews repeatedly, because of their failure to comply with the covenants made repeatedly with Yahweh. In the lapses between judges, the younger generation would forget and walk away to worship other gods. It is something of a refrain at the end of the life of each judge.

Aside from the figure of Elijah the Prophet, there is a story in the book of *Judges* that is of great interest to us at this juncture. The judges of Israel were not judges as we think of them today – judicial officials. They were instead non-hereditary leaders of the Israelites who were for the most part chosen by the Lord. That is, several of them were visited by 'an angel of the Lord' and told that they would be the new 'deliverer' of the Children of Israel from the oppression of the Gentiles and their kings. Or, we are told that the Lord 'raised up' a judge as a deliverer.

We meet the judge Ehud in *Judges* 3. It describes a time when the Israelites are said to be sorely oppressed by the Moabite king Eglon for eighteen years. It begins at verse 15. The story will be paraphrased here somewhat:

> But when the children of Israel cried unto the Lord, the Lord raised them up a deliverer, Ehud the son of Gera, a Benjamite, a man lefthanded: and by him the children of Israel sent a present unto Eglon the king of Moab. But Ehud made him a dagger which had two edges, of a cubit length; and he did gird it under his raiment upon his right thigh. And he brought the present unto Eglon king of Moab: and Eglon was a very fat man. And when Ehud had made a end to the offering of the present, he sent away the bearers of the present. But Ehud himself turned again from the quarries that were by Gilgal, and said, "I have a secret errand unto thee, O king". The king replied to him to hold his silence, until he sent away all his officials and the others in the room.
>
> Eglon and Ehud were sitting in a summer parlor that the king had made for his own pleasure. Ehud spoke to the king saying, "I have a message from God unto thee. And he arose from out of his seat. Then Ehud put forth his left hand, and took the dagger from his right thigh, and thrust it into Eglon's belly. The haft went in after the blade and the fat closed over it so Ehud could not draw the dagger from the king's belly, and all his entrails and filth fell out. Then Ehud went out of the garden and locked the doors behind him. When the servants came after Ehud left, they saw that the doors were locked and presumed that the king wanted to be alone in his chamber. They waited and waited until they began to have doubts. When they opened the doors finally, they found their king dead on the ground. In the meantime, Ehud has made

> good his escape and gone to Seirath. There, he ascends the mountain and blows a ram's horn to summon the people to tell them that they have been delivered from the oppression of the Moabite king.

This story ties so many things together. The author of this story emphasizes that Ehud was "left handed." Not once, but twice. This is significant, pointing directly to the role of Severity and Judgment in this act. Added to this is the name of the "deliverer" sent by the Lord - Ehud. Ehud's name means 'union'. This is simply an alternate spelling of Yahad. The fact that he girds the dagger on his 'right thigh' is symbolic of both Chesed, the Lord's Mercy on his children, and Victory or the sephira of Netzach. The name Eglon means 'young bull' and he was a very fat one, we are told. The weapon that Ehud made was in recognition of the fact that there were many layers of fat to cut through to gut the Moabite king. Eglon was the sacrifice that was made to release the Hebrews from their servitude. Ehud's paternity is given as the son of Gera, which is an alternate spelling of Girra, the Sumerian god of Fire. The name Benjamin, which is given as his tribe (Benjamite), is sometimes translated as "the right hand of God." But it is the "left hand of God" demonstrated by fire and judgment (Geburah) which is the hallmark of the 'angels of the Lord'.

This, combined with both Elijah and Elisha later working behind the scenes to manipulate, make and break kings can only lead to one conclusion. The Yahad was more than a group of very learned men who kept or wrote scrolls and lived out in the wilderness. They wrote in several different languages, including a cryptic script where certain symbols took the place of Hebrew letters. These documents were clearly meant only for the initiated. They knew the history of all the peoples around the Middle East, Egypt and Asia Minor, as well as the Greeks. They also knew their mythology and religions. These men were exceptional in the standard of their day. They would be exceptional, even now.

It seems that the Yahad had been around a lot longer than second century BCE. According to the story of Ehud, they had been around since at least the time of Joshua's death - only one generation out of Egypt, when this story takes place. It is thought by most biblical scholars that the Exodus took place in the mid 14th century BCE. That is, if the Yahad did not re-write the Old Testament to suit their own version of the history of the Jews. As we saw earlier, *Genesis* and *Exodus* were being re-written as the *Book of Jubilees*. We saw that there are two rather different versions of *Jeremiah*, and that *Daniel* was written around the same time as the *Book of the Watchers*, using a sort of short-story called *The Healing of King Nabonidus* as its basis or 'inspiration'. We have been told that *Ezekiel* was probably later glossed by another group "*that added a deeper understanding to the prophecies*". The ability to prophesy is always 20-20 in hindsight. We must therefore question many things about these books and others, in light of this information – which has only come to us in the last 70 years.

In Chapter 6 of *Judges*, we meet Gideon, whose name means 'destroyer'. Gideon was one of those visited by an 'angel of the Lord'. The angel tells Gideon to bring him a present, or an offering. Gideon brings the flesh of a kid goat and some unleavened cakes. He places them on a rock. We are told:

> *21 Then the angel of the Lord put forth the end of the staff that was in his hand, and touched the flesh and the unleavened cakes; and there rose up fire out of the rock, and consumed the flesh and the unleavened cakes. Then the angel of the Lord departed out of his sight. 22 And when Gideon perceived that he was an angel of the Lord, Gideon said, Alas, O Lord God! for because I have seen an angel of the Lord face to face. 23 And the Lord said unto him, Peace be unto thee; fear not: thou shalt not die. (Judges 6:21-23)*

Gideon's first thought, and indeed the first thought of several others when they are visited by an 'angel of the Lord' in the Old Testament is that *they are going to die*.

The third story in *Judges* that is of interest is that of Samson. Please see THE STORY OF SAMSON in a separate chapter.

The prophet Elijah, who was said to have lived in the 9th century BCE during the reign of king Ahab is God's instrument of judgment against the Israelites because of their idolatrous ways. After besting the priests of Baal at Mount Carmel with yet another display of pyrotechnics, Elijah orders them slaughtered, incurring the wrath of Ahab's queen Jezebel. More can be read about Elijah and his successor, Elisha in the article entitled TWO PROPHETS & A KING NAMED HAZAEL.

Like Samson, Samuel the last of the judges, and John the Baptist are all Nazarites. Possibly Elijah and Elisha are Nazarites, as well. The prophets, who seem to be unaffiliated with anyone but the Lord, move through the stories of the Old Testament performing as many or more miracles than Jesus. The angels of the Lord also perform miracles, which invariably involve fire. Elijah's 'hairiness' would seem to indicate that he had long hair and a beard. Both might mark him as a Nazarite.

The Nazarites were persons who took vows to separate themselves from certain worldly things and consecrate themselves to God. They did not cut their hair, unless they broke their vows, at which time they shaved their heads. Nazarites did not drink wine and could not eat even grapes or raisins. Neither did they shave their beards. The third edict of their vows was that they were to avoid contact with the dead. Samson, Samuel and John the Baptist were "Nazarites from birth", meaning that they were under these edicts all their lives. The root of this word, *nazar* means: to hold aloof, i.e. to abstain from food and drink, from impurity, and even from divine worship - i.e. to apostatize; specifically, to set apart for sacred purposes, i.e. devote: consecrate, separating the self from sinful actions and activities. The Ismaili Nizari sect of Islam has similar attributes and we shall investigate all of this in a few moments. But all in all, both Elijah and Elisha would seem to be precursors of, or characterizations of the traditions of the Yahad.

Looking into the future, one cannot help but notice the parallels between the ideas presented here and the famous Nizari sect of assassins formed by Hassan-i-Sabah in the twelfth century CE as a splinter group of the Moslem faith. The *fadai* or assassins of Hassan also used daggers as their instruments of choice, because they were easily concealed. They often worked alone, or in pairs, when the success of the mission was critical. If one did not succeed, the other did. One of the most important concepts to the Nizari is something called *Tawid*. This word means "the unity of God" -- that there is one and only one God. This is exactly the meaning of Yahad - "unity."

It has been mentioned previously that the Yahad were associated through the 364 day solar calendar of Qumran with the Sicarii, who were the last defenders of Masada. The Sicarii, or 'dagger men' employed short curved Roman daggers called *sicae* to assassinate those who were friendly to the Romans. Upon the commission of this act, they would often begin to lament in the crowd in loud voices to escape detection and seem to be a part of the crowd. Josephus writes of them in *Antiquities Book XX, Chapter 3:*

> 6. These works, that were done by the robbers, filled the city with all sorts of impiety. And now these impostors and deceivers persuaded the multitude to follow them into the wilderness, and pretended that they would exhibit manifest wonders and signs, that should be performed by the providence of God. And many that were prevailed on by them suffered the punishments of their folly; for Felix brought them back, and then punished them. Moreover, there came out of Egypt about this time to Jerusalem one that said he was a prophet, and advised the multitude of the common people to go along with him to the Mount of Olives, as it was called, which lay over against the city, and at the distance of five furlongs. He said further, that he would show them from hence how, at his command, the walls of Jerusalem would fall down; and he promised them that he would procure them an entrance into the city through those walls, when they were fallen down. Now when Felix was informed of these things, he ordered his soldiers to take their weapons, and came against them with a great number of horsemen and footmen from

> Jerusalem, and attacked the Egyptian and the people that
> were with him. He also slew four hundred of them, and took
> two hundred alive. But the Egyptian himself escaped out of
> the fight, but did not appear any more. And again the robbers
> stirred up the people to make war with the Romans, and said
> they ought not to obey them at all; and when any persons
> would not comply with them, they set fire to their villages,
> and plundered them.

It is of interest here that we see something similar to this story told in the New Testament book of Matthew:

> And Jesus went out, and departed from the temple; and his
> disciples came to him for to show him the buildings of the
> temple. 2 And Jesus said unto them, See ye not all these
> things? Verily I say unto you, There shall not be left here one
> stone upon another, that shall be thrown down. 3 And as he
> sat upon the mount of Olives, the disciples came unto him
> privately, saying, Tell us, when shall these things be? And
> what shall be the sign of thy coming, and of the end of the
> world? 4 And Jesus answered and said unto them, Take heed
> that no man deceive you. 5 For many shall come in my name,
> saying, I am Christ; and shall deceive many. 6 And ye shall
> hear of wars and rumours of wars ; see that ye be not
> troubled; for all these things must come to pass, but the end
> is not yet. (Mt. 24)

Was this "Egyptian" the one who was called Jesus? We are told that Jesus' family fled to Egypt, to escape the wrath of Herod. Indeed, the Coptic Church (in Egypt) relates several stories of the infant/child Jesus in their scriptures.

Again, in the same chapter and book of Antiquities, Josephus goes on to relate more about the Sicarii:

> 8. About this time king Agrippa gave the high priesthood to
> Ismael, who was the son of Fabi. And now arose a sedition
> between the high priests and the principal men of the
> multitude of Jerusalem; each of which got them a company of
> the boldest sort of men, and of those that loved innovations
> about them, and became leaders to them; and when they
> struggled together, they did it by casting reproachful words
> against one another, and by throwing stones also. And there
> was nobody to reprove them; but these disorders were done
> after a licentious manner in the city, as if it had no
> government over it. And such was the impudence and
> boldness that had seized on the high priests, that they had
> the hardiness to send their servants into the threshing-floors,
> to take away those tithes that were due to the priests,
> insomuch that it so fell out that the poorest sort of the priests

died for want. To this degree did the violence of the seditious prevail over all right and justice.

Might this relate to Jesus chasing the moneychangers from the Temple? The Temple itself was built on the threshing floor of Ornan, a prince of the Jebusites, who lived in Jerusalem before the Jews came. The city was in fact called Jebus, which means 'threshing floor'. It is written that King David purchased this land from Ornan, and there built an altar to the Lord. Later, the Temple was built there. The moneychangers were 'bankers' who exchanged one currency for another and often charged exorbitant rates for doing so. They operated in the Court of the Gentiles at the Temple. All the monies given to the Temple had to be in Tyrian silver coin. Every Israelite over 20 was required to pay a half-shekel of silver to the Temple as an annual tax. In their first revolt against Roman rule, in 66-70 CE, the Jews coined their own silver shekels.

Josephus continues in Chapter 9 of the same book:

> 3. But now the Sicarii went into the city by night, just before the festival, which was now at hand, and took the scribe belonging to the governor of the temple, whose name was Eleazar, who was the son of Ananus [Ananias] the high priest, and bound him, and carried him away with them; after which they sent to Ananias, and said that they would send the scribe to him, if he would persuade Albinus to release ten of those prisoners which he had caught of their party; so Ananias was plainly forced to persuade Albinus, and gained his request of him. This was the beginning of greater calamities; for the robbers perpetually contrived to catch some of Ananias's servants; and when they had taken them alive, they would not let them go, till they thereby recovered some of their own Sicarii. And as they were again become no small number, they grew bold, and were a great affliction to the whole country.

Ananias was appointed as the High Priest by Herod around 48 CE. Ananias was also the one who spoke before the Roman governor Felix against Paul (see Acts 24:1). In about 52 CE, Ananias was sent to Rome by the governor of Syria to be tried for the Jews violent treatment of the Samaritans. Through Agrippa's influence, Ananias was acquitted of the charges, and returned to his place as High Priest in Jerusalem. Ananias was known as a collaborator with the Romans and was murdered by a mob at the beginning of the Jewish-Roman war (66-70 CE).

The Latin term *sicarius* is a common term for an assassin. These men were not only seditionists, but rabble-rousers as well. While the Zealots and Sicarii were tyrannical and cruel, resorting to murder when they deemed it necessary, they were not exactly 'robbers' as

Josephus characterizes them. Josephus also names three men who are their leaders, Eleazar ben Dinai is one of them. Another is Tehina the Essene, known as a pious man who later became a 'fierce Zealot'. The third is a man named Amram. Din is another form of the word *dan* or judgment. Of Eleazar ben Dinai and Amram it is said "*they desired to urge the Messianic deliverance of Israel, but fell in the attempt.*" *(Jewishencyclopedia – Sicarii)*

The Zealots are well known to Jewish historians. Josephus, following his sources, bestows the name of "robbers" upon all the ardent patriots who would not endure the reign of the usurper Herod and who fled with their wives and children to the caves and fortresses of Galilee to fight and to die for their conviction and their freedom. All these "robbers" were in reality the Zealots.

Two of Jesus' compatriots are Simon the Zealot and Judas Iscariot. In *Luke* he tells his companions:

> *Then said he unto them, But now, he that hath a purse, let him take it, and likewise his scrip: and he that hath no sword, let him sell his garment, and buy one. (Luke 22:36)*

We then see the new order of the Yahad, later become the Zealots and Sicarii with the idea of the Messiah or the 'Son of Man' appearing in the text of the *Book of Parables*, which has been dated as being written at the time when the Savior, Yeshua ben Joseph is said to have lived. Ezekiel is continuously addressed throughout his book as 'Son of Man', but he is not our Savior. We hear Jesus say in *Matthew*:

> *Think not that I am come to send peace on earth: I came not to send peace, but a sword. (Mt. 10:34)*

We have learned that the leaders of the Zealots desired to promote the Messianic deliverance of the Jews, but failed to do so. Amongst the *Dead Sea Scrolls*, we find texts entitled *The Inheritance of the Firstborn, the Messiah of David, A Collection of Messianic Proof Texts, The War of the Messiah,* and *The Last Days: An Interpretation of Selected Verses.* We find a quote from *Isaiah* in the scroll entitled *The War of the Messiah:*

> *…just as in is written in the book of Isaiah the prophet, "And the thickets of the forest shall be cut down with an ax, and Lebanon with its majestic trees will fall. A shoot shall come out from the stump of Jesse and a branch shall grow out of his roots (Is. 10:34 – 11:1) This is the Branch of David. Then all forces of Belial shall be judged, and the king of the Kittim shall stand for judgment and the Leader of the nation – the Branch of David will have him put to death. Then all Israel shall come out with timbrels and dancers and the High Priest*

> shall order them to cleanse their bodies from the guilty blood of the corpses of the Kittim... (4Q285, Frag. 5)

The term "Kittim" refers to the Romans, but is sometimes used as a generalization for 'the enemy'.

The tree symbolism used here is quite similar to the dream of the giants in the *Book of Giants*:

> 4Q530, Col. 2 Thereupon two of them had dreams and the sleep of their eyes fled from them, and the arose and came to... and told their dreams, and said in the assembly of their comrades the monsters.... In my dream I was watching this very night and there was a garden... gardeners and they were watering... two hundred trees and large shoots came out of their root... all the water, and the fire burned all the garden... They found the giants to tell them the dream....

We see the tree, root and branch symbolism used in *Isaiah*, one of the most vehemently inflammatory books of the Old Testament. We also see the tree, branch and root symbolism used rather extensively in *Jeremiah, Ezekiel,* and *Daniel*. The phrase "said in the assembly of their comrades" sounds very much like something a member of the Yahad would write. Any student of literature knows that authors may be identified by certain 'turns of phrase' or ideologies present in their writing. We have here an example of that. Another word that sounds much like *nazar* (Nazarite) is the word *netzer*, which variously means 'root', 'descendent' or 'branch'. The shoots or branches coming out of the roots of the trees represent the giants, as the offspring of the Watchers. Another, similar word is *nazir*, which means: consecrated, as a prince or a Nazirite/Nazarite; figuratively 'an unpruned vine', i.e. an unshorn Nazirite. Note that the word *notzar* or *natsar* also means 'to guard' in the sense of protecting, maintaining, or obeying. In another sense, it means 'to conceal', as in hiding or keeping something. It is also another word for Watcher. In the plural, it is rendered as *notzirim*.

Strong's Hebrew Bible Dictionary makes an interesting observation about the Nazarites:

> the name of such Israelites as took on them the vow prescribed in Num. 6:2-21. The word denotes generally one who is separated from others and consecrated to God. Although there is no mention of any Nazarite before Samson, yet it is evident that they existed before the time of Moses.

This statement has a ring of validity to it. There are those who believe that the Essenes did in fact originate in Egypt, possibly under the auspices of the 'heretical' pharaoh Ankh-en-aten, who revoked the worship of all gods in favor of the worship of Aten, the sun god, and established a new seat of power at Amarna. The name Essene may in fact derive from the Egyptian word *kashai* which means 'secret'. There is a similar word in Hebrew, *chshai* also meaning 'secret' or 'silent'. The phrase 'Sons of Light' by which the Essenes/Yahad refered to themselves is derived from the Hebrew word *eeshanee* which is said to translate as 'sons of the sun', but also means 'men of convicition' who lived by a certain creed.

In Fragment 10 from *The War of the Messiah*, we read a continuation of the idea of the angelic tower commanders from the *War Scroll:*

> ...for the sake of His name...Michael, Gabriel, Sariel and Raphael...and with the chosen of heaven...

The *Collection of Messianic Proof Texts*, translated by John Allegro, show the Yahad's expectations of a prophet like Moses, a royal son of David to lead them in their war and a proper, uncorrupted High Priest.

Aside from calling themselves the 'Sons of Light', the Yahad also referred to themselves or to their initiates as the 'Children of Dawn'. It is no secret that they saw themselves as the upholders of the righteous life, as God's 'left hand of judgment and retribution'. It is the greatest of ironies that their texts were apparently taken and further expounded upon, altered and developed by the later Christians and the *Church of Rome*, for the Romans were their worst enemies. Herein is the difference between the Messianic Jews and the Christians, for the Messiah of the Yahad never came. Or did he?

THE WATCHERS

THE NAMES OF THE WATCHERS

The names of the Watchers mentioned in the *Books of Enoch* have their own significance in understanding their story. Who are they? Where did they come from? What do their names mean? These and many other questions will hopefully be addressed and answered in this section. Few of them are well-known to anyone other than scholars or 'affectionados' of Enoch. In spite of the fact that many names are given throughout the text, several of those names refer to the same Watcher. There are names that look almost the same but are spelled differently. Some of the Watchers named remain a mystery. In those cases, possibilities will be offered where there is any shred of information available. This is the only place in the text where the actual spellings of the names are shown – i.e. with carat marks.

The common ending of –el has been explained previously and will not be recapitulated here. The names of the Watchers are listed in alphabetical order (English).

****

Anânêl (ענונאל) uhn AHN ehl
Hanânêl (הנונאל) ahn AHN ehl

This Watcher first appears in Chapter 6 and is named again in Chapter 69. In neither reference are we told his knowledge. His name is said to mean 'grace of God' or 'mercy of God', but the word *anan* means 'cloud' rendering his name as meaning 'cloud of God'. These two translations may not be mutually exclusive, for in the heat of the Middle Eastern summer, a cloud providing a cover over the sun might seem a mercy to those suffering from the heat on the ground. It seems odd that Ananel is not the Watcher 'whose knowledge is of the clouds'.

Arâkîba (ערקיבה) uh ruh KEE bah
Araqiêl (ערהקאל) uh RAH kee el
Artâqîfâ (הרתהקפה) ahr tuh KEE fuh

Appears in Chapter 6 as Arakiba, as well as in Chapter 8 as Araqiel and in Chapter 69 as Artaqifa.

The Hebrew word *arak* means "deserter", while *kheebah* is translated as "affection" or "fondness", rendering the meaning of Arakiba as "deserter of the affection (of God)". The name Araqiel would mean "deserter of God", while Artaqifa translates as something like "filled with desire" or "pregnant with desire".

More prosaically, this Watcher's name is said to mean "one who has dominion over the earth". The genius of Araqiel appears to be geomancy, and the signs of the earth. Were he Chinese, he might be said to be a Feng Shui master.

Geomancy has two aspects. Both are a form of divination. The first form of geomancy is divination by making lines of random numbers of dots in the sand. The Arabic name for geomancy, "'ilm al-raml" means "the science of the sand." The dots or points are drawn from left to right in 16 lines. From the dots or points, the geomancer draws a series of figures which are arranged into the geomantic tableau. There are sixteen possible figures consisting of single or pairs of points. Each figure has a name, associations with the elements, planets, etc., and good or bad qualities. Interpretation depends on the meanings of the figures in particular locations in the spread, and is related to the practice of astrology. There is an even more primitive form of geomancy, where handfuls of earth or sand were cast onto a table or other surface and the patterns that they made were interpreted by the diviner's art – rather like reading tea leaves.

The second form of the geomantic art has to do with dousing for water, piezometric and piezoelectric currents in the earth. A dousing rod and an astrolabe are used for this purpose. In locations where these currents run strong or cross one another, you will generally find temples and other such holy sites. The menhirs of Britain and Europe are said to have been placed to mark these locations. These currents have also been dubbed as 'ley lines'. Feng-shui masters call them 'dragon lines'.

Armârôs (ארמרוס) ahrm UH rohs

Appears in Chapter 6 as Armaros, as well as in Chapters 8 and 69 as Armaros.

The name means 'cursed one' or 'accursed one'. The name 'Armaros' is possibly a Greek corruption of what may be an Aramaic name; Armoni is possibly the original. According to R.H. Charles, the translator of this version of Enoch, the name may be a corruption of Araros.

The genius of Armaros is 'the resolving of enchantments'. Some interpret this to mean that he knew ways to reverse spells that went awry. In this, he seems to be a counter-part of Shemyaza.

Armên (אַרְמוֹן) ahr MUHN

Armen is mentioned only in Chapter 69, listed as the third Watcher. We are told nothing about his knowledge there. His name may mean 'the one from Hermon'. It may also mean 'palace'. It is possible that it is a duplication or a variation of Armaros. There appear to be a few duplications within the names of the Watchers given – often in the same chapter.

Asâêl (אָסִיל) ay SAY ehl

We are not told of this Watcher's particular knowledge in the text. His name in Chapter 6 is thought by some scholars to be an alternate for Azazel. The name Asael means 'made by God'.

Asbeêl (אָסבִּיל) as BAY uhl

This Watcher's name is said by some scholars of Enoch to mean 'deserter of God' and to be a variant on Araqiel. As Asael means 'made by God', Asbeel would seem to mean 'made by Baal'. It may be that he deserted God and went over to the worship of one of the ba'alim, but 'deserter of God' is not the literal translation of his name.

He appears in Chapter 69 and is said to have led the sons of God astray with his council. His name may refer to the son of Saul, Esh-baal, who was also called Ishbosheth (man of shame). Saul was the first king of Israel. Ishbosheth reigned for two chaotic years in Mahanaim, while David reigned as the king of Judah in Hebron. At that time, only the tribe of Judah acknowledged David as king. The other eleven tribes remained loyal to Saul's line and Ishbosheth. However, Ishbosheth made a fatal error in accusing Abner – the very man who had proclaimed him as king – of sleeping with Saul's concubine. Angry at the charge, Abner switched his allegiance to David. Ishbosheth was assassinated by two captains of his own guard, Baanah and Rechab. They took his severed head to King David, who then had Ishbosheth buried along with Abner in his tomb. David ordered the assassins put to death.

Ishbosheth was the last of Saul's lineage...and the last true king of the line of Benjamin. We are not told why Baanah and Rechab slew Ishbosheth. This is an important story, for if Ishbosheth had not falsely charged Abner, and Abner (who had some considerable influence with the tribes) had not switched his allegiance to the King of Judah, history may have taken quite another turn. David was the son of Jesse, *not* a Benjamite as pointed out above.

Jesse was an Ephrathite – of the tribe of Ephraim. Ephraim was the second son of Joseph by his Egyptian wife, Asenath the daughter of an Egyptian priest at On. He was not one of the sons of Jacob, of the original Twelve Tribes, but along with his elder brother Manasseh, replaced Reuben and Simon. Reuben and Simon had been disowned by Jacob for the sins of lust and murder, respectively. Ephraim and Manasseh were half Hebrew and half Egyptian. The tribe of Ephraim occupied the city of Jerusalem and the surrounding territory.

Azazel (עזאזל) uh ZAY zuhl

The true etymology of the name is unknown. Commonly, you will see that it may come from the Hebrew word *uz* or *ez* which means 'goat' and another Hebrew word *azel* which means 'to depart'. This idea comes from the scapegoat used in an old ritual of Yom Kippur or the Day of Atonement. On the Day of Atonement, two goats were chosen, one for Yahweh and one for Azazel. The goat for Yahweh was a sacrifice to God. The sins of the tribe or the people were spoken over the 'goat for Azazel'. A red cord was tied about his horns, so that any who saw this animal knew what it was. Early on, the goat was then turned out into the wilderness. Later, it was led or forced over a cliff. From this change in the ritual , it would appear that the goat sometimes wandered back into the village or town. Not an auspicious sign. Presumably, the sins of the tribe died with the unfortunate goat.

In a play on this idea in Chapter 10:8-9 of Enoch, it is said: "And the whole earth has been corrupted through the works that were taught by Azazel: to him ascribe all sin." In Chapter 8: 1-2 of Enoch, we are told: "And Azazel taught men to make swords, and knives, and shields, and breastplates, and made known to them the metals of the earth and the art of working them, and bracelets, and ornaments, and the use of antimony, and the beautifying of the eyelids, and all kinds of costly stones, and all colouring tinctures." Here, we have a play on words or in this case, letters - the two *zayins* or z's in Azazel's name. The letter *zayin* symbolizes a sword or knife because of its shape. The letter *ayin* which begins his name is said to be composed of a *zayin* and a *vau* which is symbolic of a nail - all things of metal. The letter *ayin* is also 'the eye' or eyes, playing into the Watcher myth.

In Semitic mythology Azazel is also thought to have been the chief of the Se'irim or goat demons who inhabited the desert.

Before the advent of Mohammed and Allah, the planet Venus was worshiped as a trinity of goddesses known as al-Uzza, Allat and Menat. In the early days of Islam, these three were declared to be the 'daughters of Allah'. They were later removed from such high places, as their worship constituted a remembrance of earlier pagan rites and worship. However, it remains to this day disguised as the worship of the Kaaba stone.

In Islamic legend, Azazel is called Iblis and is the ruler of the Djinn. The djinn are made of fire (like the *seraphim* chora of angels) and are extremely long-lived. There are good and bad djinn and they live their lives much like humans, being born, marrying and giving birth. They are said to be invisible but they can appear to humans in any form they desire. They frequently appear as serpents. In Persia, there is a similar spirit called a Djann. These are described as being half wolf and half hyena. The Djinn are said to equate with the Rephaim. The Rephaim are known as giants, ghosts of darkness, or as the spirits of the dead in Sheol. The Rephaim may be the same as Remphan (see Remiel). They are also called the Chiun or Kiun, as well as the Anakim. We find an interesting reference in *Amos* that ties in with this:

> *Have ye offered unto me sacrifices and offerings in the wilderness forty years, O house of Israel? 26 But ye have borne the tabernacle of your Molech and Chiun your images, the star of your god, which ye made unto yourselves. (Amos 5:25-26)*

The Palmyrians of Syria worshipped the morning star and the evening star, which they called Azizos or Aziz and Arsu, respectively. They are portrayed as both riding a camel...rather similar to the Knights Templar and their two knights riding one horse. This is quite similar to the Canaanitish sons of El, Shalim and Sharir, who also represent the morning and evening star – Venus. Venus has been referred to throughout history (in the Vedas and other ancient texts) as a 'hairy star', a 'smoking star' or a 'bearded star'. The term 'se'irim' means 'hairy ones' as well as being related to goats. It is this terminology that prompted Immanuel Velikovsky's theory that Venus came into our solar system from 'somewhere else', having the appearance of a comet, as it came. The 'train' of a comet is called a 'coma' and they are referred to as 'hairy stars'.

Venus in her many guises in Mediterranean and Middle Eastern lore is often shown with horns, referring to the crescent phases of the planet. When Venus appears to us in both its aspects as the morning and evening star, at its furthest elongation of orbit, it is extremely brilliant, fully reflecting the sun's light, rising either ahead or falling behind the sun. The only brighter objects in the sky at these times are the sun and moon. Venus is, of course, a planet and not a star. The brightest *star* in the sky is Sirius in Canis Major.

The path of Venus as it makes its curious orbit through the sky, appearing to move away from and toward the sun is reflected in the geometric figure of a pentagram. The five-petal dog rose is also symbolic of Venus' transits. Thus, the pentagram and the number five are associated with Azazel as the 'Light Bringer'. In the goddess aspect of Venus, the symbology is the five-petal dog rose.

There is a passage in the *Zohar* that refers to Venus/Azazel/Lucifer:

> Rabbi Hiyya said, "See the face of the East, how it shines! Now all the children of the East, who dwell in the mountains of light, are bowing down to this light, which shines on behalf of the sun before it comes forth, and they are worshiping it. Of course once the sun comes forth, there are many who worship the sun; but these are those who worship this light, calling this light, 'God of the shining pearl,' and their oath is by 'Allah of the shining pearl.' Now you might say: "This worship is in vain!' But since ancient, primordial days they have discovered wisdom through it. When the sun begins to shine, before coming forth, the deputy in charge of the sun comes forth, with the holy letters of the high holy Name engraved on his forehead. With the power of those letters, he opens all the windows of heaven, knocking them open, then moving on. That deputy is in charge of gold and rubies, and they worship his image there With points and signs inherited from the ancients, from ancient days, they come to know the points of the sun and find the location of gold and gems!" (Zohar, The Golden Calf)

Here, Venus is referred to as "the deputy in charge of the sun" and is said to have the "holy letters of the high, holy Name engraved on *his* forehead". Clearly, in the ritual of the Day of Atonement, Azazel is seen to be something on a par with Yahweh, for there are the offerings of the goats made to them both. At one time Venus as the goddess Ashteroth was worshipped as the Matronit or the Shekinah of Yahweh. This was most likely an incorporation of the worship of the Canaanitish deities Baal and Ashteroth into the early (pre-exilic) Hebraic religion. The Ashteroth was commonly represented by a large wooden post or even a carven tree trunk that was placed or sat in the sacred groves of the 'high places' beside the altar of the regional Baal. This idol was most likely the idol raised by King Asa's mother, Maachah (see commentary on Chapter 13).

As we have seen in the commentary on Chapter 9, Azazel, or Azazil is also associated with Melek Ta'us, the Peacock Angel of the Yezidi. The reference above from the Zohar refers to Venus as "God of the shining pearl". This would appear to be a cross-reference to Melek Ta'us, or Azazil. God created Azazel or Azazil as the first angel according to the Meshaf Resh. He was the first Son of God and by default of legend becomes synonymous with Lucifer (the Light-Bringer) as the most beautiful and beloved of all God's angels. In the Jewish version of the story of Azazel's fall from grace, he is kicked out of heaven for refusing to bow down to man or worship man at God's request. This was taken up by Islam and incorporated into the Quran. In the Yezidi version of the story, things are a bit different:

> *When the great God created the heavens, he put all the keys of the treasuries and the mansions there in the hands of Melek Ta'us, and commanded him not to open a certain mansion. But he, without the knowledge of God, opened the house and found a piece of paper on which was written. "Thou shalt worship thy God alone, and him alone shalt thou serve." He kept the paper with him and allowed no one else to know about it. Then God created an iron ring and hung it in the air between the heaven and the earth. Afterward he created Adam the first. Melek Ta'us refused to worship Adam when God commanded him to do so. He showed the written paper which he took from the mansion and said, "See what is written here." Then the great God said, "It may be that you have opened the mansion which I forbade you to open." He answered, "Yes." Then God said to him, "You are a heretic, because you have disobeyed me and transgressed my commandment."*
>
> *From this we know that God speaks in the Kurdish language, that is from the meaning of this saying, "Go into the iron ring which I, thy God, have made for whosoever does contrary to my commandment and disobeys me."*
>
> *When one criticizes such a story as this by saying that God drove Melek Ta'us from heaven and sent him to hell because of his pride before God the most high, they do not admit that such is the case. They answer: "It is possible that one of us in his anger should drive out his child from his house and let him wait until the next day before bringing him back? Of course not. Similar is the relation of the great God to Melek Ta'us. Verily he loves him exceedingly. You do not understand the books which you read. The Gospel says, 'No one ascended up to heaven but he who came down from heaven.' No one came down from heaven but Melek Ta'us and Christ. From this we know that the great God has been reconciled to Melek Ta'us, who went up to heaven, just as God came down from heaven and went up again. (Meshaf Resh – Appendix to Part I)*

The Jewish version of the story was perhaps intended to portray an affrontery to mankind, and discourage the worship of Venus in its many forms. It is echoed in the words of Yahweh to Enoch in Chapter 15: "You should intercede for men, and not men for you."

Azazel's particular genius involves metallurgy and chemistry or alchemy, which is applicable to one's will, character and spirit. The metal of a fine sword is hammered and folded, thrust into the fire and hammered some more. Water cools and tempers the blade. Our will, character and spirit is like this, forged by our life-experiences and our assimilation of the lessons learned. We do not learn, unless we are tested. On this note, some scholars equate Azazel with the *bene Elohim* known as *ha shaitan* or 'the adversary' from the book of Job.

Azazel's association with the planet Venus in her many incarnations as Inanna, Ishtar, Asherah and Ashteroth as well as the Greek Aphrodite and the Roman Venus, may also be the root of the idea that he taught the daughters of men about beautifying themselves with shadows and powders. While this idea may seem contrary to some regarding his more masculine side as a worker of metals, the concoction of these things is still a matter of alchemy and is intimately related to metallurgy. Venus, Aphrodite, Ishtar, etc. are also viewed as goddesses of both fertility and war. In essence, Azazel embodies many extremes, and so is the most complex of the Watchers named in Enoch.

As has been noted elsewhere in this text, the Hebrews saw the animal symbolizing the Greeks as a goat. It might be of interest to note here that in the MUL.APIN, the Babylonian guide to the constellations and stars, the constellation of Hercules (another 'giant' in the sky) is known as UZ.GU.LA, the Goat.

Barâqîjâl (ברכאל) BAR ahk ee ehl
Barâqêl (ברכל) BAR ahk ehl

The name of the astrologer Watcher comes from the Hebrew word *barak*, which means 'lightning'. His name means 'lightning of God'. Baraqijal is mentioned in the *Book of Giants* as the father of the giant Mahway. He is mentioned in Chapter 6 as one of the 'chiefs of tens', and again briefly in Chapter 8 which says "Baraqijal taught astrology". In Chapter 69, he is listed as the ninth Watcher Baraqel.

The science of astrology may supersede its apparent beginnings in ancient Sumer, for the movements of the heavenly bodies has fascinated man as long as he has lived upon Earth. The MUL.APIN mentioned in the commentary on Chapter 14 is of Babylonian origin, but its contents and references point to an earlier genesis. Astrology is generally thought to have come to its height in Chaldea through the Magi, and indeed there were great astrologers amongst the Magi. The Magi may be synonymous with the masters of the art in the ancient world, the Sabaeans. According to legend, these star-lords once lived in southern Mesopotamia, but some time in the first millennium BCE they migrated to Abbysinia (Ethiopia) and there established the kingdom of Axum.

According to legend, the first king of Abbysinia was Menelik I, the son of the Queen of Sheba and King Solomon. This story can be found in the *Kebra Negest*. The worship of the Sabaeans is said to have been focused on the trinity of Heaven, Sea and Land in the deities Astar,

Beher and Medr. To these were added the tribal gods of Aksum (Axum) and Mahrem (identified as Mars). Astar is none other than Ishtar or Venus. These Sabaeans were said to have erected obelisks to their deities, however, the oldest of the obelisks found at Axum has been dated from 5000 to 2000 BCE. This is far older than the supposed migration of the Sabaeans from Mesopotamia.

All this being said, one would expect to find Baraqijal amongst the Mesopotamian gods. In fact, there is a Babylonian god called Baragulla. Baragulla was a son of Ea/Enki and said to foretell the future by oracles. The nature of these oracles is not defined, but the cross-referencing of Baragulla to Baraqijal may indicate that they were astrological in nature. Please note that in transliteration between languages, the letters 'g' and 'k' are often transferred one to the other.

Astrology may well be said to be the 'science of destiny'. In some systems of belief, there is a destiny mapped out for us the moment we become flesh and 'the moving finger having writ, moves on' - we are unable to change it. This destiny is reflected in the orbits of the planets through the houses of the zodiac and their position at the time of our birth. We are what we are and nothing can change that. Other systems posit that no matter what we chose to do, we were meant to do that very thing and the choices we make are simply an illusion. A third option is that we do have free will and we do have the ability to change our situations, and mould our own 'realities'. That is to say, we make our own destinies. Free will is a latent topic of great import within the story of the Watchers, for by their free will, they left the first estate of Heaven and became as men. However, the second idea – that whatever choices we make are illusory is also alluded to in Chapter 9, when the archangels approach Yahweh. They tell him that in spite of his omnipotence, he has allowed this to happen...as if it were meant to be, and the Watchers only *thought* they were acting of their own free will.

Batârêl (בוט(ש)ראל) bat AHR el
Batarjâl (בושריל) bat AHR yuhl

Little is known of this Watcher. He is mentioned in Chapters 6 and 69 in the two variations shown here. Nothing is told of his knowledge. He is listed as the twelfth Watcher in Chapter 69. His name is said to mean 'valley of God' and is thought to be Babylonian in origin. The name Batariel appears in Talisman 4 of the *Sage of the Pyramids*. He appears from this to have been invoked in rites of ceremonial magic.

Busasêjal (בושסיעל) boo SAS eh yehl

This Watcher's name is one that has caused great controversy amongst the translators and scholars of *Enoch*. The text is damaged where his name appears and so it is uncertain what it is exactly. It may be that he was also named in Chapter 6, but Reverend Charles did not include him – again, because of textual damage. Some alternates that have been given are Basasael and Bezaliel. Bezaliel (bay ZAH lee ehl) is mentioned as one of the angelic guardians of the gates of the North Wind in the *Ozar Midrashim*. His name is said to mean the 'shadow of God'. The name Busasejal may be a combination of two Hebrew words. The first word, *booshah*, meaning 'shame' or 'disgrace' is from the same root as the word *bosheth*, which also means 'shame'. The word *yael* is translated as 'mountain goat'. The words taken together mean 'the disgrace of the goat'.

Dânêl (דנאל) DAN uhl
Danjal (דניל) DAN yuhl

Like the prophet of the same name, this Watcher's name means 'judgment of God' or 'God is my judge'. This name appears in both Chapters 6 and 69. We are not told of his particular genius in either reference. The inclusion of his name in both these chapters seems to dispute my theory of the names of Ezeqeel, Zaqiel and Sariel having been removed from Chapter 69 as some of the 'chiefs of tens' (see commentary on Chapter 69). However, there is evidence written above that this Watcher's name may refer to the tribe of Dan, with whom the authors of *Enoch* had issues, and that the name has nothing whatever to do with the prophet Daniel.

Êzêqêêl (אזאכאל) ee ZEE key uhl

Again, we have a Watcher's name that is similar to the name of a prophet. The name is translated as the 'strength of God'. Ezeqeel is mentioned in both Chapters 6 and 8, first as one of the 'chiefs of tens' and then to tell that he taught "the knowledge of the clouds". He is missing from Chapter 69 and is replaced by Neqael, which may be a corruption of Ezeqeel. See NEQAEL.

It is uncertain here if "knowledge of the clouds" means a type of augury from the clouds or if this Watcher is a sort of early meteorologist. It could be said there is a little of each mixed into this art.

Augury is first mentioned in Homer's *Illiad* written around 700 BCE. Augury came to Rome about one hundred years later. It is said that

Romulus and Remus were *augures.* Augury is different from haruspicy, which is augury from animal entrails, said to have been introduced to the Romans by the Etruscans. Augury interprets the signs of nature – most specifically from the calls or actions of certain birds, as well as from clouds, thunder and lightning, precipitation types and celestial signs such as comets, rainbows and the occultation of the sun or moon (eclipses). This mantic art does not foretell the future, per se, but looks for signs that are auspicious (or not) from the gods, who are in control of these things. These signs are in fact called *auspices*. This is not as far-fetched as it may seem. If we see birds congregating together on utility lines, rural fence-rails or in trees, it is a sign that a storm is coming. We know too that modern meteorologists track cloud formations as well as pressure systems to predict the weather.

Gadreel (גדראל) gad REE uhl

Gadreel appears to be another name for Azazel. The name Gad (also one of the sons of Jacob) means 'fortunate' but it also means 'a camp' or 'an army'. Here we are told that he also led Eve astray, equating him with the Serpent of Eden. There is an interesting commentary on this in *The Old Enemy – Satan & the Combat Myth:*

> *What is significant about the casual but momentous addition to the activities of the lustful Watchers is that, first, Eve is seen to be parallel to the 'daughters of men' who attracted the angels, and second, that the tempting serpent is simply absent. Eve's seducer too is an angel.* (Forsyth, pg 223)

Gadreel appears in Chapter 69. We are told that he is the one who "showed the children of men all the blows of death". This is presumed by many scholars to mean that he showed men how to use the weapons that were made by Azazel. If Gadreel is not another name for Azazel, then he would seem to be a sort of military expert. Azazel has also been said to have been the Serpent in the Garden of Eden who led Eve astray and fathered Cain. As has previously been pointed out, in the commentary on Chapter 10, this 'honor' was also bestowed upon Ea/Enki or Ushumgal, the Great Serpent who was the Sumero-Babylonian god who created humans.

Jeqôn (יקון) YEH kohn

This appears to be an alternate name of Shemyaza given in Chapter 69, meaning 'the inciter'. It was Shemyaza who incited his comrades to leave Heaven and take wives from amongst the daughters of men. The *qoph* or 'q' in his name might be an indicator that he is acting on the impulses of the lower part of his brain and not the higher to disseminate his seed – symbolized by the *yod* at the beginning. The final 'n' or *nun* of his name also suggests a fertilized seed or ovum – a creature developed from a fertilized egg or *zôon*.

Jetrêl (ישראל) YEHT rehl

Jetrel is listed as the 17th Watcher in Chapter 69. He does not appear anywhere else in the text. His name may mean 'privilege of God'. We are not told of his knowledge.

Jômjâêl (יומיאל) YOHM yay ehl

This Watcher's name means 'day of God'. He is mentioned as one of the 'chiefs of tens' in Chapter 6 and does not appear elsewhere in the text. We are not told his knowledge.

Kâsbeêl (כסבאל) kass BAY uhl

Possibly an alternate name for Kasdeja, seen in Chapter 69. Please see the commentary there in reference to this name. It will not be repeated here, as it must remain in place within the commentary in order to make sense within the context of which it is written.

Kâsdejâ (כשדיה) kass DAY uh or kash DAY uh

Kasdeja appears in Chapter 69. The first syllable of his name 'kas' may point to him being a member of one of three peoples – the Chaldeans, the Kasserites or Egyptians. As we have seen earlier, a certain group of people living in Chaldea (Ur Kasdim), the Sabaeans, are said to have migrated from there to the northern part of Ethiopia at Axum. This was at one time part of the great Egyptian empire. This might explain why both Chaldea and Egypt are referred to as Cush or Kush in ancient texts.

We are told that he taught "the children of men all the wicked smitings of spirits and demons, and the smitings of the embryo in the womb, that it may pass away, and the smitings of the soul, the bites of the serpent, and the smitings which befall through the noontide heat, the son of the serpent named Taba'et".

In ancient cultures, disease was thought to be the result of demons or improper actions on the part of the patient. A diviner was often employed to discern the cause of the problem, which was then handled by a physician-priest. Magic was often used, i.e. rituals and incantations to drive out the offending evil spirits, along with decoctions or infusions of herbs, poultices, enemas and ointments to cure the patient – "the smitings of spirits and demons".

Manifestations of psychological disturbance were also seen as the result of sin – "the smitings of the soul". The name Taba'et comes from the Hebrew word *taba'at*, which means 'ring'. This is most likely a reference to the 'ring' made by the sun as it travels through the sky – often symbolized by the Ouroboros, or the serpent biting its tail. We know this today as 'sun-stroke' – the 'smiting' which occurs in the noontide heat.

Perhaps this oath mentioned in Chapter 69 is also a punning reference to the Hippocratic Oath of physicians? Hippocrates was born on the island of Kos in approximately 460 BCE. The name of his birthplace, Kos, is a Greek name might be rendered as Kas in Hebrew. The suffix '-*deja*' (dey-uh) may be an attempt to transliterate the Greek *theo* or *deo* into Hebrew. This would make Kasdeja's name translate to something like 'the god of Kos'. Given the breadth of knowledge that is displayed in the text of *Enoch* and other Old Testament writings which may be attributed to the same authors, and that groups of these people were healers, it is not unreasonable to assume that they knew of Hippocrates *and* his oath.

Below is a translation from the Greek of the Classical Hippocratic Oath by Ludwig Edelstein:

> *I swear by Apollo Physician and Asclepius and Hygieia and Panaceia and all the gods and goddesses, making them my witnesses, that I will fulfill according to my ability and judgment this oath and this covenant:*
>
> *To hold him who has taught me this art as equal to my parents and to live my life in partnership with him, and if he is in need of money to give him a share of mine, and to regard his offspring as equal to my brothers in male lineage and to teach them this art - if they desire to learn it - without fee and covenant; to give a share of precepts and oral instruction and all the other learning to my sons and to the sons of him who has instructed me and to pupils who have signed the covenant and have taken an oath according to the medical law, but no one else.*
>
> *I will apply dietetic measures for the benefit of the sick according to my ability and judgment; I will keep them from harm and injustice.*
>
> *I will neither give a deadly drug to anybody who asked for it, nor will I make a suggestion to this effect. Similarly I will not give to a woman an abortive remedy. In purity and holiness I*

> will guard my life and my art.
>
> I will not use the knife, not even on sufferers from stone, but will withdraw in favor of such men as are engaged in this work.
>
> Whatever houses I may visit, I will come for the benefit of the sick, remaining free of all intentional injustice, of all mischief and in particular of sexual relations with both female and male persons, be they free or slaves.
>
> What I may see or hear in the course of the treatment or even outside of the treatment in regard to the life of men, which on no account one must spread abroad, I will keep to myself, holding such things shameful to be spoken about.
>
> If I fulfill this oath and do not violate it, may it be granted to me to enjoy life and art, being honored with fame among all men for all time to come; if I transgress it and swear falsely, may the opposite of all this be my lot.

We see here that part of this oath states that the physician will not provide an abortive remedy to a woman. It is quite curious that this is mentioned at all in the text, and may again be a sort of pun on the words *nefallem* (aborted fetus) and *nephilim*. It is curious, because this mention proves that such things were known as far back as the 5th century BCE, and that at least Hippocrates was against this practice. But the modern Jews themselves have no particular taboo against it. Rabbi Balfour Brickner, National Director of the Commission on Interfaith Activities, states:

> "Jewish law is quite clear in its statement that an embryo is not reckoned a viable living thing (in Hebrew, bar kayama) until thirty days after its birth. One is not allowed to observe the Laws of Mourning for an expelled fetus. As a matter of fact, these Laws are not applicable for a child who does not survive until his thirtieth day."

As we know, the symbol of healers and physicians has been the caduceus for a very long time. Traditionally, it is the wand of Hermes, who was syncretized with the Egyptian god Thoth (or sometimes the divinized royal architect Imhotep) and became Hermes-Trismegistus (Hermes the Thrice-born) the patron god or god-man of the wise men of Alexandria, alchemists and healers. Asclepius, who probably originated in Egypt was also a divinized man who became the god of healing and medicine. Like Hercules and other heroes, he was the son of a god – Apollo and a nymph named Coronis. He was said to have been taught medicine by the Centaur Cheiron and credited with such abilities as raising the dead. This upset Zeus and a few other gods - notably Hades, who was worried he wouldn't be getting any new 'guests' in the Underworld. Zeus thought to kill him, but Apollo interceded. Zeus relented and placed Asclepius in the sky as the constellation Serpentarius, better known as Ophiucus, the Serpent Holder – another 'giant' from the heavens. Sometimes, Asclepius is shown as a serpent. In his human appearance, he is depicted as a benign looking man carrying a staff upon which is entwined either one or two serpents.

There is another interesting story regarding Asclepius that has to do with Medusa and her blood. After she was beheaded by Perseus, the blood was drained from her body. Presumably, it was Athena, Perseus' divine guide in the expedition to slay the Gorgon, who did this. Presumably, because later, Athena gives Asclepius two vials of Medusa's blood. One vial is life-giving and healing, said to have given him the power to raise the dead. The other vial of Medusa's blood caused instant death. These vials of blood were said to have been taken from her right and left arteries. Which was which depends upon the version of the myth you're reading.

As it has been noted before, some of the first hospitals were located within the temple precincts of the Egyptians. While they might have been referred to as 'magicians' in the tale of *Exodus* with the rods and serpents, they may have been physicians.

> 10 And Moses and Aaron went in unto the Pharoah, and they did so as the Lord had commanded: and Aaron cast down his rod before Pharoah, and before his servants, and it became a serpent. 11 Then Pharoah also called the wise men and the sorcerers: now the magicians of Egypt, they also did in like manner with their enchantments. 12 For they cast down every man his rod, and they became serpents: but Aaron's rod swallowed up their rods. (Exodus 7)

As far back as Sumer and Babylonia, sin and illness were thought to go hand in hand. The Sumero-Babylonian physicians were referred to as magicians or wise men. It was common practice to use 'white magic' to heal patients of their illnesses. Illness could be caused by demons, 'sinful actions' (arsu), or even unwitting negligence. The sick person might not even know which deity he or she had offended. It was up to the diviner or augurer to determine this through various auspices, and relate the information to the physician. One who was ill was just as much a 'patient' as one who had sinned.

This emphasizes the view that sin = disease. Sin could be transmitted by relatives or inherited from parents. Here we have the implication of 'original sin', inherited from one's ancestors, i.e., Adam and Eve – a superstition we still live with today. Sin could be 'caught', like disease, from touching or wearing something worn or touched by a tabooed person or a 'sinner'. We know today that there are such things as congenital diseases, which (as the name states) we inherit from our parents or grandparents. We can contract viral and bacterial borne diseases by contact with one who is a carrier – that is, they are infected with these diseases and we are infected in turn. The common cold or the flu is a good example of this. We can also contract other diseases by contamination from various substances, but to believe that we do so because we have 'sinned' or offended any deity is sheer superstition that remains from ancient times.

The previous story from *Exodus* would seem to be a way of saying that Moses and Aaron had more power, or more pull with their god than did the Egyptian wise men with their gods. In the following story from *Numbers* we clearly see that the people thought they were sick because they'd sinned. This viewpoint continued in popular thought well into the 19th century, and may be found even today. As a hold-over of this, we still *bless* people when they sneeze, saying "Gesundheit!" (Health!).

> 6 And the Lord sent fiery serpents among the people, and they bit the people; and much people of Israel died. 7 Therefore the people came to Moses, and said, We have sinned, for we have spoken against the Lord, and against thee; pray unto the Lord that he take away the serpents from us. And Moses prayed for the people. 8 And the Lord said unto Moses, Make thee a fiery serpent, and set it upon a pole: and it shall come to pass, that everyone that is bitten, when he looketh upon it, shall live. 9 And Moses made a serpent of brass, and put it upon a pole, and it came to pass, that if a serpent had bitten any man, when he beheld the serpent of brass, he lived. (Numbers 21)

The wise man or physician/magician had not only to be familiar with diseases and their causes, but the cures. The cures included not just herbal remedies, but knowing how to propitiate offended gods, a little psychology, and a hefty repertoire of spells and rituals. Things haven't changed much in all these thousands of years. The Roman Catholic priests still 'exorcise' demons on occasion, using holy water, ritual incantations and the cross.

Kôkabiêl (כוכביאל) koh KAH bee ehl

Kôkabêl (כוכבאל) koh KAH behl

Mentioned as one of the 'chiefs of tens' in Chapter 6, we are told in Chapter 8 that his knowledge is "of the constellations". Kokabel is in effect, another astrologer Watcher, his name meaning 'star of God'. The Hebrew word *kokh* means 'star', 'planet' or 'comet'. Kochab, the second brightest star in the constellation Ursa Minor (the Little Bear or Little Dipper) was the polestar in the 8th to 7th centuries BCE.

Kochab and Perkab, the star just below it in the 'bowl' are called the Guardians of the Pole.

There was little distinction between astronomy and astrology in ancient times. The study of the movements of the stars, constellations and planets is an ancient art that was important for keeping track of proper days for observing festivals, the holy days of deities, planting and harvest. This art was also used to augur or divine the most auspicious times for coronations and other civic events, including the erection of public buildings, temples and tombs. Many of the ancient monuments that we find today, such as henges, barrow-mounds, and temples are laid out to accommodate the rising of certain heavenly bodies on important days. The most important of these seem time and again to be the Sun and Venus, as well as the nodes of the Moon. That is not to say that the other planets, stars and constellations were not carefully observed and marked, as well. We also see references to the precession of the sun in the 'ages' of man and the gods in ancient literature and art forms. Lunar and solar eclipses or occultations were also predicted in this manner.

The word 'planet' comes from a Greek word, 'planētēs', which means 'wanderer'. These wandering 'lights' moved through the heavens, seemingly contrary to the movements of the fixed stars and constellations. To the ancients, they appeared to have their own agendas and purposes. Planets were deified and anthropomorphised stories fabricated about their exploits to explain their actions in the heavens. The famous tale of Inanna's Descent into the Underworld is more than likely an explanation for why Venus seems to disappear from the heavens at certain times during the year. Each planet/deity had definitive characteristics and its position in relation to the Earth, to the constellations of the Zodiac and other planets created a 'circumstance' which was believed to be reflected here in the mundane world. It was the art of the astrologers to understand these relationships between the heavens and man, and to advise the leaders of empires when and when not to act. They saw conjunctions of planets and 'fixed' stars as particularly potent signs which incorporated the attributes of the deities and the constellations of the Zodiac to give a scenario which they would then relate to their people or leaders. Like physicians, astronomers and augerers, the astrologers were often of the priestly class.

Comets were seen to be portents of social unrest, collapse of government, outbreaks of violence and 'the death of princes'. They are also seen as harbingers of plagues and various miseries. Of comets in his time, Pliny wrote:

> *"A fearful star this comet is, it appeared at the civil troubles when Octavius was consul; also a second time at the war of Pompey and Caesar; and about the time that Claudius Caesar was poisoned and left the empire to Nero, in the time of*

> *whose reign and government there was a blazing comet continually seen."*

The births and deaths of kings and princes were also supposedly attended by comets. Seven days after the death of Julius Caesar, a comet appeared in the northern sky. This was taken to mean he had become immortal and received into the realm of heaven.

Eclipses are likewise seen to be harbingers of change, unrest or doom and destruction. It was therefore quite important to know when these events would occur. There also seem to be some occurrences of using fore-knowledge of these events to establish one's 'influence' with the gods and impress the natives.

Horoscopic astrology is a very specific and complex system that was developed in the Mediterranean, specifically in Ptolomeic Egypt sometime around the late 2nd or early 1st century BCE – around the same time the *Book of the Watchers* was written. We know that the members of the Yahad were also interested in astronomy and astrology, for we see scrolls with such titles as: *The Phases of the Moon, Calendar of the Heavenly Signs, An Aramaic Horoscope* and *An Annalistic Calendar*.

Kokabiel's knowledge may be a pun on both the words *kokh* and *kaabah* the Arabic word which means 'high or lofty place'. The *beth* or 'b' in his name means 'house'. As we know, the position of the constellations at one's moment of birth define the houses in which the positions of the planets are read to foretell our fate.

Nêqâêl (נקיאל) neh KAEY ehl

The text is damaged at this name. It is probably an alternate or replacement name for the Watcher Ezeqeel. Named as the eighth Watcher in Chapter 69. Neqael does not appear in any other chapters of *Enoch*. His name may mean 'incorruptible of God' from the Hebrew word *nekee*.

The Neqa'el are said to be Egyptian and/or Greek cat demons who could assume human form. Cats were considered to be temple guardians, as well as minor deities. It is not clear whether this has to do with the Watchers, but it may refer to Bast, to whom cats were sacred. Bast was sometimes represented as a ferocious lion-headed goddess and was said to be the daughter of the Sun god, Ra and in some cases, the wife of Set in his form known as Bes. Lion imagery is often symbolic of the Sun. Bast was also sometimes seen as a male divinity connected with Bosheth (Ba'al).

Penemue (פנימוי) peh NEHM way

Penemue is listed only in Chapter 69. Some scholars have posited that Penemue is an alternate name for Kokabel, but this doesn't seem likely, as their respective knowledge-bases are quite different.

Penemue is a strange name in comparison to the names of the other Watchers. While *peney* is a Hebrew word meaning 'face of' or 'surface of', can we find anything else of the name in the Hebrew language? There is a phrase *mee peney mah* which is translated as 'why? on what account?'. If this is indeed the root of his name, we may again be seeing a kind of pun on the author's feeling of hopelessness, identifying himself with the Watcher who is one of the 'curers of the stupidity of man'.

There has been much discussion as to what it means that Penemue "taught the children of men the bitter and the sweet". It is interpreted in *The Ashes of Angels – The Forbidden Legacy of a Fallen Race* in this way:

> One of their number, Penémûe, taught 'the bitter and the sweet', surely a reference to the use of herbs and spices in foods, while instructing men on the use of 'ink and paper', implying that the Watchers introduced the earliest forms of writing. (Collins, pg. 26)

The *peh* or 'p' that begins Penemue's name represents the mouth - a head with a tongue inside – the *yod* symbolizing the tongue. It may also represent eating or devouring. Knowing this, we can see that his teaching of the 'bitter and the sweet' is a pun on the meaning of the letter *peh* – for it is by the tongue that we apprehend the attributes of the food we eat. The *peh* is also the letter of Mercury, the Greek messenger of the gods, whose astrological attributions are: intelligence, perception and cleverness.

Râmêêl (רמיאל) RAHM ee ehl
Râmîêl (רמיאל) RAHM ee ehl
Rûmjâl (רמיל) RUHM yahl

Rameel or Ramiel is listed as one of the 'chiefs of tens' – apparently twice, in Chapter 6. He is mentioned again in Chapter 69 as Rumjal, the sixth Watcher. We are never told his particular knowledge. The name may be translated as 'high one of God'. His name may also be translated as 'thunder of God' from the root word *ra'am*. The name(s) of this Watcher may be a covert reference to Rimmon or Ramman, the Babylonian god of thunder and storms.

As Ramiel, this Watcher appears in the Syriac *Apocalypse of Baruch*. He instructs Baruch (whose name is of the same root as Baraqijal: Barak = 'lightning') in the meaning of his vision. Ramiel is said to be the chief of thunder, as is the angel Uriel.

Ramiel has been equated with the angels Uriel, Phanuel and Yerahmeel. He may also be the same Watcher as Remiel, who appears in Chapter 20, verse 8 as "one of the holy angels, whom God set over those who rise". This would be yet another pun, this time on the first meaning of this Watcher's name.

Samjâzâ (שמיחזה) shahm YAkH zuh
Sêmîazâz (שמיחזז) shehm ee kHAH zahz
Semjâzâ (שמיחזה) shehm YAkH zuh

We see the leader of the Watchers as Semjaza in Chapters 6, 8, 9 and 10. He is also listed as Semiazaz in Chapter 6, in the list of the 'chiefs of ten'. In Chapter 69, he is called Samjaza. These are all merely variations on his name. It is preferred to use Shemyaza here, as has been throughout the commentary. The Ethiopian corruption of his name is Amezerak. His name is said by some scholars to mean 'the (in)famous rebellion' or 'arrogance'. The word *shem* can mean 'name' or 'famous'...or 'infamous', as when one 'makes a name' for themselves – one way or another. However, the word 'rebellion' is *mereedah*. The word 'uprising' is *heetkomemoot.* The Hebrew word for 'arrogance' is *shakhtsanoot.* Hebrew hasn't changed so much over the centuries that we would suppose these words might be that much different. Michael Knibb gives the meaning of his name as 'he sees the name', which appears to be in reference to the story of Shemyaza knowing the ineffable name of God. The word *shem* means 'name', but 'to see' is *leer'oot.* This has been addressed in the commentary on Chapter 69.

The most obvious translation of the name Samyaza would go back to Zoroastrianism and the Avestan word *yaz-* which is a verbal root that means 'to worship', 'to venerate' or 'to honor'. Sams or Shams was the sun god of northern Arabia, probably derived from Shamash or Shemesh. Putting these together, Shamyaza would translate as something like 'he worships the Sun'. Given the apparent solar implications of both Enoch-Metatron, and Shemyaza's apparent relationship to Samson, this makes more sense.

Shemyaza's name as it is spelled in Hebrew letters may be a pun on the word 'relations', which is *yekhaseem.* (Remember to exclude the *shem* portion of the name when looking at this). Shemyaza would then be translated as '(in)famous relations' - as in 'human relations', 'family relations', 'public relations' and 'sexual relations'. All of these ideas are certainly applicable to the leader of the 'fallen angels'. It might be pointed out here, as well that the word *yakhad* – i.e. Yahad – is the root of this word, and not only means 'unity', but 'togetherness' or 'together'.

In his *Dictionary of Angels – Including the Fallen Angels*, Gustav Davidson gives Shemyaza's name translated as 'the name Uzza' or 'Azza'. Uzza means 'strong', which, and as it has been noted, may refer to the story of Samson. The name Uzza is another one of Metatron's many epithets. In some ways, Shemyaza also seems like a 'dark' counterpart of Enoch-Metatron...the 'eclipsed Sun' or the sun of winter as opposed to the summer sun. This comes down to us later in the mythology of the Oak King and the Holly King of the summer and winter solstices, which may also be linked to the ancient worship of Janus, the guardian deity of gateways and doorways.

In the chapter previous to this, we have seen that the Nazarites abstained from 'sinful actions', including the drinking of wine and even eating certain foods. The Yahad were said by some, including Josephus, to have been vegetarians. We saw that both of the 'angels' who came to Samson's parents, and to Gideon refused the food offered them and made the meat given them an offering to God. If the members of the Yahad took a wife, she was put 'on probation' for three years, according to the reports of Josephus. If she did not stray or quit her betrothed before that time and proved herself to be a 'righteous' woman, the man would marry her. Sexual relations were restricted to certain times and only for the purpose of procreation – providing an heir. They abstained from all other sexual activity.

What we have here in the Yahad is a strict group of 'pious men'. The actions of Shemyaza and his companions flaunt these rules of living in the extreme direction. This is a circumstance that the writers of *Enoch* witnessed going on all around them by the 'barbarians' and those Jews who were influenced to behave other than how the Yahad thought people should act. We see how the members of the Yahad thought people should comport themselves time and again in their writings – the sectarian scrolls found in the caches at Qumran. While there were several groups of this 'sectarian association' scattered about Israel, Samaria, Palestine and even Egypt, they were in the minority.

Shemyaza is nominally the leader of the fallen Watchers, however in Chapter 10, we see the 'blame' for all of this shifted to Azazel. This and an apparent similarity between parts of their names has caused many to wonder if they are not the same being. This does not seem to be the case. Azazel's knowledge is far different from Shemyaza's and so too are their punishments.

We are told that Shemyaza "taught enchantments, and root-cuttings". The word 'enchant' is defined as "to cast under a spell, or bewitch". One might do this magically or through personal charisma, being a charming or delightful personality...one capable of convincing others to do something they might not otherwise do. The term 'bewitchment' can be a dire word, often used in the past by over-zealous Inquisitors and puritanical preachers to accuse purported witches of manipulating other people into committing evil actions or causing them to become ill, lame or insane. Calling Shemyaza an 'enchanter' may have its basis in this idea – effectively calling him a 'sorcerer'. For surely – in their eyes - unless someone cast some sort of black charm upon the other Watchers, they would not have done what they did.

We are also told that Shemyaza's knowledge extends to "root-cuttings". This may again be a pun on the propagation of heirs, or of removing the 'roots' of the Yahad by taking two hundred plus of the membership out with him. Significantly, grapevines are most efficiently propagated by root-cuttings – dividing the plant at the branches of the roots from the parent plant to create a new plant. We have seen the reference to the related words *nazir* (an 'unpruned vine'), from which comes Nazirite, and *notzir*, meaning Watcher or guardian.

This association with grapevines may also point to Shemyaza as a Dionysian figure. Dionysus is a fertility god or earth god, as well as a god of wine, ecstasy and prophecy. The most popular rendition of his origins say that he was the son of Zeus and Semele. Semele was a human woman - a priestess by some accounts – with whom Zeus became infatuated one day while watching her sacrifice a bull. While she was with child, jealous Hera appeared to her as her nurse and convinced her that she should appeal to the changeling god Zeus to reveal himself to her in his true form. Semele begged and prayed that Zeus would appear to her. He attempted to dissuade her from this folly, but Semele would not listen. When he did appear to her, Semele was unable to endure the brilliance of the god's divine form and went up in flames. Hermes, the physician god, was able to save her unborn child and Dionysus was sewn into Zeus's thigh (i.e. testicles), from which he was later 'reborn'.

In another version of the story, Dionysius is the son of Zeus and Persephone, the goddess of corn and the underworld. Here, Dionysus is snatched away from his mother and eaten by the Titans. Zeus was able to save the child's heart and later served it to Semele in a drink, by which she became pregnant. These stories earned Dionysius the epithet of 'twice born'. As the god of the vine, the heart of Dionysius most likely refers to the grape and the drink was the wine of the grape. In Christianity, we see the Dionysian reference to wine as 'the blood of Christ'. Wine was considered the blood of Dionysus well before the advent of the Christian Savior, and used mixed with various other ingredients as the sacrament of the Orphic, Samo-thracian and Cretan mysteries.

This story is important for several reasons. It is the root of the idea that none can behold the face of Zeus/God for all it's divine brilliance, without being burned to ashes. This is the reason why both Jacob and Gideon fear that they will die, because they have beheld an angel, or 'the face of God'. This story also has a parallel in the Vedic myth of the anti-gods – the *asuras* – stealing the soma (the sacrament of Shiva and Persian mystery cults – i.e. haoma) from the gods and thus becoming more wise than the gods. In the story of Dionysius, it is the Titans or giants (the anti-gods of the Greek pantheon) who steal the child and devour him, after ripping him to pieces. The adepts of the aforementioned mysteries became gods by the virtue of the transcendental visions they received from the sacrament of the wine.

Dionysus' divinity was said not to have been recognized immediately, and so he wandered the earth, much like Gilgamesh and Osiris, spreading his teachings. The reason for this is said to be that Dionysus is actually a far older god than the gods of Olympus, and was a mushroom-god before he was the god of the vine. The sacrament of the mysteries was originally a concoction of hallucinogenic mushrooms and other ingredients, that was later replaced by wine. The Greeks believed that mushrooms and toadstools were engendered by lightning, rather than seed, like other fruit. Lightning is the weapon of both Zeus and Yahweh, as storm-gods. As Dionysus wandered the earth, he gathered a great following. We see Shemyaza gathering a great following as well, as he and his companions reveal the 'secrets of heaven' to mankind, making them as wise as those in heaven.

What we see here is a pre-cursor to the story of Adam and Eve eating the fruit of the Tree of Knowledge and becoming wise. We see this Tree in Chapters 24 and 25 of the *Book of the Watchers*:

> And amongst them was a tree such as I had never yet smelt, neither was any amongst them nor were others like it: it had a fragrance beyond all fragrance, and its leaves and blooms and wood wither not for ever: 5 and its fruit is beautiful, and its fruit resembles the dates of a palm. Then I said: 'How beautiful is this tree, and fragrant, and its leaves are fair, and its blooms very delightful in appearance.' 6 Then answered Michael, one of the holy and honoured angels who was with me, and was their leader.
>
> [Chapter 25] 1 And he said unto me: 'Enoch, why dost thou ask me regarding the fragrance of the tree, 2 and why dost thou wish to learn the truth?' Then I answered him saying: 'I wish to 3 know about everything, but especially about this tree.'

In *The Old Enemy – Satan & the Combat Myth* we are told:

> The first Adam books may have been composed as early as the first century B.C. and probably circulated among some of the same sectarian Jewish groups (scattered throughout the diaspora but especially strong in Palestine itself and in Alexandria) among whom the Enoch literature was popular. It seems to have been a development of redemption theology in sectarian circles like Qumran which encouraged this new emphasis on Adam and his brood. On the one hand, these Adam books show strong links with the apocalyptic Enoch tradition; on the other, they already contain many of the redemption ideas that were soon to be so radically developed in Gnosticism. (Forsyth, pg. 227)

In other words, the Adamic literature was written *after* the *Book of the Watchers*. The *Book of Parables/Similitudes* was written at a later date than the Adamic literature, as if the authors were trying to find a story that would resonate with those they wished to redeem or convert to their way of thinking. If the idea of fallen angels didn't resonate with people, perhaps the idea of fallen humans who might be redeemed would strike a chord.

Casting Shemyaza as a Dionysian figure by the implication of his knowledge of root-cuttings points again to the Greeks. It also points to him rejecting The Way of the Nazirites or the Yahad, who are forbidden to touch the fruit of the vine because of its consecration to the god of the Greek mysteries. We know little or nothing about the exact nature of the mysteries of the Yahad, or if they had their own version of a sacrament that produced transcendental visions.

It has been mentioned throughout the text that Shemyaza may also be a caricature of Samson the judge. Like Samson, Shemyaza is also said to have been a judge in heaven before his fall.

The curious inverted angel at Rosslyn Chapel in Scotland is called Shemyaza, referring to the rabbinical legend that as his punishment for revealing the holy name of god to the maiden Ishtahar, he is suspended upside down between heaven and earth in the constellation of Orion, with one eye closed. Like Samson, who reveals the secret of his strength, Shemyaza is a revelator of secrets and for it is punished for the transgression. Samson is literally blinded – "because he followed his eyes too often", while Shemyaza is portrayed as choosing to close one eye to what he has given up by leaving his divinity behind for the world of the flesh.

Before Samson was a judge in Hebraic literature, he was a sun-hero or sun-god of the Philistines. The name of Samson in Hebrew is Shimshone, which means *sunlight*. We could extend this to be 'son-light' or 'light of the sun/son'. Samson was similar in many attributes to the sun-hero Hercules, who was not only wise, charming and strong, but said to be a glutton, a drunk and a man of great sexual prowess. These same attributes are implied in Shemyaza's name, as well as his knowledge and his deeds. We find an interesting reference to Samson in *The White Goddess*:

> *'Must all things swing round and round again for ever? Or how can we escape from the Wheel?' This was the problem of the blinded Sun-hero Samson when he was harnessed to the corn-mill of Gaza; and it should be noted that the term 'corn mill' was applied in Greek philosophy to the revolving heavens. Samson resolved the problem magnificently by pulling down both posts of the temple so that the roof collapsed upon everyone. (Graves, pg. 140)*

In his own way, Shemyaza also brings down the Yahad's 'Living Temple' by leaving and taking many members of its foundation with him. As in the letters of Azazel's name, we see the same sort of spelling pun with the letter *cheth* representing the doorway or gateway of the Temple and the letter *heh* which looks nearly the same, but has a chink (the window) in the left upright, which would cause that doorway to collapse. (See GEMATRIA.) The left pillar of the Temple doorway was called Boaz, and said to represent 'strength' as well as representing the southern kingdom of Judah. These pillars stood at the eastern doorway of the Temple in Jerusalem, facing the rising sun. As the first rays of the morning sun shone into the Eastern or Golden Gate of the Second Temple, the priests began their recitation of the *Shema* – the holy names of God.

Samsâpêêl (שמשפיאל) sam SAH pee ehl
Shamsiêl (שמשאל) sham SHE ehl
Sîmâpêsîêl (שמהפסיאל) shim ah PEE zee ehl

Listed as one of the 'chiefs of tens' in Chapter 6. We are then told in Chapter 8 that Shamsiel taught "the signs of the Sun". In Chapter 69, he is listed as the sixteenth Watcher. Simapesiel may mean 'idol of the Sun' from the word *peesel*, which means 'carved' or 'sculpture'; and the word *pession*, meaning 'statue' or 'figurine'. Shamsiel can be translated as 'light of God'.

In spite of the many variations on his name in the text, this Watcher's name seems to refer to the name of the Sumero-Babylonian sun god, Shamash. Shamash has been discussed previously in the section THE MAN WHO WALKED WITH GOD.

What does it mean that Shamsiel taught man the signs of the Sun? Today, we think of sun-signs as the signs of the Zodiac, but we already have two Watchers who are teachers of astrology and the constellations. What is most likely meant here is that Shamsiel knew the times of the solstices and equinoxes, as well as the laws of

Precession of the Equinoxes - the movement of the sun through the 'great years' of the Zodiac. A 'great year' is a period of 25,868 years which the Earth takes to pass through influence of each of the signs of the Zodiac. Due to a bit of a wobble in the Earth's rotation, the constellation showing behind the Sun at the vernal equinox changes gradually through the centuries. The 'great year' is the period of time that it takes for the *same* constellation to appear behind the Sun that appeared at the beginning of the 'great year' there. There are 'great months' of the 'great year' as well. It takes about 2,000 years for the sign that appears behind the Sun to be replaced by the next sign. The Greek astronomer Hipparcus of Nicaea (190-120 BCE) is said to be the first to discover this principle. Hipparcus' original writings are lost, but partially preserved in Ptolemy's *Almagest*. Some astro-archeological scholars are of the opinion that the Chaldeans may have known about precession around 330 to 315 BCE. Hipparcus' theory of precession was based upon a geocentric model – that is, the idea that the Sun and the constellations rotated around the Earth.

Shamsiel might have also known how to predict solar eclipses. His knowledge would have gone hand in hand with the knowledge of Kokabiel, Baraqiel and Sariel. He might have also been the one who calculated when to add intercalary days to the 364 day solar calendar each year at the vernal equinox. The 'signs of the Sun' are related in Chapter 72 of the third book of Enoch, *The Book of the Heavenly Luminaries*. The rule of the intercalary days is mentioned in Chapter 75.

Sariêl (זהריאל) sah REE ehl

This Watcher appears in Chapter 6, listed as one of the 'chiefs of tens'. In Chapter 8, we are told that Sariel taught "the course of the moon". He is not named again in the *Enoch* writings, but shows up as a Wing Commander in the army of the Sons of Light in the *War Scroll* of the Yahad.

One might ask, "How is Sariel both fallen and exalted?" The answer may lie in what was already posited – that he was written originally as a member of the fallen Watchers, but in later chapters was replaced with another name, because of his 'new position' within the ranks of the Sons of Light. This makes Sariel both a Son of Darkness and a Son of Light. This could also – rather obviously – point to the full and dark phases of the moon.

His name is sometimes translated as 'prince of God', from the word *sar* meaning 'prince' or 'minister'. However, his name is not spelled with a *samekh*, but with a *zayin*. It would appear that his name is a pun on the word *zreeah*, which means 'sowing'. In Sariel's case the *zayin* at the beginning of his name does not represent a sword or dagger, but a dibble – a pointed gardening instrument used to make holes in the ground in which to plant seeds. A dibble is also similar in shape to the letter *zayin*. While the Yahad had discontinued using the 354-day lunar calendar in favor of a solar calendar, the phases of the moon were still important to planting. Crops that grew above the ground were planted by the light of the full moon, while crops that were tuberous or grew underground were planted by the dark of the moon. The Hebrew word for barley is *se'or* which comes from the root *sa'ar*.

The Hebrew calendar begins with the first new moon after the barley attains ripeness. Ripened barley is called *abib* and the first month of the Hebrew calendar was Aviv in pre-exilic times. Later, it became Nissan, as the Jews elected to use the names of the months in the Babylonian calendar. The period between one year and the next is 12 or 13 months. The state of the barley crop was checked at the end of the twelfth month, and if it was ripe at this time, the following new moon marked the beginning of the first month of the year. If the barley was still not ready for harvest, another month was added to the calendar called Adar Bet. This constituted a Jewish 'leap year', not to be confused with the leap-year of the Gregorian calendar. In the time of the Second Temple, the beginning of each lunar month was decided by two eyewitnesses or watchmen testifying to having seen the new crescent moon and reporting this to the priests.

The *sar* portion of Sariel's name may also be related to Osiris as Au-Sar. Osiris was originally an Egyptian vegetation god, who later became the Lord of the Underworld and the Resurrected God. It is little known that Osiris was also a moon god called Iu-wen. As the story goes, it was Isis who discovered wheat (emmer) and barley growing wild in the fields. Osiris then taught mankind the art of agriculture, harvesting and planting. We can readily see the parallels of both the yearly resurrected vegetation god with the monthly 'resurrected' moon god, who waxes to darkness and then returns to fullness. Osiris' brother Set represents the dark side of Osiris or the new moon. Here again, we might see why Sariel is both a fallen angel as well as an archangel.

The harvesting of the wheat or barley was seen as the 'death' of the vegetation, as well as its 'dismemberment' – being ploughed down, gathered, winnowed and then ground into flour. A similar legend can be found in the English story of John Barleycorn. The story of Set dismembering Osiris into either 13, 14 or 16 parts (depending on the version of the story) may also refer to the phases of the moon. The lunar month is 29.53 days long. The lunar year is approximately eleven days shorter than the 365 day solar year. The 'course of the Moon' is related in Chapter 73 and 74 of the third book of Enoch, *The Book of the Heavenly Luminaries*.

Tâmîêl (תמיאל) tam EE ehl
Tûmâêl (שומיאל) too MAY ehl

Tamiel appears in Chapter 6 as one of the 'chiefs of tens'. The Watcher listed as the eighteenth in Chapter 69 is Tumael. They are most likely one in the same. We can note an interesting shift in the spelling and meaning of the two names in this. One seems to be the opposite of the other. Tamiel means the 'perfection of God' or 'innocent of God' from *tamah* meaning both 'naïve' or 'complete' in the sense of being all something should be. Tumael, on the other hand, means 'defilement of God' or 'impurity of God' from the Hebrew word *toomah*. It is as if in the later book, the author made the decision to take Tamiel's 'perfection' away by slightly altering the spelling.

We are not told what is the knowledge of this Watcher. Tumael may be a reference to the Egyptian god of the setting sun, Tum, who presides over the darkness.

Tûrêl (שוראל) TOOR ehl

Turel is first mentioned in Chapter 6 as one of the 'chiefs of tens'. Curiously, he is shown in Chapter 69 twice, as the fifteenth and nineteenth Watchers. The text is damaged at the name of the fifteenth Watcher, but not at the name of the nineteenth Watcher. This same anomaly occurs with the name of Azazel, listed as both the tenth and the twenty-first Watchers – also because of textual damage at the twenty-first Watcher's name. The name Turel means 'rock of God' or 'column of God', referring to a supportive structure. We are not told what is the knowledge of Turel in the text.

There exists a curious little volume called *The Secret Grimoire of Turiel* which was purportedly written in 1518. As the story goes, it was sold to the man who came to possess it in 1927 – one Marius Malchus - by a strange, dark little man claiming to have once been a priest. In it, Turel or Turiel is named as one of the messengers of Jupiter. Turiel's amulet appears at the end of the document. Turiel is also said to be the messenger of the angel 'Setchiel', of whom nothing is known.

Zaqiel (זכאל) zah KEY ehl

Zaqiel is listed only in Chapter 6 as a 'chief of tens'. He does not appear anywhere else in the text and we are never told of his knowledge. The name means 'purity of God' from the word *zakh*, which means 'pure' or 'clear'.

In what may be an alternate spelling of his name, the angel Zakiel is invoked with the angels Michael, Gabriel and Sarphiel in Syrian binding rituals from *The Book of Protection*. He may also be the same as Zakkiel, an angel governing storms.

****

There are those who will say that the Watchers were a race of alien beings who came from the stars and begat a race of giants with the women of human-kind. And it seems that at least some of them *did* come from the stars – the star 'giants' and deified heroes ("mighty men of old") in the night sky, such as Orion, Perseus, Hercules and Ophiucus – perhaps Cephus and Boötes, as well. Some of them seem to be linked with popular pagan deities of the time in which these texts were written.

Why would the authors of *Enoch* do this – i.e. make angels or Watchers of the gods of the people with whom they felt themselves at odds? The answer to this question seems to lie in what is said in Chapter 10 of *Jubilees*:

> 5 And Thou knowest how Thy Watchers, the fathers of these spirits, acted in my day: and as for these spirits which are living, imprison them and hold them fast in the place of condemnation, and let them not bring destruction on the sons of thy servant, my God; for these are malignant, and 6 created in order to destroy. And let them not rule over the spirits of the living; for Thou alone canst exercise dominion over them. And let them not have power over the sons of the righteous 7,8 from henceforth and for evermore.' And the Lord our God bade us to bind all. And the chief of the spirits, Mastema, came and said: 'Lord, Creator, let some of them remain before me, and let them harken to my voice, and do all that I shall say unto them; for if some of them are not left to me, I shall not be able to execute the power of my will on the sons of men; for these are for corruption and leading astray before my judgment, for great is the wickedness of the sons of men.' 9 And He said: Let the tenth part of them remain before him, and let nine parts descend into the 10 place of condemnation.' And one of us He commanded that we should teach Noah all their 11 medicines; for He knew that they would not walk in uprightness, nor strive in righteousness. And we did according to all His words: all the malignant evil ones we bound in the place of condemna- 12 tion and a tenth part of them we left that they might be subject before Satan on the earth. And we explained to Noah all the medicines of their diseases, together with their seductions, how he 13 might heal them with herbs of the

> earth. And Noah wrote down all things in a book as we instructed him concerning every kind of medicine. Thus the evil spirits were precluded from 14 (hurting) the sons of Noah.

As we have read here, post-exilic Judaic religious thought was heavily influenced by the duality of Zoroastrianism that was learned and absorbed during their captivity in Babylon. It is said by scholars of what are the earliest documents of Zoroastrianism, that not even Zarathrustra himself was as extreme in his doctrines of Light versus Darkness as the later developments – specifically of the post-exilic rabbis and the descendents of their tradition, the Yahad. The period in which the *Book of the Watchers* was written was one of great eclecticism, where the rule of the day seemed to be 'anything goes'. Church and state went hand in hand. The regents, and kings of the foreign dominators had the priests firmly under their thumbs. The priesthood was bought and sold like a garment in the market-place, more often than not to those who were known to 'sympathize' with the leaders of the occupation, or were at least 'malleable'. Religion itself was undergoing tremendous metamorphoses during this period with the influx of ideas, philosophies and mystery teachings. These were all poured and well mixed with conflicting systems of morality, culture, and lifestyles into the seething alembic of the Holy Land to create – among other things – this highly dualistic view of the universe.

If Yahweh was to rise above his many competitors, an adversary - a Prince of Darkness - was required like Angira Mainyu was to Ahura Mazda. Mastema/Satan filled this role, the two names meaning Enmity and Adversary, respectively. The authors of these texts understood that the world was full of evil and much of what they found evil in it was connected in some way or another with the worship of these gods and the consequent 'morals' of those people who worshiped them. What better way to discredit them, than to make them demons who caused all the ills of the world and mankind, like the spirits trapped in Pandora's Box or Solomon's vessel? Who better to give command of their dark spirits than Yahweh's opponent in the affairs of men than Mastema/Satan? Once the Adversary and his demons have been established, Yahweh is no longer responsible for the ills and tribulations of mankind. These become the works of the Devil and his minions.

GEMATRIA

GEMATRIC TABLE OF HEBREW LETTERS

Letter Name	Hebrew Figure	Letter Value	English Equivalent	Symbology
Aleph	א	1	A, Eh	Ox
Beth	ב	2	B, Bh	House
Gimel	ג	3	G, Gh	Camel
Daleth	ד	4	D, Dh	Door
Heh	ה	5	H, Ee	Window
Vau	ו	6	V, U, W	Nail
Zayin	ז	7	Z	Sword/Weapon
Cheth	ח	8	Ch	Fence/Barrier
Teth	ט	9	T	Serpent
Yod	י	10	Y, I, J	Hand/Seed/Sperm
Kaph	כ ך	20/500	K, Kh	Palm of hand
Lamed	ל	30	L	Ox-goad, Watchtower
Mem	מ ם	40/600	M	Water/Womb
Nun	נ ן	50/700	N	Fish
Samekh	ס	60	S	Prop
Ayin	ע	70	O, Aa or Ng	Eye/Eye & Nose
Peh	פ ף	80/800	P, Ph, F	Mouth
Tzaddi	צ ץ	90/900	Tz	Fish hook
Qoph	ק	100	Q	Back of head
Resh	ר	200	R, Rh	Head
Shin	ש	300	S, Sh	Tooth/Fire/Ether
Tau	ת	400	T, Th	Seal/Cross/Earth

When written large, the value of a Hebrew letter is increased to one thousand times its normal value. A large *aleph* is counted as 1000, a large *beth* is counted as 2000, etc.

The A, I, O, U and H are considered consonants, a mere basis for vowels. The vowels are not used in gematria.

Five letters have both medial and final forms. That is, they are written differently if they occur in the beginning or middle of a word as opposed to occurring at the end of the word.

THE SYMBOLOGY OF HEBREW LETTERS

Each letter of the Hebrew alphabet contains a symbology of its own, which is relevant in some cases to the names of the Watchers. The meanings of the letters composing their names often make a pun on their particular knowledge, while the names themselves can point to other aspects of their identification and their knowledge. The gematric value of their names or parts of their names may also point to other words, which define them as well.

> **Aleph**: an Ox, because the shape of the letter suggests the shape of a yoke. This letter also symbolizes the union of higher reality (the upper *yod*) with lower reality (the lower *yod*) by means of a transverse *vau* (a nail). "As above, so below." Commonly pronounced as 'eh', but may also be pronounced as the 'a' sound in *father*. Mother letter: Air, Breath.
>
> **Beth**: a House, the letter showing the roof, wall and floor. It can also represent a temple or a cave. Is inter-changeable in some cases with *peh*. Double letter: Moon, Wisdom, Sunday.
>
> **Gimel**: a Camel, the letter being composed of a shortened *resh* (a head) and a lateral which represents the in-folded leg of the camel at rest. It is also thought to represent a man walking. In either case, it signifies a traveling from 'here' to 'there', in either exoteric or esoteric terms. Double letter: Mars, Wealth, Monday.
>
> **Daleth**: a Door, the shape resembles the porch of a doorway or a tent-flap extended over the entrance. Also symbolic of the sub-conscious. Double letter: Sun, Seed, Tuesday.
>
> **Heh**: the gap between the two strokes (walls and roof) is a Window. Pronounced sometimes as 'ee' or a soft 'h' sound, as in *house*. Sometimes silent. Simple letter: Aries, speech.
>
> **Vau**: the shape of the letter suggests a Nail – something that fastens things together. May be pronounced either as a V or a U sound. Simple letter: Taurus, thought.
>
> **Zayin**: this letter resembles a Sword or Knife, therefore symbolizing a weapon. Simple letter: Gemini, motion.
>
> **Cheth**: the crossbar on the uprights of the letter (posts) suggests a Fence. It is also representative of the two uprights and a lintel of a Gateway through which one enters and exits. Pronounced gutterally, as in the word *loch*. Simple letter: Cancer, sight.

Teth: the shape of the letter is suggestive of a Serpent, representing the law of vibration/resonance and transformation. What is appears on the exterior is not necessarily significant of what is contained on the interior. Pronounced as more of a palatal 't' sound, as in *daughter*. Simple letter: Leo, hearing.

Yod: represents a Hand, the means of action and creativity. It also represents the Divine Spark and the spermatazoon. May be transliterated as an I, J or Y, thus Jared, Ired and Yared are the same word. Pronounced as the 'y' in *year*. Simple letter: Virgo, action.

Kaph: represents the Palm of the Hand or a Grasping Hand, the shape of the letter suggesting the form made by the palm, fingers and thumb when taking hold of something. The final form suggests an open hand. Pronounced like the 'k' in *kitten*. Double letter: Venus, Life, Wednesday.

Lamed: suggests an Ox-goad, forming an implicit relationship with the letter *aleph* (as in El). Also considered representative of a Watchtower because this is the only Hebrew letter that rises above the script-line of the other letters; also because of the upper portion of the letter resembling the watchman standing in or on the look-out tower. Simple letter: Libra, coition.

Mem: the form of this letter represents various bodies of Water, including the Womb of both woman and all manifest existence (exoteric and esoteric meanings). The sound of the letter 'm' in most languages is the basic sound of 'mother'. Many words for the ocean or sea also begin with the letter 'm' (mar, mer, mir). Moving water is suggested by the medial form and still water by the final form. Mother letter: Water, Fluids.

Nun: the form is suggestive of a Fish moving through the Water – or the sperm moving through the womb, the manifestation of creation and the changing nature of material existence. The final form of the letter suggests a tadpole or a fertilized seed/ovum. Simple letter: Scorpio, smell.

Samekh: suggests a Prop – that is something temporarily bolstering up something else, like a pillow or a stone. It is also representative of a temporary shelter and a ring or circle – something where the point of beginning and ending converge, like the circle of the sun. Pronounced as a hard 's' sound, as in *sort* or as a hard 'c' sound, as in *certify*. Simple letter: Sagittarius, sleep.

Ayin: the form of this letter suggests an Eye or the two Eyes and Nose of a face. It is also said to represent the head of a goat with its two horns and nose. Is pronounced as an 'uh' sound, as in *up* or can be pronounced as a long A sound, as in *aaah*. Occasionally used as the nasal 'ng' sound, such as the 'n' in *monkey*. Simple letter: Capricorn, anger/aggressiveness.

Peh: represents the Mouth, a head with a tongue inside – the *yod* symbolizing the tongue. It may also represent eating or devouring. Being composed of a *kaph* (a palm) and a *yod* (a hand) it is also said to represent practical action. The final form, composed of an extended *resh* (a head) and a *yod* (a seed) may be suggestive of the contemplation of ideas. This letter may be pronounced as either a P or F sound and is sometimes inter-changeable with *beth*. Double letter: Mercury, Dominance, Thursday.

Tzaddi: the shape of this letter represents a Fish-hook. Being composed of a bent *nun* and a *yod* this letter is also said to represent the dimensions of form (potential) and matter, which exist simultaneously in all created reality. Pure form shapes matter. This letter is pronounced like the 'ts' in *tsar*. The final form may suggest matter rising into its purer form, or pure form descending into matter. Simple letter: Aquarius, taste.

Qoph: the shape of the letter represents the Back of the Head, wherein is contained many of our primal instincts, as well as the seat of our intuition, or spontaneity – the corporeal intelligence. This letter is pronounced like the 'q' in *quit*. Simple letter: Pisces, laughter.

Resh: represents the Head as the collective intelligence of man. In shape it is an extended *yod* implying that the brain is an extension of the sperm. Double letter: Saturn, Peace, Friday.

Shin: generally said to represent the three prongs of a molar, this letter represents a Tooth in its exoteric sense. Esoterically, this letter represents three tongues of Fire or the Trinity of Binah, Chokmah and Tiphareth – the Mother, Father and Son (the three *yods*), which is implied in the Tetragrammaton, therefore the first letter of the word meaning 'the name' - *shema*. It can also represent the element of Ether or Spirit – a reaching heavenward. This letter is pronounced as a sibilant 's' as in *less*, or commonly as the 'sh' sound in *share*. Mother letter: Fire, Ether.

Tau: this letter is said to possess nothing of its own, being the culmination of all the letters before it – therefore representing the sacrifice of the Tau Cross. It is composed of an extended *yod*, with a downward stroke, like the *vau*, *daleth* and *resh*. It completes all the *nun*-like letters, also known as 'vessel' letters (manifestation). This letter combines the imaginative powers of the subconscious (*daleth*) with the power of change and manifestation (*nun*). It is therefore said to represent the transformational power of the Universal Mind and the Seal of the completion of the Great Work. This letter is pronounced both as a hard 't' sound, as in *time* and as a 'th' sound like *truth*. Thus you may see words ending in this letter, like *Tiphareth*, transliterated sometimes as *Tipharet*. Either one is acceptable. Double letter: Jupiter, Grace, Sunday/Sabbath.

BRANCHES, KNOTS & SPIRALS

TWO PROPHETS AND A KING NAMED HAZAEL

The city of Damascus in Syria, is the oldest continually inhabited city in the world, according to Lockyear's Bible Dictionary. Syria was called Aram or Aramea in those days. Damascus was the capital of Aram and is still the capital of modern Syria. It lies north of the Sea of Galilee and it is near to Mount Hermon. The founder of Damascus was said to be Uz, the grandson of Shem, Noah's eldest son. Aram was the name of Uz's father. Lockyear's dictionary goes on to tell us this:

> Shortly after Solomon's death, the king of Damascus formed a powerful league with other Aramean states. This alliance resulted in many years of conflict between Israel and Damascus. First Ben-Hadad of Damascus defeated King Baasha of Israel (1Kin.15:16-20; 2 Chr. 16:1-4). Later, God miraculously delivered King Ahab of Israel and his small army from the superior Syrian forces (1Kin. 20:1-30).

Even after this miraculous deliverance, Ahab made a covenant with Ben-Hadad II against God's will (1 Kin. 20:31-43). Ahab was killed a few years later in a battle with Syria (1Kin. 22:29-38).

> In the midst of these wars, the prophet Elisha was instructed by God to anoint Hazael as the new king of Damascus (1Kin. 19:15). King Joram of Israel successfully opposed Hazael for a time (2 Kin. 13:4-5), but the situation was eventually reversed. Hazael severely oppressed both Israel and Judah during later years (2 Kin. 13:3, 22).

Elisha is the spiritual son or heir of Elijah the Tishbite. Elijah was a formidable prophet with great powers. He is described as "an hairy man, and girt with a girdle of leather about his loins" (2 Kin. 1:8). Elijah is constantly on the move, for he lives in the time when Jezebel, who was the wife of Ahab, has declared death to all prophets of the Lord. He does not die when his time on earth is up, but is taken into heaven by a fiery chariot drawn by horses of fire - or a whirlwind...or both. Before he goes, he asks his 'son' what he would have of him. Elisha asks "let a double portion of thy spirit be upon me." Elisha becomes twice as powerful as his master. In *Kings I*, it is Elijah whom the Lord tells to anoint Hazael the King of Syria, but it is Elisha to whom the deed actually falls.

Uz? Hazael? These names sound familiar, don't they? Little is known about Uz, but we do know a few things about Hazael. Hazael was an official of the court of Ben-Hadad I. Ben-Hadad was ill and he sent Hazael to Elisha to ask God if he would recover from his illness. Elisha told Hazael that he, himself was destined to become the king:

> And Elisha said unto him, Go, say unto him, Thou mayest
> certainly recover: howbeit the Lord hath shewed me that he
> shall surely die. And he settled his countenance stedfastly,
> until he was ashamed: and the man of God wept. And Hazael
> said, Why weepeth my lord? And he answered, Because I
> know the evil that thou wilt do unto the children of Israel:
> their strong holds wilt thou set on fire, and their young men
> wilt thou slay with the sword, and wilt dash their children, and
> rip up their women with child. And Hazael said, But what, is
> thy servant a dog, that he should do this great thing? And
> Elisha answered, The Lord hath shewed me that thou shalt be
> king over Syria. (2 Kin. 8:10-13)

The next day Hazael put Ben-Hadad out of his misery by smothering him with a thick wet cloth, and took over the throne.

Ben-Hadad means "son of Hadad." For the king to take such a name is similar to the practice of the pharaohs, whose names translate into similar epithets of Ra, Horus, Amen and Set. Hadad (the thunderer) was a storm god worshipped by both the Syrians and the Phoenicians. He was later known as Rimmon, the son of Dagon (Ea). We sometimes see Rimmon mentioned as one of the fallen angels (see Ramiel). To the Syrians, Hadad was a god of lightning, rain and fertility. He resembled the Egyptian god Resheph, as a thunder god. Resheph was known in Egypt as a warrior god, who is the same as the Semitic Aleyin/Amurru. This god is depicted wearing a crown of gazelle horns. He carries a club, spear and shield. In the Babylonian pantheon, Reshef and Hadad were equivalent to Nergal, who was the lord of the Netherworld as well as a war god and a healing god. Nergal controlled many demons called such things as Flashes of Lightning, Croucher, Scab, Stroke and Lord of the Roof, as well as the gallu-demons and umu-demons. Nergal is sometimes a son of Ea. The Canaanites called Hadad 'Ba'al' - Lord.

It is easy to see here how interchangeable were the gods of the various regions of the Middle East. This is an important idea to keep in mind, when studying mythologies. Hadad is later compared to Zeus, of the Greeks and Jupiter/Jove of the Romans, who both wield lightning bolts as godly weapons. The idea of both El Elyon and Jehovah wielding lightning bolts comes from these earlier gods. Scholars look at the "attributes" of these gods, which includes weaponry; colors and sigils or signs associated with them; and the similarities of their personal myths.

Long before this time, the Syrians (Aramaeans), Mitanni, Hittites and Hivites possessed chariots and horses, which made them formidable and nearly always victorious in battles. They were expert bowmen, using compound bows. Some of the finest craftsmen in the known world lived within their borders. They had relatively well-tempered bronze swords and good shields. They may have learned the art of sword-making from the Mycenaen Greeks, as we shall later see. At one time, the craftsmen of Damascus were well-known for their beautiful, supple and deadly blades. Other weapons included daggers, spears, pikes and maces.

Many scholars believe that the Syrians or Aramaeans were the Hyksos kings who invaded Egypt and ruled there beginning in about 1650 BCE. An amulet of one of the Hyksos pharaohs shows him with a full beard and a decidedly Syrian looking nose. At the time of this story, about 800 years have passed from the time of the Hyksos kings. While these 'masters of war' continued to do battle with the Egyptians, they never regained their foothold in Egypt. The Egyptians had learned too much from these mighty men about the art of war. Here, we can see the link with Azazel as he who "taught men to make swords, and knives, and shields, and breastplates, and made known to them the metals of the earth and the art of working them... (Enoch 8:1)

The kings of Judah (Ahaziah) and Israel (Joram) were wicked men, we are told in later verses. They conspire between them to make war on Hazael in Ramoth-gilead. King Joram of Israel was seriously wounded in that battle by the Syrians, and retired to Jezreel to be healed. Ahaziah went down to Jezreel see him during his recuperation. While Joram is recuperating, Elisha sends a man to Jehu in Ramoth-Gilead, and has the man anoint Jehu as the new king of Israel. Jehu then goes to Jezreel and slays Joram, and wounds Ahaziah, who eventually dies of his wounds. During the reign of Jehu's successor, Jehoahaz, Hazael oppressed Israel because "the anger of the Lord was aroused against Israel." King Jehoash or Joash of Judah (who was the only decent one of the lot) made a gift of personal and Temple treasures to Hazael, as an assurance that he would not attack Jerusalem, itself. The plan seemed to have worked. We are told that Hazael turned his troops around and went home. Joash had a vested spiritual interest in seeing that the Temple of Solomon was not damaged, since he was the one who ordered the priests to repair it after long years of neglect during the reigns of Ahab and Joram.

The enigmatic Hazael moves through the eighth through thirteenth chapter of *II Kings* like a specter of Judgment. This seems to be intentional. Unlike just about everyone else in the book, we are told little or nothing of the King of Syria as a person. The name "Hazael" itself seems to me to be a contraction of *ha'azael* – 'the one whom God makes strong'.

Elisha is not happy about making Hazael king, but it is God's will. Elisha never does one thing to undermine Hazael's reign - although it seems that he could have. Instead, it seems that he is busy trying to correct the wrongs done by the house of Ahab. These chapters are filled with the treachery and scheming of five Israelite kings and one queen, Athaliah. King Jehu - the one Elisha has anointed, is not of the house of Ahab. Jehu begins his reign all about taking care of the Lord's business. He slays the worshippers and priests of Baal, and wipes out the remaining "seventy sons" of Ahab so none of them might try to reclaim the throne in their father's name. He is the king who orders Jezebel thrown down from her palace window and to be trampled to death by horses. In the end, Jehu proves himself to be no better than those he has mercilessly slaughtered in the name of the Lord, wandering away from the covenant he made with the Lord and worshipping heathen gods, himself.

In the beginning, Hazael himself cannot conceive that he would do such things as Elisha prophesies. Yet, he does not hesitate to smother his ailing lord and take his throne. Perhaps this is all symbolic of the coming destruction of Baal's (Hadad's) temples, worshippers and priests. Elisha's words that "he shall surely recover" are prophetic in the fact that no matter how many times their temples are torn down and they are massacred, Baal's worshippers keep coming back.

The duration of the kingships for this period are given in a somewhat confusing manner, but it seems that Hazael reigned for nearly a hundred years. We are told that he was finally defeated in battle and his son, Ben-Haddad II took over the throne. Talk about "mighty men of old"!

Job was said to live in the Land of Uz, and it is purported by biblical scholars that Azazel was the *bene elohim* who was the Adversary or *ha shaitan* who took Job's situation before Yahweh to be tested. However, many scholars believe that Job lived in the same approximate time as Abraham, when ones wealth was measured by the size of one's flocks and herds of animals - not in precious metals or possessions. This seems to me to be a reasonable deduction. If we take all of this as literal history, we can see Hazael being a 'real life' angel of the Lord's judgment against Israel. All of this happened around 845 BCE to 744 BCE -- five to six hundred years before the Qumran settlement and about two hundred years before the Babylonian captivity of the Hebrews...and long after the Flood.

Both Ben-Hadad and Hazael were still worshipped in Damascus as late as the first century CE. Kings of men become gods, who live long in legend. Surely, the memory of his reign of suppression and the similarity of his name to the Peacock Angel heard during the captivity in Babylon offered a tempting parallel to the authors of these texts with the idea of judgment and the concept of the "angry (and punishing) spirit."

Recall that Hazael, when he first goes to visit the prophet on behalf of his lord, calls himself Elisha's servant - or the Lord's servant. Elisha was seen as an earthly emanation or 'son' of the Lord, and the spiritual heir to one of his most important prophets. Possibly this is simply a common display of respect for the holy man. We are never told whom Hazael worships, and because he is a Syrian we are left to presume that he worships 'foreign gods'. But why does he call himself a servant of Elisha and his god?

Aside from being a seer or prophet, we are told in Kings II that Elisha performed healings, a bit of magic with an axe-head and even the resurrection of several children. However, he also sets bears upon a large group of children who make fun of his baldness and "fourty-two" of them are ripped to pieces. It is only when Elisha is dying that he gives the then reigning king the power to smite the Syrian armies and Hazael through acts of sympathetic magic. All his life, like his predecessor before him, Elisha dabbled behind the scenes in the politics of the region, making and breaking kings. He is not the first to do this, nor is he the last.

THE STORY OF SAMSON

When we think of Samson, we generally think of his love and nemesis, Delilah. But there is a lot more to the story of Samson than his disastrous relationship with the Philistine priestess who betrayed him.

Samson was the hero of the Tribe of Dan. He was born to be the liberator of Israel from the fourty year oppression of the Philistines. Samson is described as a giant of a man, great in strength and capable of performing feats no ordinary mortal could manage, like the Greek Heracles. Samson was said to be so strong that "he could uplift two mountains and rub them together like two clods of earth" (Targum, *Sotah* 9b). His shoulders were said to be sixty ells wide. He sounds rather like a Nephilim, doesn't he?

A NAZARITE FROM BIRTH

Samson's story begins much like several other significant stories in the Bible. His parents were getting on in years and childless. They are visited by an "angel of the Lord" who tells them they will conceive and have a son. As one reads through the Bible, this scenario seems to be a way of pointing out those who are to become involved in some way with the mysterious Nazarites. With the exception of Mary, who is quite young, most of the parents are older. They have demonstrated to those who watch that they are not of a "beastly nature." That is, they are not involved in mindlessly pro-creating themselves and hold to the sacred nature of the sexual act. They have also demonstrated their fidelity to one another by having been together for a long period of time.

Both of these ideas are of central importance in Jewish mysticism. God made Adam and Eve "one" and as such, the union of a man and wife is supposed to be eternal. At least while here on earth. Possibly also through incarnations, meeting up with one another again in the next life. It is not a generally known fact, but the Jews do believe in reincarnation. In the twenty-fourth verse of *Genesis* 2, we are told:

> *Therefore shall a man leave his father and his mother, and shall cleave unto his wife: and they shall be one flesh.*

At the time the angel appears to Manoah and his wife, the children of Israel have been under the control of the Philistines for fourty years. In biblical times, fourty years was the span of a generation. Manoah means 'quiet' - one who does not speak secrets. We are never told the name of Samson's mother. Manoah and his wife live in Zorah, which means a 'place of hornets'. Manoah's paternity is given as being of the Danites. This ties the father to Judgment, which is also called Din or Dan.

The angel tells Samson's future mother that she is not to drink wine or any other strong drink, nor to eat any unclean thing.

> *For, lo, thou shalt conceive, and bear a son; and no razor shall come on his head: for the child shall be a Nazarite unto God from the womb: and he shall begin to deliver Israel out of the hand of the Philistines. (Ju. 3:5, KJV)*

Manoah is not present when the 'angel' comes to visit his wife. After she returns home and tells him about her visitation, Manoah prays to the Lord to have the 'man of God' return and tell them how they should raise the child. The angel returns and repeats what he has told the wife to Manoah.

Being an hospitable man, Manoah offers to dress a kid for the man, so that he may eat. He declines the offer, saying that he will not eat of their bread. Rather, he tells Manoah that if a burnt offering is to be made, it should be made to the Lord.

> *So Manoah took a kid with a meat offering, and offered it upon a rock unto the Lord: and the angel did wondrously; and Manoah and his wife looked on. For it came to pass, when the flame went up toward heaven from off the altar, that the angel of the Lord ascended in the flame of the altar. But the angel of the Lord did no more appear to Manoah and to his wife. Then Manoah knew that he was an angel of the Lord. And Manoah said unto his wife, We shall surely die, because we have seen God. But his wife said unto him, If the Lord were pleased to kill us, he would not have received a burnt offering and a meat offering at our hands, neither would he have shewed us all these things, nor would as at this time have told us such things as these. (Ju 13:19-23)*

Samson isn't even born yet and already, things are quite interesting. We have an angel disappearing into the fire! Very magical, indeed. We also have here an important catch-phrase in "We shall surely die, because we have seen God." This is repeated often, throughout the Old Testament. In *Genesis*, this is Jacob's relief after wrestling with an 'angel' all night -- "For I have seen God face to face, and my life is preserved." Physical death at the appearance of an angel of the Lord seems to be a given result of such visitations. In the light of my hypothesis that the Nasoreans or Nazarites considered themselves to be the "Left Hand of God" or the punishing and testing arm of God, this makes a whole lot of sense.

Samson is then born in the twenty-fourth verse, after the quote above. Another interesting circumstance, as one of the gematric meanings of the number 24 is "to give substance to; a body." It is also significant of a vessel or shell. The two numbers added together make 6, which is the mystic number of Binah, the Mother, as well as the number of the manifestation of the flesh.

We are told that Samson is to be dedicated to the Nazarites from birth. "No razor shall touch his head." His hair is not to be cut. But is Samson to be one of these 'angels of vengeance'? He could have been one of these, but fate seems to have designed for him more the role of a pawn. It is through his love of pagan women (Philistine women, in particular) that his troubles are created.

As a young man, Samson first becomes enamored of a Philistine girl and wishes to marry her. His parents are very much against this union and try to dissuade him. But Samson, being the mighty man he was, prevailed over their wishes. They travel to Timnath to ask for the girl's hand. Samson kills a lion there and when he returns to the carcass later in the day, he sees that it is full of honey. He eats the honey and takes some to his parents to eat.

Timnah, or Timnath is a town in the kingdom of Judah that lies about 20 miles west of Jerusalem. We are told in Joshua, Chapter 19 that Timnath, or Thimnathah as it is called there, was part of the original inheritance of the tribe of Dan. In other words, Samson was returning to the land of his tribe's inheritance to wed – the land that they left behind, purportedly due to it not being of sufficient size to hold the tribe of Dan.

At a feast for the men of the community, Samson makes a bet with the men there that they cannot guess the answer to a riddle. They must guess the answer within seven days. If they fail to do so, they must give him "thirty sheets and thirty change of garments." If they guess it, he must give them the same. The riddle is based upon his encounter with the lion:

> *And he said unto them, Out of the eater came forth meat, and out of the strong came forth sweetness. (Ju. 14:14)*

After three days, the men find themselves stumped. They go to Samson's bride and ask her to get the answer from Samson. If she doesn't, they threaten to burn down her house, along with her and her family. In the face of this threat, she goes to Samson and cries and tells him that he doesn't really love her, or he would tell her the answer to the riddle. She keeps this up for the rest of the week until Samson is vexed to the point of telling her the answer. She then goes to the men and tells them the answer.

> *And the men of the city said unto him on the seventh day before the sun went down, What is sweeter than honey? and what is stronger than the lion? And he said unto them, If ye*

> had not plowed with my heifer, ye had not found out my riddle. (Ju. 14:18)

Notice that Samson's answer is another riddle, in itself. Honey is often taken to be symbolic of wisdom – or, as 'in the land of milk and honey' as symbolic of abundance. In Revelations 10:9, we read:

> And I went unto the angel; and said unto him, Give me the little book. And he said unto me, Take it, and eat it up; and it shall make thy belly bitter, but it shall be in they mouth sweet as honey.

What is stronger than a lion? Obviously here, it is Samson who is stronger than a lion, for he slew it with his bare hands. The lion is also symbolic of the Sun, its golden color and eyes relating to the 'gold of the sun'; its mane being seen as the rays of the sun. Since Samson is a sun-hero or sun-king, this may be seen as a 'new sun' or the winter solstice sun 'slaying' the 'old sun' of the summer solstice. The summer (old) sun reaches its strength in the sign of Leo, which falls between July 24th and August 23rd. It is at this time that the heat of the sun is most intense and the 'dog days' come with the rising of the Dog Star, Sirius. This could be what is meant below, regarding Samson setting fire to the fields in retribution – the heat of the sun 'burning' the crops.

Samson's wrath is kindled against the men and he goes down to Ashkelon and slays thirty other men as 'scapegoats' for the men who "plowed with" his bride. He takes the belongings of the men he kills and gives it to those who cheated him, as payment of his debt – because they guessed the answer to his riddle, albeit by collusion. In the meantime, the bride's father gives her away to another who was a friend of Samson's.

The 'thirty men' may refer to the 30 degrees of each sign of the Zodiac. If Samson is here the waning or 'old sun' who is later reborn, his 're-gifting' of the belongings to the thirty men he killed to the thirty groomsmen may signify the beginning of a new year and a new round of the Zodiacal wheel. His bride might be seen here as the 'Queen of Heaven' (i.e. Venus) who wanders through the signs of the heavens in the company of the sun. The father giving her away to a 'friend' of Samson's might be interpreted that the 'friend' is Samson's alter-ego, the 'new sun' where Venus appears as the Morning Star ahead of the new winter sun. During the summer, Venus appears lagging behind the sun as the Evening Star.

When Samson discovers this duplicity, he is again angered. His retribution is to gather three hundred foxes or jackals and tie fire-brands to their tails and set them loose in the grain fields, destroying all their source of grain. Commentary in Lockyear's Bible Dictionary says that evidently Samson had not learned that vengeance belonged to the Lord. But Samson was a part of the vengeance of the Lord. He was a Nazarite. And this was only the beginning.

THE JAWBONE OF AN ASS

The men of the town come and take their own vengeance on the bride and her family, burning them in their house. This is in retribution for having caused this calamity to come upon their fields. They then go and ask Samson why he has done this thing -- burning their fields. He tells them that he will have his vengeance on them for what they've done and he proceeds to slaughter them. After this, he goes into Judah and dwells on a mountain called Etam. Etam is translated as 'a place of birds of prey'. Birds of prey are commonly associated with eagles, which would indicate that he went back to the original lands of the tribe of Dan. Recall that the symbol of Dan was first a serpent and then an eagle.

Those who are left pursue him into Judah, to capture him. When the men of Judah ask the Philistines why they have come, they tell them it is to bind Samson and take him back for punishment. They talk the men of Judah into going and getting him and bringing him to them.

The Judeans approach Samson and tell him why they are there. He makes them swear that they themselves will not harm him. They tell him that they will not and bind him with two new cords, then take him to the Philistines. The Philistines take him to Lehi, which means 'jawbone'. The ropes that bind his arms "melt like flax burned in a fire" and he breaks free from his bonds, snatching up the jawbone of a dead ass and slaying a thousand Philistines with it.

The story of him killing a thousand Philistines with the jawbone of an ass is of particular interest. Can we take this literally? Only if we stretch our imaginations. There are many legends and mythic characters who are connected with the donkey or ass. In late Roman times, to call someone a donkey or an ass was to call him a fool - much as it is today. Clearly, Samson has been a fool. But this doesn't tell us anything about the significance of killing a whole lot of people with a donkey's jawbone. In Samson's day, the most well-known figure associated with a donkey was the supposedly 'ass-eared' Egyptian god Set. (Baal-Peor did not appear until sometime later, if we are to accept the chronology of the Bible.)

The later incarnation of the Nazarites, the Nasoreans were known to be Gnostics. The Gnostics considered themselves the Children of Seth, Adam's oldest son. Adam was taught all the secrets of heaven and earth by the angel Raziel. Adam, in turn, taught all these things to his son Seth. These wisdoms can be found in a book called *Sepher Raziel Ha'malech* - The Book of the Angel Raziel. This book contains not only instructions in astrology, the elements, and the secret names of God (to name a few of the many subjects covered) ... it also contains many spells, ciphers and magical diagrams. It is a grimoire of sorts. The practice of magic is forbidden by the *Torah*, the Bible and the Koran, yet Moses and Aaron, Abraham and Mohammed all were portrayed to have practiced magic. So too did the later prophets and that "angel of the Lord" that announced Samson's birth.

Set is also called Seth, and the priests of Set were known to be magicians of great and dark powers. When one thinks of a jawbone, the idea of talking - or 'flapping' one's jaw comes to mind. Could it be then that what is inferred here is that Samson actually uttered spells he knew from the Setian based wisdoms of the Nazarites to slay a thousand men? No one can answer that for certain, but it *is* something to contemplate.

One would think that Samson might have learned something from his first wife. As big and strong as he is, he is weak in resisting the temptations of the flesh and does not learn his lessons. In this way, he could be considered arrogant, as well as a fool.

In this regard, the story of Samson is very much like the story of the Watchers in Enoch. It is by their lust for women that they fall from their first estate of heaven.

DELILAH

After his escape from the Philistines, Samson goes to Gaza. It is there that he meets Delilah, who is described as "an harlot." Contrary to what has become the meaning of this term today - a woman who sells her sexual favors for money - a harlot was a temple priestess of certain pagan divinities. The Greeks called them 'hierodules' and they acted as vehicles to ecstasies and presumably revelations of a divine nature in much the same context of what is known today as 'sex-magic'. In Mesopotamia, the High Priestess also was 'married' to the current king once a year as the representative of the god, to insure the fertility of the people and the land. Describing Delilah as a harlot also points to the 'Queen of Heaven' in the form of Inanna/Ishtar, in whose temple women served as prostitutes. As the goddess of love, Inanna was the protectress of prostitutes and her temple was euphemistically referred to as 'a tavern'. This was also the case with the temples of Aphrodite and Astarte, who are simply other 'faces' of the ancient goddess Inanna.

Delilah is most likely the High Priestess of the Temple of Dagon. Dagon has long been associated with Ea, the Sumerian god who was also called 'the Great Serpent' Ushumgal. The epithet of the Great Serpent appears to be a reference to the constellation Draco, which is 'coiled' around the northern ecliptic pole – the axis of the 'corn mill'. The word *dagan* is commonly used in the language of the Canaanites and Hebrews for 'grain' or 'corn'. One tradition holds that Dagon was the inventor of the plough, which is seen in the northern sky as the the constellation of the Great Bear or *Ursa major*, the Big Dipper or the Wain. Dagon was a west Semitic corn god. His position as a god of vegetation was usurped around 1500 BCE by the various Baals. The consort of Inanna/Ishtar, Dumuzi or Tammuz was also a vegetation god. At one point, the Philistines stole the Ark of the Covenant and kept it at Ashdod in the Temple of Dagon there. Delilah then is a symbol of the Goddess, the Divine Feminine portrayed as working her 'wiles' on the sun-king Samson.

Because of what he had done previously in Timnath, the Philistines decide to use Samson's infatuation with this priestess to find out the secret of his strength. He'd been tricked once before and it seemed to work. They go to Delilah and bribe her to get from Samson the secret of his great strength. We are not told how many of them there are, but they tell her that they will each give her eleven hundred pieces of silver. An extremely tempting offer, no doubt. One that Delilah does not refuse.

Working her feminine wiles on him, she confronts him in much the same manner as his first wife, telling him that if he truly trusted and respected her, he would tell her the secret of his strength.

First, he tells her that if he is bound with new ropes (or un-dried reeds) - *withies*, he would be like anyone else. We know, this doesn't work, but she doesn't. Some of the Philistines are lying in wait in their chamber, while Delilah binds him. As before, when they fall upon him, the ropes were broken off from his arms like a thread. The second time she asks him, he tells her that if "thou weavest the seven locks of my head with the web" that he will be as weak as any man. This too proves to be false. The third time, she pesters and vexes him to the point that he finally tells her the truth. If his hair is shorn from his head, he will be weak....

> *That he told her with all his heart, and said unto her, There hath not come a razor upon mine head; for I have been a Nazarite unto God from my mother's womb: if I be shaven, then my strength will go from me, and I shall become weak, and be like any other man. (Ju. 16:17)*

Delilah then lulls Samson to sleep in her lap and calls for a man to come and shave his head.

Esoterically, in relation to Samson as a sun-hero or sun-deity, the shearing of his hair – which gives him his strength – would be symbolic of the waning strength of the sun after the autumnal equinox. As the sun moves toward the winter solstice, it becomes more feeble. That is, it's rays are not as strong.

As to the exoteric meaning of this: In ancient times, as well as now, anything directly from a person's body contained their essence. Those familiar with casting spells of various sorts know these things. If one possesses an article of clothing or a favored possession belonging to someone, this gives the possessor power over that person. Even better is to possess something directly from the person's body, such as hair or fingernail clippings, bodily fluids or waste.

We know today -- thanks to all the spectacular publicity generated from rape and murder cases -- that our DNA is contained within our hair, sputum, nails, blood, sexual fluids, urine and other by-products of the body. Our ancestors weren't so far out in their beliefs. These items do contain our essence. The shearing of Samson's dreded locks gave those who possessed them power over him.

We are told that he had seven locks of hair. Seven is significant of so many things in mythology, magic and religion that it would be difficult to uncover the exact meaning of the seven locks. In light of the fact that Samson was a Philistine sun deity before becoming a sort of anti-hero of the Hebrews, the seven locks may represent the seven days of the week. It may also have something to do with the seven sacraments, or something similar by which Samson was bound to the Nazarites through a ritual or rituals that included baptism, anointing, circumcision, the reception of his name, etc., that 'sealed' him to the Nazarites. Considering that Samson failed in his duty and had fallen into what is perceived as a sinful life of lust by the Nazarites, it is only fitting in their view that he should be shorn and the 'locks' or seals undone.

The Philistines finally capture Samson, and put out both of his eyes. Here, we have a connection with Samael, as 'the blind god', or the 'old sun', blind and feeble in its age. They take him to Gaza and bind him with fetters of brass and he is set to grinding grain or corn like a donkey in the prison house. Donkeys were often used in this capacity. They were either blindfolded or blinders were applied to their harnesses to keep them looking and walking straight ahead - i.e., around in a circle. Making Samson a 'donkey' points to him as being a fool, and may even equate him with Set, the 'ass-eared Egyptian god' of the desert and the fierce heat of summer. As it has been mentioned previously, the turning of the sun and stars about the earth were seen as a 'corn mill', with the pole of the ecliptic being the axis of the mill. The circle is symbolic of the sun and its journey through the heavens.

While he is imprisoned, Samson's hair begins to grow back. He realizes this and he also realizes what a fool he's been. The strength of the Lord returns to him.

Once the 'new son' is born at the winter solstice, its strength (rays) gradually begin to return – it's 'mane' or 'hair' growing longer and stronger until the next solstice, when it begins 'aging' again and becomes the 'old sun'. Here, the 'strength of the Lord' is the strength of the 'new sun'.

The Philistines are having a great feast to their god Dagon and they are congratulating themselves on the fact that they have captured the mighty Samson. Once they all become quite merry (drunk), they decide that they wish to make sport of Samson and humiliate him. They have him brought from the grinding house, presumably to the temple. It is merely termed "a house", but there are said to be three thousand people standing on the roof and that the house was full of many, many people. In any event, we get the impression that this is a very large and important building. The temple of Dagon seems the most logical assumption.

Samson asks them to stand him between the two pillars that support the roof of the house. The people jeer and make sport of him in the meanwhile.

> And Samson took hold of the two middle pillars upon which the house stood, and on which it was borne up, of the one with his right hand, and of the other with his left. And Samson said, Let me die with the Philistines. And he bowed himself with all his might; and the house fell upon the lords, and upon all the people that were therein. So the dead which he slew at his death were more than they which he slew in his life. (Ju. 16:29-30)

Esoterically, the "two middle pillars upon which the house stood" would be the solstices – the furthest points north and south that the sun travels in the sky in its yearly journey. We know these as the Tropic of Capricorn and the Tropic of Cancer. This imagery is used in Egypt, symbolized by the two obelisks or stelae that represent northern and southern Egypt, as the Egyptians saw their country as a microcosm of creation. The guardians of the pharaoh, Wadjet (serpent goddess) and Nekhbet (vulture goddess) symbolize both northern and southern Egypt, as well as the solstices. This idea was 'borrowed' by the Hebrews, when Jacob established two pillars in the northern and southern kingdoms, Israel (Samaria) and Judah. To the Hebrews, the pillars of the temple also symbolized their own Boaz and Jachin, the pillars of the Eastern Gate of the Second Temple, which were symbolic of the unity of the two kingdoms, as well as the priesthood and kingship.

What is written in the Bible regarding the Philistines is rather heavily slanted and sympathetic toward the Israelites. The Philistines are depicted as cruel and idol worshiping giants (i.e. Goliath). They were, however a more advanced culture than the Israelites, and were probably of some portion of the Mycenaean peoples, or from Cyprus, Crete or Malta. The description of Goliath's battle dress and weapon is indicative of a people who had advanced knowledge of metal-working. The Philistines are named in the Amarna Letters as the Peleset, one of the tribes of the Sea People. The original lands of the Tribe of Dan encroached upon or were some part of the territory of the Palestinians. The reference to the honey of the bees found in the carcass of the lion Samson slew may point to these origins, for the Cretans and the Maltese peoples were known as keepers of bees and their honey was highly prized. Philistinian pottery bears motifs of spirals, fish and birds, which are typical Aegean and Mycenaean motifs.

THE STORY OF SOLOMON AND SHEBA

Judah is a lion's whelp. (Gen. 49:9)

The lion is the symbol of the tribe of Judah and appeared on their standards in battle. In the *Kebra Negest*, a 13th century manuscript from Ethiopia (where the *Books of Enoch* were found by James Bruce) we read the story of Solomon and the Queen of Sheba. The Queen comes to visit the great Solomon, and while she is there they become lovers. While they are together, Solomon has a rather portentous dream:

> *And after he slept there appeared unto King SOLOMON [in a dream] a brilliant sun, and it came down from heaven and shed exceedingly great splendour over ISRAEL. And when it had tarried there for a time it suddenly withdrew itself, and it flew away to the country of ETHIOPIA, and it shone there with exceedingly great brightness for ever, for it willed to dwell there. And [the King said], "I waited [to see] if it would come back to ISRAEL, but it did not return. And again while I waited a light rose up in the heavens, and a Sun came down from them in the country of JUDAH, and it sent forth light which was very much stronger than before." And ISRAEL, because of the flame of that Sun entreated that Sun evilly and would not walk in the light thereof. And that Sun paid no heed to ISRAEL, and the ISRAELITES hated Him, and it became impossible that peace should exist between them and the Sun. And they lifted up their hands against Him with staves and knives, and they wished to extinguish that Sun. And they cast darkness upon the whole world with earthquake and thick darkness, and they imagined that that Sun would never more rise upon them. And they destroyed His light and cast themselves upon Him and they set a guard over His tomb wherein they had cast Him. And He came forth where they did not look for Him, and illumined the whole world, more especially the First Sea and the Last Sea, ETHIOPIA and RÔM. And He paid no heed whatsoever to ISRAEL, and He ascended His former throne. (Kebra Negest:30)*

We are further told that the Queen of Sheba had a son by Solomon and he was called Menyelek I. Before she leaves Solomon, he gives her a ring to give to his son, that he may know him, when he returns to him. The Queen gives this ring to her son and sets him off to see his father. She tells Solomon:

> *Now there was a law in the country of ETHIOPIA that [only] a woman should reign, and that she must be a virgin who had never known man, but the Queen said [unto SOLOMON], "Henceforward a man who is of thy seed shall reign, and a*

> woman shall nevermore reign; only seed of thine shall reign and his seed after him from generation to generation. And this thou shalt inscribe in the letters of the rolls in the Book of their Prophets in brass, and thou shalt lay it in the House of God, which shall be built as a memorial and as a prophecy for the last days. And the people shall not worship the sun and the magnificence of the heavens, or the mountains and the forests, or the stones and the trees of the wilderness, or the abysses and that which is in the waters, or graven images and figures of gold, or the feathered fowl which fly; and they shall not make use of them in divining, and they shall not pay adoration unto them. And this law shall abide for ever. (Kebra Negest:33)

A retinue of Israelites returned to Ethiopia with the Queen. In both Christian and Ethiopian tradition, these Israelites were of the tribe of Dan and Judah. Menyelek is the founder of the Solomonic dynasty in Ethiopia. The Emperor of Ethiopia, Haile Selassie and other kings of Judah or the Solomonic dynasty have been called "The Lion of Judah". It is thought that the reference to "The Lion of Judah" in the Book of Revelations means Christ, the Messiah of the Davidic line. Lions are an animal that represent both kings and queens. Even today, we call the lion 'the King of Beasts'. He represents the sun as the 'king of the angels' or the great star that lights our world. It is most likely that for this reason Enoch was chosen as the patriarch of the Ethiopian patriarchal religion. For Metatron is shown as the 'lesser face of Yahweh', the Sun, with his rays and horns.

Clearly, the story of Solomon and Sheba represents the transference of the matriarchal society and religion of the Abysinnian peoples to that of the patriarchal society and religion. This transference can also be seen in the myth of Medusa, which is discussed in the article THE DIVINE FEMININE.

THE SONS OF DAN

THE MYCENAEANS

It all begins with a "once upon a time", as do so many other things....

The most prominent hero of the Mycenaean Greeks was Perseus, who is – mythically speaking – the founder of their tribe or lineage, as well as their capitol, Mycenae. The story of his birth is a folk-tale of great antiquity that later passed into the general heroic mythology of the Greeks.

Mycenae sat around 90 km to the south and west of Athens, in the northeastern territories of the Peloponnese. In the second milennium BCE, Mycenae was one of the major centers of the Hellenic civilization and dominated much of what is today southern Greece. The original name of these peoples were the Mukanai, which is thought to be of pre-Hellenic origins. The site of Mycenae can be dated back to Neolithic times. Archaeologists have turned up potsherds that date to 3500 BCE. Later, the citadel of Mycenae was constructed on this same site and much of the earlier development and artifacts were obliterated.

In the ruins of Mycenae, archaeologists found several 'bee-hive' (*tholoi*) and shaft graves, both full of grave goods that attest to the wealth and power of the royalty buried within them. Bronze Age weapons found in the graves have been dated to 1600 BCE. The inlaid swords and daggers, as well as spear-points and arrowheads show that these people were warriors. Some of the more well known art treasures found in these graves were the Silver Seige Rhyton, the so-called Mask of Agamemnon and the Cup of Nestor. A *rhyton* is a vessel made generally in the shape of the head of a bull, a boar or even a dog. There is a hole at the bottom, from which libations may be poured in ritual, or may be used to drink from, as with a wineskin.

About 1350 BCE, the fortifications of Mycenae were rebuilt in a style called 'cyclopean masonry'. It is called thus, because the dressed stones or ashlars used are so large that those who later beheld them thought that they could only have been cut and moved by the one-eyed giants known as Cyclops. The Lion Gate is the best known feature of the city wall, named for the two stone lions which stand atop the stone lintel at the entry.

According to scholars, by 1200 BCE, the power of the Mycenaeans was weakening and seems to have been put to an end by a great catastrophe. Evidence of the burning of all the palaces in southern Greece around 1250 BCE has been traditionally attributed to the invasion of the Dorians around this time period. Another theory posits that some elements of the Mycenaean peoples, who later came to speak Doric, turned on the weakening Mycenaean dynasty and overthrew it. Whatever the case, the Mycenaean peoples scattered, some migrating to former colonies in Anatolia and elsewhere, where they came to speak the Ionian dialect.

Clearly, the Mycenaeans were a sea-going people who were known to have had contact with the Egyptians (specifically Amenhotep III, from a scarab of Queen Tiye found in the Temple at Mycenae) and the people of the Baltic regions. They were dependent upon trade with the Far East for tin for their bronze weapons and artifacts, but this trade was cut off by the Cretans. The only other alternative was to sail to the 'tin islands' of Britain for their supply of this precious metal.

THE SEA PEOPLE

The legend of Perseus states that his mother was a fair maiden named Danaë and that his father was Zeus, who came to Danaë as a shower of gold from the heavens. Danaoi is an ancient tribal name that appears to pertain to the sea-faring peoples mentioned in the Amarna letters. The Egyptians knew them as the Denyen. They were also known as the Danunites, Danaoi, Danaus, Danaids, Dene, Danai, Danaian. Martin P. Nilsson in his book The Mycenaean Origin of Greek Mythology posits that Acrisius was later added as her father to attach the genealogy of Perseus to Argos. It is thought by many scholars that the Danaoi were a group of the so-called Sea People who invaded Egypt, Anatolia, Lebanon and Palestine called the Denyen. The earliest Egyptian text to mention them is the El-Amarna letters from mid 14th century BCE. This letter tells of Pharaoh Amenhotep IV's vassal, the king of Tyre, Abimilki:

> *A letter from Abi-Milku, mayor of Tyre, to Akhenaten. (EA 151)*
> *To the king, my Sun, my god, my gods: Message of Abi-Milku, your servant. I fall at the feet of the king, my lord, 7 times and 7 times. I am the dirt under the sandals of the king, my lord. I am indeed guarding carefully the city of the king that he put in my charge. My intention has been to go to see the face of the king, my lord, but I have not been able, due to Zimredda of Sidon. He heard that I was going to Egypt, and so he has waged war against me. May the king, my lord, give me 20 men to guard the city of the king, my lord, so I can enter before the king, my lord, to behold his gracious face. I have devoted myself to the service of the king, my lord. May the king, my lord, ask his commissioner whether I have devoted myself to the king, my lord. I herewith send my messenger to the king, my lord, and may the king, my lord, send his messenger and his tablet to me, so I may enter*

> before the king, my lord. May the king, my lord, not abandon his servant. May the king, my lord, give his attention and give water for our drink and wood to his servant. The king, my lord, knows that we are situated on the sea; we have neither water nor wood. I herewith send Ilumilku as mesenger to the king, my lord, and I give 5 talents of bronze, mallets, and 1 whip. The king, my lord, wrote to me, "Write to me what you have heard in Canaan." The king of Danuna died; his brother became king after his death, and his land is at peace. Fire destroyed the palace at Ugarit; rather, it destroyed half of it and so half of it has disappeared. There are no Hittite troops about. Etakkama, the prince of Qidshu, and Aziru are at war; the war is with Biryawaza. I have experienced the injustices of Zimredda, for he assembled troops and ships from the cities of Aziru against me. Is it good that a palace attendant of my lord should become frightened? All have become frightened. May the king give his attention to his servant and return yu-sa (come forth).

The description of the palace at Ugarit being burned by fire is significant of the widespread destruction that occurred toward the end of the late Bronze Age. As we have seen, this also happened at Mycenae – which was at one time the home of the Sons of Danaë. Perhaps it has been overlooked that some group of them had left the Peloponnese and moved further south, then returned to find the Dorians or others living in their city, and burned it. As we shall see, burning cities was a favored technique of another group who may have been the Danuna.

Figure 6: The captured Denyen from Medinet Habu relief

The Danuna appear later in a relief on the mortuary temple of Ramesses III at Medinet Habu. The story there relates that there was a confederation of Peleset (Philistines), Tjeker, Shelelesh, Denyen and Weshesh that united to attack Egypt.

In the Harris Papyrus, dated to about 1164 BCE – also in the reign of Ramesses III, we are told:

> *I slew the Denyen in their islands, while the Tjeker and the Philistines were made ashes. The Sherden and the Weshesh of the Sea were non-existent, captured all together and brought into captivity in Egypt like the sands of the shore. (Pritchard, pgs. 260-261)*

There are also Hittite and other sources which mention the Danuna. And 8th century BCE bilingual inscription from Karatepe tells how king Azitwadda expanded the Plain of Adana and restored his people, the Danunites (Pritchard, pg. 262). We also have a clue in the story of Io and her son by Zeus, Epaphus, who became the king of Egypt and founded the city of Memphis.

There are at least three theories on the origin of the Danuna. One is that they came from Cilicia in Anatolia. This is argued by the fact that there is a sea-port city called Adana, which exists to this day. Adana lies just to the north of Crete and about 100 miles northwest of Aleppo, Syria. King Telepinus whose reign is now dated at 1525-1500 BCE mentions the Adaniya. The Denyen of the Egyptian sources as well were the inhabitants of the Cilician Adana, without any connection with Greece. The "islands" where Ramesses III situated the Danuna were tiny islets and capes of the Cilician coast. The second theory is that they came from mainland Greece and were the Danaoi. Scholars associate the Danuna with these Greeks because of Homer's many referrences to the Greeks as the Danaans in the *Illiad*. The third theory holds that they were originally the inhabitants of Canaan and returned there with the other sea-peoples such as the Philistines, Tjekker and Weshesh as a counter migration. It is uncertain as to the identity of the two later-named peoples.

In these theories, we see that whatever their origin, the Danuna were associated with the Greeks and may have even been some of the original inhabitants of Canaan. They were a coastal people who were sea-going and did at one time inhabit Egypt. This would explain the judge Deborah's question in 5:17 of *Judges*: "...and why did Dan remain in ships?" Even if they lived in Cilicia at some point, it's a short hop and a skip into Syria. The division of the lands of the Twelve Tribes seem not so much decreed by Moses, Joshua or Yahweh, but the natural lands and abodes of the peoples absorbed into the 'Israelites'. This may also explain the determination of Samson to have himself a Philistine bride, and to spend his time there in the land of the Philistines.

The Hyksos kings of Egypt may have been the Sea People, reigning roughly between 1650 and 1540 BCE. 1650 BCE is the general date given for the eruption of Thera, which may explain why the Mukani left the original site of Mycenae – with some of them possibly returning to it 50 – 100 years later. Many scholars have thought that they were the Hebrews – and in some respects that might be true, from what we now know. The Hyksos have been wrongly known as the "Shepherd Kings", but 'Hyksos' is now thought to be from the Egyptian phrase *heka khasewet* which means 'rulers of foreign lands'. This word *heka* is quite similar to the word of the oath given in Chapter 69 of the *Book of Similitudes* – Akae. This may also refer to the Greeks, as they referred to themselves as the *Hakhaioi*. We have seen that in Hebrew, this word *hakh* means to 'strike' or 'smite', and indeed this is what the Hyskos did to the Egyptians, according to Manetho. Manetho only lists six Hyksos kings, which are later reported by Josephus. These names are said to bear strong similarities to Canaanite names – i.e. Phoenician. However, the names cannot be known with any certainty because they appear only in bits and pieces on reliefs, jar lids and scarabs.

What is known, is that the first of the Hyksos kings, variously known as Salitis, Salatis or Sheshi established his seat at Memphis, the very city that Io's son Epaphus was said to have established. In Manetho's *Aegyptiaca* we read:

> from the regions of the East, invaders of obscure race marched in confidence of victory against our land. By main force they easily overpowered the rulers of the land, they then burned our cities ruthlessly, razed to the ground the temples of the gods, and treated all the natives with a cruel hostility, massacring some and leading into slavery the wives and children of others. Finally, they appointed as king one of their number whose name was Salitis. He had his seat at Memphis, levying tribute from Upper and Lower Egypt, and leaving garrisons behind in the most advantageous positions. Above all, he fortified the district to the east, foreseeing that the Assyrians, as they grew stronger, would one day covet and attack his kingdom.
>
> In the Saite [Sethroite] nome he found a city very favorably situated on the east of the Bubastite branch of the Nile, and called Auaris (= Avaris) after an ancient religious tradition. This place he rebuilt and fortified with massive walls, planting there a garrison of as many as 240,000 heavy-armed men to guard his frontier. Here he would come in summertime, partly to serve out rations and pay his troops, partly to train them carefully in manoeuvres and so strike terror into foreign tribes. (frag. 42, 1.75-79.2)

The name of the city or fortress established here as *Auaris* may be a corruption of the root of the name Horus. The name 'Horus' means 'foresighted' or 'farsighted'. The root of Horus' name is *her*, which means 'above'. Auris or Avaris is also known as Hauar, which is an Arabic word from the root *hoor*, which means one possessed of 'large luminous eyes'. The Hebrew word *hur* means 'lofty' or 'highly placed'. Clearly, Aurais was meant to be a *watch*-point established by Salitis against any invasions from the east.

Josephus continues the story:

> After a reign of thirteen years, he was followed by one whose name was Beon [2], who ruled for for forty-four years. After him reigned Apachnas [3] for thirty-six years and seven months. After him Apophis [4] was king for sixty-one years, followed by Janins for fifty years and one month. After all these Assis reigned during forty-nine years and two months. These six were their first kings. They all along waged war against the Egyptians, and wanted to destroy them to the very roots. (Against Apion: Book 1, Section 73)

Avaris was known to be a city of 'Typho', according to Josephus reporting Manetho's writings. This is most likely Typhon, another name for Set or Seth. It is known that the Hyksos kings promoted the worship of Set. One of the Hyksos kings is named Apophis, which is the Underworld deity of darkness, mist, storms and night that is often confuted with Set. Apophis' form is that of a great serpent, who is the enemy of Ra, the Sun god, and attempts daily to displace him from the heavens in his travels. When Apophis is successful, an eclipse occurs – the dragon swallowing the sun motif. Apophis' servants are called "the children of rebellion".

Typhon is a distinctly Greek god, who is the demon of the whirlwind and a volcano god. He is said to be the giant son of Tartarus and Gaea. His legend was most probably 'born' with the eruption of Thera on Crete. The Greeks equated Typhon with Set. During the Nineteenth and Twentieth Dynasties, Set was seen by the Egyptians as a benevolent god who restrained the forces of the desert. He was the patron god of the Ramesside kings, notably the Setis. However, by the Twenty-first Dynasty, he was once again seen as the god of evil. Josephus probably used Typho in place of Set, as Manetho – an Egyptian historian – clearly refers to the nome as Saite (Set).

THE TUATHA DE DANANN

I would be remiss, if I did not mention yet another name to the long list of epithets for these doughty sailors of old – the Tuatha Dé Danann, the Children of the Goddess Danu. There is no doubt, from what is written in the *Lebor Gabala Erren*, the Book of Invasions of

Ireland, that the Tuatha Dé Danann were Greeks. In fact, it says so quite plainly. The 'invasion' of Ireland by the Sons of Dan(u) was not the first time they'd been to that part of the world. In *Invasions* we are told that like the Firbolg people, the Tuatha Dé Danann were the descendents of the Nemedians and their progenitor, Nemed. Nemed was said to be a descendent of Noah, through Japheth and Magog. According to Invasions, Magog had settled in the country of the Scythians, in southern Russia. Nemed left there because of the oppression of the Scythians and a plague, and sailed to Ireland with members of his family and tribe. After the war with the Fomorians, the surviving Nemedians left Ireland. Nemed's son, Fergus Lethderg went to Alba (Scotland) and settled there. Nemed's great-great grandson, Semion returned to Greece. There, they became the Firbolg. After eleven generations, they returned to Ireland. Iobath, the great-grandson of Nemed and son of Beothach migrated to the northeastern portion of 'the island' of Greece – perhaps meaning the Peloponnese, where the Mycenaeans lived. Iobath was the ancestor of the Tuatha Dé Danann. A point of interest here is that Nemed's wife's name was Macha – a name quite like Maachah, the mother of the Hebrew kings Abijam and Asa (see the commentary on Chapter 13 of Watchers). Nuada's consort was also named Macha.

The Tuatha Dé Danann came to Ireland under the leadership of Nuada, a son of Danu. Among the Danaans were also Dagda, Oghma, Goibhniu and Bres. Keep in mind that being a 'son of' in ancient terms does not necessarily mean that one is born directly from a certain man or woman. It simply means that this is their lineage – that they are of that family. In spite of the fact that they were related to the Tuatha Dé Danann, the Firbolg decided they didn't want to share the land with the newcomers and declared war. It is said that the Tuatha Dé Danann won the first battle of Moytura because of their superior weapons and their knowledge of magic. In spite of their win, Nuada lost his right hand in the battle. With this 'blemish' he could not become king. The Tuatha Dé Danann decided that Bres should be king, but Bres was tyrant. He made Dagda and Oghma do menial work and harrassed the two battle heroes in many ways, going so far as to starve Dagda.

Bres' rule became so unbearable, that the people were sorry they'd made him king. They wanted Nuada to rule them, instead. The physician of the Tuatha Dé Danann, Dian Cécht had kept Nuada's severed hand in a jar of preserving liquid. Their smith Goibhniu fashioned a hand of silver to match Nuada's severed hand, and Dian Cécht attached it to Nuada's arm with 'magic' and surgery. (Possibly the world's 'first' bionic man.) His hand thus restored, Nuada demanded that Bres step down. Without the support of the people, Bres had no choice but to vacate the throne. Nuada was then crowned king and became known as Nuada of the Silver Hand.

In a story that is quite reminiscent of Solomon, the Queen of Sheba and their son Menyelik I, Bres returns to his mother Eriu and asks her who is his father. She tells him that it is the Fomorian king Elatha. Eriu then gives her son a signet ring, given to her by Elatha, and tells him to go to his father. Bres then sought audience with Elatha and showed him the ring to prove that he was his son. Elatha recognizes him by the ring and after Bres tells him of his deposition from the throne, he promises military aid to Bres. This time, the Tuatha Dé Danann are defeated and Bres is restored to the throne, taking his vengeance on them with heavy tribute and severe oppression. He even declares that the Druids and scholars may not teach, nor their bards – basically outlawing their culture. Bres was the god of agriculture. His enforced labor of the Tuatha Dé Danann and their heroes Oghma and Dagda is probably an allusion to the fact that upon coming to this new land, they were forced to put aside their 'other' pursuits and devote much of their time to growing food to sustain themselves. The fact that Dagda starves would point to the fact that there were some hard times in the beginning. Dagda is, among other things, the 'dispenser of plenty', and the controller of the weather and crops. He may be related in some way to the earlier gods Ea and Dagon. Like Ea and Dagon, he is an omnipotent god of knowledge, life and death.

The Tuatha Dé Danann were said to know the arts of philosophy, medicine, science, warfare, magic and many crafts. Given that they were sailors, they were also quite familiar with the stars and the motions of the sun and moon, by which they navigated. They were the Druids, the lawmakers and bards of Ireland, and most likely England and Scotland, as well. Oghma was the god of eloquence and language, and said to be the inventor of the Ogham 'tree' alphabet. The alphabet of the trees is written about extensively in Robert Graves' *The White Goddess*. All of this and the story of Dian Cécht restoring Nuada's hand is rather reminiscent of the story of the Watchers and their various wisdoms. It seems that no matter where they went, they were bound for trouble, these Sons of Dan.

The Tuatha Dé Danann later became the Fairy Folk – the Sidhe of Ireland. They pronounce it 'shee'; the Scotish Gaels pronounce it as 'sith'. The Sídhe or Sìth are variously believed to be the ancestors, spirits of nature, or the gods and goddesses, themselves.

Like the sun-hero Samson was to deliver the Hebrews from the oppression of the Philistines, the sun-hero of the Tuatha Dé Danann, Lugh, was to deliver them from the oppression of the giant Fomorians. The Fomorians had a great warrior named Balor, who had only one eye, and that eye was a terrible weapon that shot forth fire and lightning. Balor slew many of the Tuatha Dé Danann, but he was old and he soon grew tired. His eye fell shut and in this lull, Lugh hurled a stone from his sling and hit Balor's eye, killing him. Sounds a bit like David and Goliath, doesn't it?

THE DIVINE FEMININE

LIONS, BEES & SERPENTS

Timnah or Timnath is the place where Samson goes to seek his bride and kills a lion, whose carcass is then filled with honey by the bees. Bees were the emblem of Egyptian royalty in pharaonic times. It is of interest here to point out that the *tholoi* or hive-shaped tombs of Mycenae were prepared only for their royalty – so perhaps bees were the symbol of Mycenaean royalty, as well.

The ancient Minoans of Crete, as well as the Mycenaeans of circa 1500 BCE worshiped a goddess known as Potnia Theron. She was called by the epithets 'Mistress of the Wild Animals', as well as 'Queen of the Wild Bees'. The Minoans gave her the name Britomartis, which means 'sweet virgin'. Potnia was the foremost Mycenaean female deity and later came to be associated with Artemis, the Greek virgin goddess of the Moon.

Figure 7: Inanna/Ishtar and lion from an Akkadian cylinder seal

Images of the Minoan Mistress of Animals are found on ring seals. They often show the goddess attired in a Minoan-style skirt. More often than not, she is shown in a frontal position with raised hands, and the lower part of her body is turned. These images are often symmetrical in their composition, showing her flanked by two goats, two lions, two gazelles, or two gryphons. In some images, she is flanked by two goats and standing on a lion. There is generally a 'serpent frame' over her head, with a double-headed axe set in the center of the serpents, which marks her as divine. In some images, she is shown with wings. A Theban storage jar (*pithos*) from the early Archaic Greek period shows her flanked by two lions and two small human figures. Necklace plaques from late 7th century BCE show her with wings, flanked by lions, or as having a body composed entirely of bees and no other animals present. Later jars or vases show her holding a lion or a deer. The deer is the sacred animal of Artemis.

There is one image in particular that stands out in relation to the Mistress of Animals motif that dates from around 2000 BCE. This is the famous terracotta plaque that depicts what has variously been described as a *lillitu* demon, Lillith or Inanna. It is most likely an image of Inanna, for lions are associated with Inanna and she is seen in other images with her foot resting on one, as seen above.

Figure 8: The Neumann Plate

Here, Inanna is winged and shown holding the ring and rod symbol of measuring or power. Her feet are like the feet of the owls and she is shown standing atop two lions. The owls are symbolic of death and the underworld. In Mesopotamian literature, lions are symbolic of war-like kings and fierce deities – most often associated with Ninurta and Inanna. There were two great stone lion-guardians at the entrance to Ea/Enki's temple in Eridu. The rod and ring motif is also symbolic of kingship, which is bestowed upon man by heaven. Her horned cap or 'crown' is symbolic of her divine status in Anu's heaven. All taken together, she is here depicted as the 'Queen of Heaven, Earth and the Underworld'.

While the Neumann Plate and others similar to it are taken by some scholars to be the 'template' of the Mistress of Animals motif, there is clearly other symbolism at work in the Inanna plate that has only to do with animals in as much the goddess figures in them are associated with these particular animals as part of their attributions.

We see a similar image in this stela of the child Horus, also known as Harpocrates:

Figure 9: The Child Horus as a Master of Animals

Here, Harpocrates is shown holding a donkey and a scorpion by their tails in his right hand, along with two serpents. In his left hand, he holds a lion by the tail and two additional serpents. On the right pillar sits a falcon, the symbol of the adult Horus, while the left holds what appears to be two obelisks, which symbolize Upper and Lower Egypt. It was Horus who was said to have united the northern and southern kingdoms. The child stands on two crocodiles, much like Inanna stands on the backs of two lions.

These Mistress of Animals images spread westward through the Mitanni culture (upper Iraq and eastern Anatolia) into Syria and later into Palestine and Cyprus. With all the trading, conquering and 'foreign-exchange' programs of various Assyrian and Babylonian rulers, this is not surprising. Cyprus was an important trading center in the Bronze Age, because of its rich copper deposits. Copper was necessary to make bronze, as was tin. Yet, Potnia Theron is a distinctly different goddess – always virginal. And yet, many of the goddesses depicted in these motifs are considered as deities of fertility.

Mycenaean royalty did identify themselves with bees and worshiped the Queen of the Wild Bees in earlier times. The name of the (only) female judge in *Judges* is Deborah, which means 'bee'. Samson's riddle to his 'companions', the story about the lion and the bees may be a covert reference to the Danites being Mycenaen. The gate to their citadel at Mycenae is crowned by two rampant lions.

Figure 10: Typical Minoan Snake-goddess figure

We know that the Minoan (Cretan) society and religion was matriarchal in nature. No Minoan *god* statues or idols have been found in the ruins of their cities or temples – only goddesses. The Minoan goddess was a 'snake goddess', commonly depicted with a serpent in each hand and often with serpents wrapped about her upper arms and sometimes around her girdle. The Minoans are said to have borrowed some elements of their culture and worship from the Egyptians, with whom they were known to have been in contact from Egyptian artifacts found in Minoan ruins, as well as Egyptian motifs and symbols found in their frescos.

We see a certain similarity with the stela of the child Horus, also holding serpents in both hands. Possibly, the Minoan snake goddess is somehow connected with the Egyptian snake goddess Wadjet, who was symbolic of Lower Egypt (northern Nile delta) and appears as the cobra or *uraeus* on the head-dress of several goddesses and the pharaoh. As the *uraeus* Wadjet was identified as the Eye of Re or Ra, the sun god. She is sometimes depicted with a lion's head surmounted by a solar disk and a *uraeus*. Wadjet or Uatchit was seen as the protectress of the pharaoh, who would spit flames at his enemies. She is also known as 'the Woman of Flame'. The goddesses Tefnut and Bast or Bastet were also identified with the Eye of Ra. Both of these goddesses were often shown as lion-headed or cat-headed, and in fact are thought to be forms of the ferocious lion-goddess Sekmeht. During the holy festival of Bast, lion-hunting was forbidden. If you will note, a small figure of a sacred cat sits upon the head-dress of the Minoan snake goddess. Cats were sacred to the Egyptians.

The Mycenaeans conquered Knossos on Crete apparently sometime after the eruption of Thera. The eruption of Thera generated a massive tsunami which wiped out the Cretan navy that had previously defended the island – not to mention the vast quantity of pyro-clastic ejecta that was spewed into the surrounding area. Crete was then controlled by mainland Greece until the Romans took it in 69 BCE.

Did the Mycenaeans then adopt elements of the Minoan culture and religion? It is possible, but it is just as possible that they already knew of these elements, having traded with the Cretan Minoans *and* the Egyptians in the past. Certainly the Mycenaean culture was also matriarchal at one time, for the rest of the tale of Perseus, the 'founder' of Mycenaean civilization seems to tell of the transition between the matriarchy and the growing patrilineal societies and religions spreading from the east.

We come now to the tale of Medusa.

THE GORGON

In the Greek version of her story, Medusa was said to have been born from the waters of Lake Tritonis in Libya, the eldest daughter of Phorcys and Ceto. Phorcys or Orcus was a very ancient sea god, also known as 'the Old Man of the Sea'. Ceto was his sister and said to be a monster of the sea. Their children were the great serpent Ladon, the three Gorgons, Echnidna, Scylla (of Scylla and Charibdis) and the three Graeae. Medusa's two sisters were Euryale (Universality) and Stheno (Strength). The Graeae were something like the Three Fates, born as old crones who shared one eye and one tooth between them. Ladon was the great serpent who was the watcher of the garden where the Golden Apples were kept. He was slain by Hercules. Echnidna is like the Gorgons, half nymph and half serpent, and said to be the wife of Typhon. Scylla is said to be a sea-monster and seems to be confuted in many ways with Medusa, as their stories are quite similar.

We have here a mythical family of serpent-people, not considering the Graeae. While that is all very fascinating, the Libyan origins of Medusa are a bit different. Medusa was originally the serpent goddess of the Libyan Amazons. Some images of her from Libya show her with dreded-locks, which translated in the Greek mind to serpents. Medusa was what is known as a triple-goddess. Medusa was seen as symbolic of the Divine Feminine, or 'sovereign female wisdom'. As a serpent goddess, she represented the cycles of Time: past, present and future. Her 'cyclical' nature also extended to represent the cycles of life, death and rebirth, as well as creation, destruction and transformation. She was also seen as the Mediatrix between the three worlds, the Underworld, Earth and Heaven. Medusa was also revered as a guardian of gateways – beginnings and endings, and a Mistress of Animals. In short, she typified all feminine wisdom – that which was forbidden to men to know.

Her frightening face was thought to be a mask worn by her priestesses to frighten men away from their temples. The head of Medusa was also carven in stone on gateways and at cave-shrines sacred to her, to warn the uninitiated to keep away, as well as a guardian figure. But there is more than this to the idea of her 'terrible visage'. The mask of Medusa commonly shows her with boars tusks, with her tongue lolling out between them. She is the Devourer, Time. This image is very much like the frightening face of the Tantric goddess Kali-Ma, who is also symbolic of Time and the Great Mother. As she destroys and devours all things through her mouth, she also gives birth and rebirth through her womb. At the temple of Neith in Sais is found the inscription: "I am all that has been, that will be, and no mortal has yet been able to lift the veil that covers me." This same maxim has been applied to the Divine Mother Isis, more often than not in her aspect as Black Isis. To look into the eyes of Medusa is to see one's own mortality, to see 'beyond the veil' of illusion that is this reality into the ultimate reality. She rips away all delusions and dualities, revealing the wholeness of creation. To look into her eyes and understand what she knows would be a descent into madness for those unprepared to witness the Truth.

As a triple-goddess, she is the Maiden, the Mother and the Crone – much like Hecate. As the Maiden, Medusa is a fair young girl symbolic of all the potential and beauty of creation. In this aspect, she is possessed of long, beautiful hair, a fair form and luminous eyes. She is seen as irresistable to men and gods. As the Mother, she gives birth to all things. She is the creative principle. She is also seen as giving birth to or creating speech and letters, for it is by words that we form our ideas and descriptions of reality. In this aspect, she is shown in a birthing position or as squatting down, displaying her genitals. The Mother is also the Protectress. As the Crone, she is the wisdom of age personified, when there is no more need to engender and create 'in the flesh', for she has come to realize that the cycles which she represents take care of all of that. Her daughter is the new Mother, and her grand-daughter is the new Maiden. She is the Mistress of her own powers of darkness and light, for although the Crone is often associated with the darkness, she has crossed the line of illusion that separates this world from the next. The three old crones, the Graeae represent the Crone aspect of Medusa. Stheno is significant of the Maiden aspect – the young woman in her prime...Strength. Euryale, as the concept of Universality is symbolic of the Mother. Medusa is all of these, but unlike her sisters, she is mortal and can be slain.

Like Hecate, Medusa is seen as a moon-goddess, the phases of the moon representing her three aspects – the Full Moon being the Maiden, the Waxing and Waning Moon as the 'pregnant' Mother, and the Dark Moon as the Crone. Like Hecate, Medusa is also seen as a goddess of the Underworld, as her serpentine form indicates. The serpentine form is also indicative of the Great Serpent Mother, the Sea which encircles the earth and gives birth to all things. The serpent also represents immortality, arcane wisdom and mystery, because of its shedding its skin and being 'reborn'. Hecate, like Medusa, presides over birth, life and death and is a guardian of gateways and byways. Hecate is the goddess of the cross-roads, the Queen of Shadows and Shades, and the Night. Artemis and Diana are also moon goddesses and patronesses of the hunt.

There was a full-bodied image of Medusa at the Temple of Artemis, showing her with spiraling hair, wings and bird feet...an image that is very similar to the attributes of Inanna from the Neumann Plate. The wings, which appear on Medusa's shoulders behind her head in Greek iconography, are symbolic of her ability to move between the worlds. Her bird-feet connect her with the owl, the vulture and the corvids - all birds of death - but also birds of wisdom.

But what was for men the most bemusing and in some ways 'terrifying' aspect of feminine mysteries was their ability to bleed each month. Superstition from early times stated that if a man looked at a bleeding woman, he would turn to stone. Later patriarchal dogma claimed that women were 'unclean' at this time and so must be separated from men, and confined amongst other women. Better that than to admit they were frightened by the fact that women could lose quantities of blood once a month without dying and without being cut or wounded. This seemed quite mysterious and inexplicable – therefore dark and possibly evil.

The Neolithic association of the Goddess with the Underworld can be seen in the design of certain tomb types. This is particularly true of the long and round barrows seen in the British Isles, where the tomb itself is only accessible by crouching or crawling through a long narrow passage way that is symbolic of the birth canal. There are other barrows, which were not tombs, but used as ritual sites, where the participants crawled back 'into the womb' of the Mother, partook of the ceremony and were 'reborn' as they crawled back out. This is similar as well to the shamanic practice of burying the initiate in a pit in the earth and covering him with dirt, leaves and branches – from whence he is 'reborn' after a proscribed time as the shaman. From the Great Mother Earth we are born of the clay and to Her, we return. Dust to dust. The *tholoi* tombs of the Mycenaeans also symbolized the womb, as well as the bee-hive – for it is inside the hive that the queen bee mates, giving birth to other bees; it is where the marvelous, healing and nourishing honey is made. Honey might be equated with menstruum and/or female sexual fluids in this context. Bee propolis – which keeps the hive pure, and the royal jelly produced by the queen are known to have healing and purifying properties. One property of honey is that it allows the body to retain fluids – an important thing in a desert climate, where pure water is precious and moisture is sparse. Honey is also a highly nutritional food.

As an Amazon goddess, Medusa is equated with Neith. Neith is many things, but above all, she is the 'Divine Mother', who existed before all else, emerging from the primal waters (Chaos). She is also known as Nut, Nuit, Nyt, Tehenut (her Libyan name) and as Pallas-Athene (her Greek name). She may also be related to the primordial Creatrix Nox or Nyx, who was also born from the primal waters, much like Tiamat of the ancient Sumerian pantheon. She is a goddess devoted entirely to the mysteries and arts of the feminine: a weaver, the protectress of marriage, a goddess of childbirth, the patron deity of the arts of domesticity and an arbitrator. As the weaver, she is similar to Ariadne, who weaves the 'cloth of reality'. However, she is not exclusively domestic. She is also a goddess of hunting, warriors and mortuaries. She is the protectress of the city of Sais. As such, her early iconography was two arrows crossed over a shield or an animal hide. Later, she came to be anthropomorphized into a woman wearing a crown, holding a bow and arrows.

As the primordial Nut, she is a sky goddess whose mate is Nu an ancient water deity. Nut's lover was her brother, the Earth, Geb. This is one of the few myths where the Earth is a masculine god and the sky is feminine, which shows its great antiquity. There is an involved story about this, but to make it short, Nut becomes the mother of Osiris, Isis, Horus the Elder, Set and Nepthys. She is the 'Mother of the Gods'.

As Nuit, she is the starry goddess of the night sky, who bends over the earth. Nuit is the goddess of mystery as Amunet, the bride of Amun or Amen. Together, they create light from the primordial darkness – the stars and the planets.

To get on with the story of Medusa and Perseus, let us now review the myth itself. Any emphasis below (italics) is this author's.

Perseus is sent on his quest to secure the head of Medusa, by King Polydectes of Seriphos, where the infant Perseus and his mother

Danaë landed. Polydectes wants the now grown Perseus out of the way, because he is highly enamoured of Danaë. The feelings are not mutual however, and Perseus guards his mother from the king's unwonted advances. Polydectes figures this quest will get the boy out of his way and he might even die in the effort.

In this version of the story, Medusa had once been a beautiful maiden with long flowing hair – so beautiful that the sea-god Poseidon became her lover or raped her. It is not clear which. The act was done in the Temple of Athena. Athena, learning of this, was outraged and cast a curse upon Medusa so that she became the monstrous Gorgon with the snakey locks and horrible face.

Perseus sets off for Greece on a ship, not telling his mother where he is going. He travels there to find out where the Gorgons live. He consults the priestess at Delphi, who tells him to go to the land where they eat only acorns. He then goes to Dodona, the land of *talking oak trees*. There, he meets Hermes. It is Hermes who tells Perseus that he must go to the lands of the North, where the sun never shines and all is swathed in a cold mist, to confer with the Graeae (the Grey Ones). They have the tools that he needs to find the Gorgons. The Graeae are the sisters of the Gorgons, and so Perseus has to trick them into giving up their secret. Between the three of them, they share one eye and one tooth. Perseus is to hide and wait until he observes one of them remove the eye from her forehead, then rush them and grab it, refusing to return it until they tell him the location of the Gorgons. Before he leaves, Hermes presents him with what is variously described as an adamant sword (made of diamond), or a golden sickle which would not break on Medusa's scales. Athena then appears and provides Perseus with her *aegis* or breastplate of polished bronze which he carries on his left arm, and the sword in his right. She tells him to look at Medusa only in its reflection, to avoid being turned to stone.

Hermes then guides Perseus to the Graeae. The hero waits until the right time and then grabs the prophetic eye and tooth from the old crones. Reluctantly, they tell him where the Gorgons are. In some versions of the story, he returns the eye. In others, he takes the eye and tooth and casts them away into Lake Tritonis, after he's slain Medusa.

He and Hermes then leave for the Land of Hyperboria, the land beyond the North Wind. The Hyperborians show him great kindness and welcome him to their feast. Dancing maidens bring him the gifts he seeks. These are a) winged sandals enabling him to fly, b) a magic silver pouch that would adjust itself to the size of whatever it held, and c) a cap or helmet of darkness from Hades which made the wearer invisible. Hermes somehow now knows where the Gorgons live, so the two fly back across the Ocean and over the sea to the Terrible Sisters' Island. In other versions of the story, Hermes and

Athena give him these gifts. Hermes gives Perseus the winged sandals and it is Athena who guides him – flying through the sky to the place of the Gorgons.

Perseus comes upon the sleeping Gorgons and cuts off Medusa's head, while Athena watches. As he does this, the blood of her arteries spills on the ground and the great winged horse Pegasus, and the giant Chrysaor are born. These were the children of Poseidon. Knowing he'd best get out of there, he puts Medusa's head into the bag and escapes, pursued by Medusa's sisters.

As he is returning to Seriphos, he spies Andromeda chained to a cliff and rescues the maid from the terrible sea-monster (Ceto or Ketos) which would otherwise have devoured her. But that is another story.

He eventually returns to Seriphos and walks in on Polydectes giving a banquet for all his close friends and supporters. He tells the king that he's brought him the promised gift of the Gorgon's head. The men all laugh at him, and Perseus removes Medusa's head from the bag and turns them all to stone. This circle of stones can still be seen today on Seriphos.

This story is seen by many scholars as a parable on the transference of matriarchal society and religion to patriarchal society and religion. Perseus, the son of Olympian Zeus, slays the Mother Goddess, so that the Olympians now have free reign, with Zeus at the helm. Athena is often seen by feminists as a 'turncoat' goddess who goes over to the patriarchal side and for this reason betrays her 'other self', Medusa. Athena and Medusa share many of the same qualities and attributes – both being goddesses of wisdom and battle.

Robert Graves in *The White Goddess* sees the story as something else. The reference in the story to "the land of talking oak trees" is seen by Graves to refer to the Alphabet of the Trees, the Druidic Ogham alphabet. The head of Medusa and the serpents are the letters of the alphabet, words or the 'wisdom' of the Great Goddess. It is also signigicant that in this "land of talking oak trees", Perseus meets Hermes, who in his various forms as Hermes, Mercury, Hermes-Thoth, Thoth and Hermes-Trismagistus is said to have been the inventor of letters. I will not pretend to address this subject any further than this, as it is quite involved and beyond the scope of this article. I suggest that you read *The White Goddess* if you wish to know more about it. As was mentioned previously, language and letters was attributed to the invention of the Mother Goddess before the Olympian incursion into religion. It is She who weaves this illusion of reality and it is by words and language that we convey our impressions of this reality to one another. Letters are also said to have their own innate symbology, which we are to decipher intuitively as a path to enlightenment. This can be seen in the Chapter on the Hebrew alphabet (GEMATRIA) – which is only one of many.

This is perhaps the root of Penemue's lament, that man is not meant to write things down; speak of them or define them. For by defining or concretizing them (turning them to stone), man limits them to what is only a portion of their true meaning. The universe is a place of infinite variety, and one meaning can be woven into another so that there are layers upon layers of meaning and attributions for every thing or idea that exists. I recognize that this is in fact happening as this very moment, as I write these words. Yet, if we do not attempt to express some part of the mystery as we intuit and understand it, and cause others to consider our ideas in relation to what they know, we might remain entombed in our own little boxes of thought and never emerge 'reborn'.

THE PRIMORDIAL SERPENT DEITIES

TIAMAT

Perhaps the first primordial serpent deity ever commited to writing by man was Tiamat in the Babylonian *Epic of Creation*. That is not to say that Tiamat hadn't 'existed' before her history was written down by the Babylonians. She was the primordial goddess of the Sumerians, as well. In the beginning, according to the *Epic*, after the heavens and earth were separated, the only beings that existed were Apsu and Tiamat. Apsu was the personification of the fresh subterranean waters, while Tiamat personified the salt waters. It is said that they "had mixed their waters together" and then the gods were born to them. Their firstborn son was An or Anu, who later becomes the supreme god of the ancient Mesopotamian pantheon. Anu begat Nudimmud "in his likeness" we are told:

> *He, Nudimmud, was superior to his forefathers: Profound of understanding, he was wise, was very strong at arms. Mightier by far than Anshar his father's begetter, he had no rival among the gods his peers. (Tablet I)*

Nudimmud is the Sumerian name of Enki or Ea as a creator god. He is described as "Ea who knows everything", the "Creator of divine wisdom", and "Niššiku the far-sighted".

In a tale that is to become common-place through time, the Father of the Gods, Apsu wishes to destroy his children because they are disturbing him with their clamor and playing. Tiamat is here portrayed as the patient mother. Apsu and his vizier Mummu plot to kill the younger gods. Ea discovers the plot and tells Anu. Ea then slays Apsu, and Tiamat finally loses her patience. Thus begins a great battle between the younger gods and the Mother. Tiamat gives birth to a gallery of nightmarish monsters to aid her in her battle. In the end, she is destroyed by Marduk in the Babylonian version, and the younger gods take over.

Tiamat is described in the text as "Mother Hubur, who fashions all things". Mother Hubur is a river of the Underworld, or perhaps a subterranean river. Possibly, this 'subterranean river' is the magma, which comprises most of the Earth's substance, under the crust. It oozes out in volcanic flows, which crawl down the cone like fiery dragons or serpents. When Marduk challenges her to one on one combat, we are told:

> *She went wild, she lost her temper. Tiamat screamed aloud in a passion, Her lower parts shook together from the depths....*

> *Fierce winds distended her belly; Her insides were constipated and she stretched her mouth wide. (Tab. IV)*

Many of the monsters that Tiamat bears for her army are great serpents and various sorts of dragons. Magma that is subjected to pressure and builds up (seen as constipation), unvented, finally explodes thousands of cubic feet of pyro-clastic ejecta: fire-bombs, ash and scoria, which burn, shred and abraid, stinging the eyes and skin. In addition to the serpents and dragons, we are also told that she creates various demons, scorpion men, and rabid dogs to name a few. This is, after all, in primordial times when the earth was still being formed. It was chaos unleashed.

TYPHON

Clearly, our ancestors knew about volcanic eruptions. It is almost certain that we can take the mural at Çatal Hüyük as showing the eruption of a double-coned volcano, circa 1100 BCE.

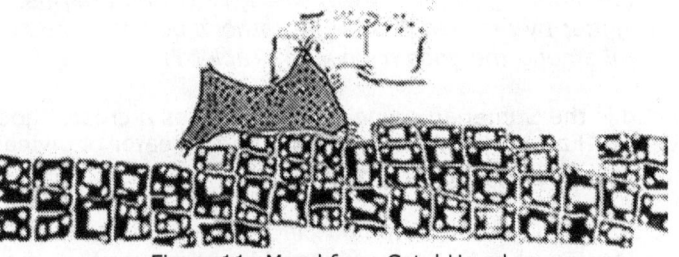

Figure 11: Mural from Catal Huyuk

Thera blew up sometime between 1650 and 1550 BCE by many guestimates, and is probably the basis of the great serpent god Typhon. Typhon is described as 'a giant monster having a hundred dragon heads each shooting flames from mouth, eyes and nostrils and uttering blood-curdling screams at the same time'. The eruption of Thera – the largest volvanic eruption in known history – spewed 30 cubic *miles* of ejecta into the atmosphere and affected the weather for many years afterward, causing a sort of 'nuclear winter' where little or nothing would grow. The sea, rivers, and lakes would have been polluted. Fields grain would have burned up or been buried in ash. Many fish and animals would have been killed, thus effectively removing all forms of sustenance from the immediately affected areas. As Andrew Collins and others have pointed out, this eruption may have been the source of the plagues of Egypt. This truly cataclysmic event may have heralded a kind of wake-up call for the peoples affected by it, perceiving that their old deities had abandoned them, and it was time for a new order of things. The story of Zeus remaining on Olympus to do battle when all the other gods had fled and eventually triumphing over the terrible Typhon may signal this 'new beginning'. It is related that Zeus finally throws Typhon 'down into Tartarus' – back from whence it came, into the bowels of the earth.

The story of Pandora's box may also be tied in with the eruption of Thera, unleashing all the plagues, ills and demons that trouble man. If indeed, as it has been suggested by others, that the pillar of fire described in *Exodus* was the column of smoke and flame from the eruption of Thera that guided the Israelites out of Egypt, it becomes understandable how Typhon and Set (the god of destruction) became confuted with Yahweh, the 'new god' of the Hebrews. To say that this event left a 'burning memory' in the minds of those who witnessed it and lived to tell the tale would be an understatement. Their children and their childrens' children would have heard about it – but time, the frailties of language and the human imagination have a way of metamorphosizing things over time, until they become something else.

There is no doubt that the eruption caused a diaspora from the areas affected, with people moving away into unaffected or less affected areas. We know from the Amarna Letters that the Sea People, who were all inhabitants of Palestine, Canaan, the Aegean and Anatolia *were* driven out of Egypt as usurpers of the land who tried to make it their own – but that was not until *after* the purported exodus of the Israelites. The Hyksos Kings (rulers of foreign lands) reigned in Egypt right around the time of the eruption of Thera, bringing with them their worship of Set and Typho(n). It is rather a literary convenience that we are never told *who* was Pharaoh at the time of the Exodus, when so many other invading and usurping kings and even their generals are specifically named in the Old Testament.

As for the noise or 'screaming', the eruption of Kraktoa in 1883 was heard as far as three thousand miles away on the island of Rodrigues. Atmospheric shock waves reverberated around the world seven times, lasting for five days. (*Wikipedia – Krakatoa*). It most likely did seem like the voice of some terrible and mighty god speaking to the inhabitants of the earth.

We know today that volcanic 'islands' grow up from the sea bed, where the crust is closer to the magma than on land. Great surges of magma have risen up from the sea, creating land masses. *This* is the dark, primoridal chaos which created and recreated the earth. This is the primordial goddesss of the salt waters. These are the 'earth-born' Titans who swallow villages, cities and entire country-sides. This is also the genesis of at least two of the great deities of destruction and chaos, Tiamat and Typhon.

WATER, FIRE & BLOOD

Serpent imagery is applicable to many things. The sea is seen as a great serpent encircling the Earth. The Milky Way is another sort of sea, river, or serpent that encircles the Earth in the heavens – 'As above, so below'. Rivers are seen as serpentine and like great serpents crawling across the earth, have been known to slowly change their courses. In this way, serpents are equated with water.

The fires of the earth are buried, concealed beneath the sea. When we don't necessarily know what something is, we describe it in terms that we do know what it is – something it resembles, so that others like us will also understand if they are not witnessing it for themselves. Above, the analogy of a magma flow crawling down a volcano was compared to a serpent. This burning, 'biting' and stinging serpent devours all in its path, finally turning to stone and burying the land beneath it, creating a new landform. We see here where the serpent is equated with fire.

The Mesopotamians, who lived in an area that was highly volatile in terms of volcanic and petrolic disturbances had several fire dragons and assorted demons that would personify these sorts of activity. It is entirely plausible that the appearance of the fiery djinn as serpents is attributable to small- to mid- scale eruptions of gases and bitumen fronts ignited by lightning or even the fires of men. The destruction of Sodom and Gomorrah, and the Mesopotamian city of Mashkan Shapir may have been attributable to such activities as well. Yet, in the Old Testament, Sodom and Gomorrah are destroyed by the fire-weilding angels of Yahweh.

Fire and water are seen not only as destructive principles, but also as nurturing, cleansing and creative principles – thus two of the four elements that comprise creation. Perhaps the two serpents in the hands of the Minoan goddess represent fire and water. Both fire and water are necessary to forge weapons, cook food and keep man sustained.

In analogy, the cone of a volcano may be likened to the womb of Mother Earth and the magma, Her bleeding. From it issues both new land-forms and in semi-dormant phases, 'rains' of ash that fertilize the tilled fields of man and the natural flora on its slopes. One has only to look at the lush vegetation of Sumatra, Borneo and Java, which are volcanic in origin to see this. In spite of the dangers of living beneath volcanos, people persist in doing so, because of the great fertility of these areas. Magma is the 'blood' of the Earth Mother, flowing under her skin, the crust. From the seas, She rises, serpentine and fiery in form – the mystical fire contained in the water.

THE GENESIS OF GODS & RELIGION

We tend in this day and age to not think of these analogies for earth-building or other primordial sorts of activities because they simply are not part of our daily lives. We take for granted that the earth is and always has been the way it is, but this is simply not so. In order to understand the allusions and allegories that have come down to us from our ancestors, we must put ourselves into their world and their frames of mind.

The most ancient gods were often forces of Nature, over which men felt powerless to control. Shamanism developed as a way to observe and interpret the signs of Nature and Her beasts. The shaman became the 'wise man' of his people, far-seeing and a mediator between the worlds. Trance and ecstatic visions enabled hir to 'see' beyond hir five senses. S/he knew the ways of the clouds, the wind, and the beasts. S/he learned what caused sickness, and what plants healed or poisoned. S/he developed a relationship with the 'spirit' of Nature in Its many forms, which acted as hir guide when traveling to other realms. This was the earliest form of what we might call 'religion' and it was tied up with healing and divination.

As man advanced, his deities became zoomorophosized and anthromorphosized as he attempted to better relate to and control the world. Man began to attempt to exert his will upon Nature and the abstractions of Time, Life, Death and Birth. He created gods to represent these concepts, as well as those functions which allowed him to live more comfortably, yet still in harmony with Nature. Hunting deities arose, because of the need for food, horn and hides in the hunter-gatherer societies. Fertility deities filled the duty of ensuring that the earth provided sufficient fruits and grains, as well as ensuring the fertility of the tribe or group and the beasts that fed them. Because Nature provided their sustenance, Nature and the Earth became the Great Mother, who was a bit more benificent than her earlier primordial counterparts like Tiamat...although She could still surprise them now and then.

Men noticed that certain animals were more sexually powerful or active than others. Some animals produced many young in one litter, or gave birth often. These became symbolic of their fertility deities. As man began to fashion implements and weapons from the materials he found in the earth, craft gods were 'born'. Attributes that made a man superior to others, such as the 'eye of a hawk' or the 'fearlessness of a lion' were deified in zoomorphic deities. Man sought to propitiate them, in order to gain these attributes for himself.

As man became settled, his gods began to become more and more like himself – divine reflections or anthropomorphizations. He told stories about his deities to explain in human terms why they 'did' the things they did; to explain why certain things happened, or why things are the way they are. As time went on, man became more philosophically inclined, delving deeper into the abstractions and their whys and wherefores. But always, no matter when or where he found himself, his greatest attraction was to the mysteries of the heavens and the night sky.

THE SUN & THE SERPENT

The sun was and still is the brightest object in our heavens. It nourishes life and warms us. Without it, we would wither and die. In this way, the sun is seen as a beneficent god. But in the lands near the equator, the sun can also be destructive, burning crops and drying up sources of water. In Chapter 4 of the *Book of the Watchers*, we see reference to this:

> And again, observe ye the days of summer how the sun is above the earth over against it. And you seek shade and shelter by reason of the heat of the sun, and the earth also burns with growing heat, and so you cannot tread on the earth, or on a rock by reason of its heat.

We are told again in Chapter 69, verses 12 and 13 of the 'evil sun':

> and the smitings 13 which befall through the noontide heat, the son of the serpent named Taba'et.

As has been told before, the serpent Taba'et refers to the 'ring' or circle made by the sun in it's daily journey through the heavens. One of the oldest symbologies of this is the serpent that bites its tail.

Figure 102: The circular Ouroboros

The serpent bites its own tail because it seems always to start and end at the same point. However, when man took a closer observation of the sun, he noticed that the sun actually moved across the sky in a rather serpentine fashion, where at the equinoxes, it crossed its previous path.

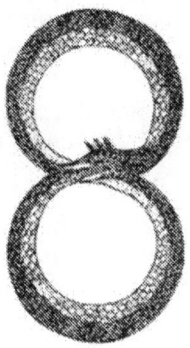

Figure 113: The lemniscate Ouroboros

The circular Ouroboros then became the lemniscate Oroboros, representing the analema or the yearly path of the sun, still biting its tail. At the new solar year, the sun does indeed appear to start where it began. However, due to the wobble of the earth and precession, it's always in a bit of a different position in relation to the constellations and stars in which it rises. Yet, there is order in all this that spans eons of time. For this reason, the sun became the ruler and measurer of Time, and the personification of Order and Law.

Another figure of interest in relation to the sun is the so-called Z-rod and Serpent that is found in Pictish rock carvings in Scotland:

Figure 14: Z-Rod with Serpent from the Bransbutt Stone, Scotland

The upward and downward 'legs' of the Z in this symbol represent the solstices of the sun, i.e. the furthest points north and south that the sun travels during the year. The serpent again represents the sun traveling through the heavens. If you will recall, in the myth of Perseus slaying the Gorgon, he begins in Greece and then travels northward, where he is welcomed in a feast and a celebration by the Hyperboreans in the Land Beyond the North Wind. He then returns south to Libya and once he is finished there with his task, he returns to Greece. This story would seem to point to Perseus being yet another solar-hero or sun-king, like Samson.

Like Samson, and the sun between the uprights of the Temple pillars Jachin and Boaz, the serpent or the sun is 'trapped' between the solstices.

The relationship between the lion iconography and the sun has previously been explained, and so will not be reiterated here. We now see the relationship between the sun and the serpent, as well. This was recognized by the Gnostics, who 'invented' the god Abraxas with the leonine head and serpentine legs, whose name adds up to 365, the number of days in a solar year.

THE WATCHERS OF "THE MYSTERIES"

The following is a listing of the Watchers as they are listed in the book *The Book of the Mysteries of Heaven and Earth* by Bakhayla Mîkâ'êl (Zôsîmâs). The chapter under which these are found is called "The Angels Who Taught Men the Arts and Crafts" and is found on page 27 of the book. You may notice a few familiar names, but most of them have quite different names. What they taught is also different in most cases and reflects a cultural difference, as well as a different time. Some of these 'occupations' are rather amusing and mundane when compared with the Watchers of *Enoch*.

[The Occupations of the Angels on the Earth (?)]

First of all 'AKARÊ who carrieth in his eyes four *'entalâm* – and this [is] the figure four:
and **PIPIRÔS** runneth with the sun;
and **RÛRÎDÊ** who smasheth the mountains;
and the inventor of the circle **ZAR'ÊL**, which is the moon (or month);
and **PÎNÊNÊ** who showed [men] the running (racing) of horses;
and **GALÊ** showed [men] how to hold the *gadab*, that is to say the *galab* (fish-hook) as it is interpreted in the Abysinnian language;
and **TÎGANA** showed [men] how to make the shield;
and **HÔRÊRI** taught [men] the harp;
and **YUEBÊ** taught [men] how to work in iron;
and **MÊGÊA** taught [men] how to ride the horse;
and **NEGÔDÎ** showed [men] springs of mineral waters and healed the sick [therewith], and the [proper] hour (or, season) when they would benefit the sick man; and one of them wished to snatch away everything the children of CAIN had taken. He took fifty *sâdâla* that is to say, fifty *entalâm*, which he carried away in his right hand.
O this thing is hard [to understand] – the gift of Him Who created both the weak and the strong!
And **GARGÊ** showed [men the pattern of] the corn grinder;
and **SÊTÊR** showed [men] how to knead dough;
and **GÎMÊR** [showed men] how to extract food from [raw] plasma;
and **ZÂRÊ** showed [men] how to milk animals;
and **HEGGÊ** showed [men] how to work in wood and make a roof for the house;
and **TENTÔREB-'AREB** (?) showed [men how to make] the door;
and **SÊPHÊR** showed [men] how to boil milk (?);
and **HALÊGÊ** showed [men] carving (or, sculpture);
and **HÊDER** showed [men] how to make the tree flourish;

and SÎNÔ showed [men] how to build;
and TÔF showed [men] how to burn clay (or, mud, i.e. how to make pottery);
and 'ARTÔRBEGÂS showed [men how to make] cutting tools;
and SBÊDÊGUÂZ showed [men] stibium (?) (eye-paint);
and ZÂRÊ showed [men] how to make must (wine);
and BÊTÊNÊLÂDÂS showed [men] the bread oven;
and NÂFÎL showed [men] the planting [of trees];
and YÂRBEH showed [men] how to saw up wood;
and ELYÔ showed [men] how to dance;
and PHENÊMÛS showed [men] architecture and writing;
and EGÂLÊMÛN showed [men how to make] yokes for cattle and the chariot pole;
and KUERES showed [men how to make] the body of the chariot and the whip (or, goad);
and 'AKÔR showed [men how to make] brass;
And there were among them some who taught [men] to work the cedar and the willow. And WASAG and ABÊRGEYÂ, whose heads shone in the clouds, showed [men] all these things; they it was who taught men to play TÂBAT. And NÊR and ZABÊRÊNÎ-GUED taught them to play 'AFÂWEMÂ, and 'AKÎS taught them the Circus.

Zar'el appears to be the same as Sariel, while Phenemus may be Penemue. You may have noticed that there are several 'angels' who teach all of Azazel's wisdoms. There is one apparent duplication in the names, that of Zare, who taught men both how to milk animals and to make wine. Zare is probably the name of Shemyaza, which in its Ethiopian rendering is Amezarek. All of these 'occupations' were shown to men – which is implied here.

Following this list is a rather short exposition of two paragraphs which explain about the Flood. I include them here as a comparison with what is written in *Enoch*.

[Men's Evil Lives Caused the Flood]
Now, it was through these men that the waters of the Flood came upon the earth; seven in the heavens, and seventy on the earth. Of great [magnitude] were the outpourings of water which were set loose in those days! Evil had multiplied and had filled the earth. Whoredom had magnified itself and even the four-footed beasts went mad. Neither a father nor his son [respected each other], for no son considered his father, and no father his son. Men consorted with the beasts. Even the earth complained and uttered lamentations.

[The Destruction of the Giants and the Flood]
And the Creator said concerning them: 'Hold [thy] peace. Mine eye seeth them, and Mine ear hath heard them, and My longsuffering hath made Me silent in respect of them.' And in

those days harlotry had increased to such an extent that it merited the taking of the vengeance which God had not hitherto commanded [1]. And in those days He took vengeance on the giants and a voice went forth which said, 'Kill ye each other with the sword.' And the waters of the Flood rose and swallowed up their bodies as far as their breasts, and they hacked off their heads with the sword. And in those days NOAH and his sons clung to righteous dealing and they were saved from destruction.

[1] i.e. it was so great that God could not possibly refrain any longer from taking vengeance.

BIBLIOGRAPHY

BOOKS REFERENCED

"The Book of Enoch the Prophet" translated by R.H. Charles, Weiser Books, York Beach, ME., 2003. Originally published in 1912 by Oxford University Press. (Enoch Texts in Public Domain.)

"Myths from Mesopotamia – Revised Edition" by Stephanie Dalley, Oxford University Press, Oxford, UK, 1989.

"Dictionary of Angels – Including the Fallen Angels" by Gustav Davidson, The Free Press – a Division of Simon & Schuster, Inc., New York, NY, 1967.

"The Dead Sea Scrolls – A New Translation" translated with commentary by Michael Wise, Martin Abegg, Jr. & Edward Cook, Harper-Collins Publishers, Inc., New York, NY, 1996.

"The Dead Sea Scrolls" by William B. Eerdmans and the Public Museum of Grand Rapids, William B. Eerdmans Publishing Co., Grand Rapids, MI, 2003.

"The Key of Solomon the King (Clavicula Salomonis)" Translated and edited from manuscripts in the British Museum by S. Liddell MacGregor Mathers, Samuel Wiser, Inc., York Beach, Maine. Published in 2000.

"Hindu Polytheism" by Alain Danielou, Bollingen Series LXXIII, Pantheon Books, published by The Bollingen Foundation, 1964.

"Dictionary of Ancient Deities" by Patricia Turner & Charles Russell Coulter, Oxford University Press, 2000.

"The HarperCollins Concise ATLAS of the BIBLE" edited by James B. Pritchard with I. Michael White, Harper San Francisco – an Imprint of HarperCollins Publishers.

"The Apocrypha – An American Translation" translated by Edgar J. Goodspeed, Vintage Books A Division of Random House, Inc. New York, 1989.

"Illustrated Dictionary of the Bible", Herbert Lockyear, Sr. Editor with FF. Bruce and R.K. Harrison, Thomas Nelson Publishers, Nashville, TN., 1986

"The Origin of Satan", Elaine Pagels, Vintage, New York, 1995

"The Egyptian Hermes – A Historical Approach To The Late Pagan Mind", Garth Fowden, Princeton University Press, New Jersey, 1986.

"Sefer Yetzirah – The Book of Creation", Aryeh Kaplan, Weiser Books, York Beach, Maine, 1997.

"The Devil" by Jeffrey Burton Russell, Cornell University Press and Cornell Paperbacks, Ithaca, NY, 1977.

"Hindu Polytheism", Alain Danielou, Bollingen Series LXXIII, Pantheon Books – A Division of Random House, New York, NY, 1964.

"Die Sterne von Babylon (The Stars of Babylon)", Werner Papke, Gustav Luebbe Verlag, Bergisch Gladbach, Germany, 1989.

"The Old Enemy – Satan & the Combat Myth", Neil Forsyth, Princeton University Press, Princeton, NJ, 1987

"Oxford Dictionary of Celtic Mythology", James MacKillop, Oxford University Press, Oxford, UK, 1998.

"The Ashes of Angels – The Forbidden Legacy of a Fallen Race", Andrew Collins, Bear & Co., Rochester, VT, 1996.

"The Ethiopic Book Of Enoch", Knibb, Michael A., Oxford: Clarendon Press, 1978, repr. 1982

"Gods, Demons and Symbols of Ancient Mesopotamia – An Illustrated Dictionary", Jeremy Black and Anthony Green, University of Texas Press, Austin, TX., 2000.

"The Hippocratic Oath: Text, Translation, and Interpretation", Ludwig Edelstein, Johns Hopkins Press, Baltimore, MD, 1943.

"The Zohar – The Book of Enlightenment" translation by Daniel Chanan Matt, Paulist Press, New York, NY., 1981

"The Ancient Near East, Supplementary Text and Pictures Relating to the Old Testament", J.B Pritchard. Princeton University Press, Princeton, NJ, 1969.

"The Amarna Letters", W. L. Moran, The Johns Hopkins University Press, Baltimore, MD, 1992.

"The New Golden Bough" by Sir James George Frasier, edited by Dr. Theodor H. Gaster, A Mentor Book, New York, NY 1964.

"The Goddess, The Grail & The Lodge" by Alan Butler, O Books, New York, NY, 2004.

"Genesis of the Grail Kings" by Laurence Gardner, Fair Winds Press, Gloucester, MA, 2002.

ONLINE SOURCES

WIKIPEDIA – The Free Encyclopedia
http://www.wikipedia.org/

SACRED TEXTS – The Internet Sacred Text Archive
http://www.sacred-texts.com/index.htm

> "The Mycenaean Origin of Greek Mythology" by Martin P. Nilsson, 1932 (Copyright not renewed).
> http://www.sacred texts.com/cla/mog/index.htm

> "The Gnostics and Their Remains" by Charles William King, 1887.
> http://www.sacred-texts.com/gno/gar/index.htm

JEWISH ENCYCLOPEDIA – The Only Free Jewish Encyclopedia on the Internet
http://www.jewishencyclopedia.com/

Lebor Gebála Érenn – The Book of Invasions (12/2006)
http://members.aol.com/lochlan2/lebor.htm

Order of Nazorean Essenes – A Buddhist Branch of Original Chritianity (12/2006)
http://essenes.net/

"The Testament of Solomon" translated by F.C. Conybeare, Jewish Quarterly Review, October, 1898. Digital edition by Joseph H. Peterson, 1997 (11/2006)
http://www.esotericarchives.com/solomon/testamen.htm

"The Secret Grimoire of Turiel" preserved by Marius Malchus (12/2006)
http://www.geocities.com/imuhtuk/occult/turiel.htm

Josephus "Antiquities of the Jews" and "War of the Jews" (11-12/2006)
http://bible.christiansunite.com/josindex.shtml

www.ingramcontent.com/pod-product-compliance
Lightning Source LLC
Chambersburg PA
CBHW020756160426
43192CB00006B/342